George Ro

Processes of the Lesser Peace

George Ronald Bahá'í Studies Series

Processes of the Lesser Peace

edited by

Babak Bahador and Nazila Ghanea

George Ronald
Oxford

GEORGE RONALD, Publisher
46 High Street, Kidlington, Oxford OX5 2DN

*A catalogue record for this book is available
from the British Library*

ISBN 0–85398–472–7

Contents

Introduction   vii

1 Bahá'í Proposals for the Reformation of World Order   1
  Jeffrey Huffines

2 The Establishment of the Lesser Peace   46
  Babak Bahador

3 The Environment and the Lesser Peace   79
  Arthur Lyon Dahl

4 The Spiritual Destiny of America and the Achievement of   107
  World Peace
  John Huddleston

5 Collective Security as a Means of Ensuring Peace Among   162
  the Nations: The Contribution of the Bahá'í Faith
  Danesh Sarooshi

6 An International Legal Order   181
  Rod Rastan

7 Global Governance: Has a Paradigm Shift in World   227
  Government Theory Brought the Lesser Peace Closer?
  Daniel Wheatley

8 'Everything That Rises Must Converge': Global   250
  Governance and the Emergence of the Lesser Peace
  Charles Lerche

Introduction

The Lesser Peace is a subject of great interest to Bahá'ís throughout the world, as it is a process that we are witnessing during our
own lifetimes. The following book is a collection of articles on the
theme of the Lesser Peace. The articles were adapted from talks
given at conferences of the Bahá'í Politics and International Law
Special Interest Group (BIPOLIG) over a five-year period (1995–
2000). BIPOLIG, a special interest group of the Association for
Bahá'í Studies English-Speaking Europe, was set up with the aim
of studying and correlating Bahá'í writings on international politics, law and related subjects to their respective academic
disciplines and in so doing engage in Bahá'í scholarship.

The eight articles in this book look at the Lesser Peace and elements often associated with it from different angles. The first two
articles largely take a macro approach to the subject, providing
overviews on Bahá'í proposals that have promoted peace and references throughout Bahá'í history on the Lesser Peace. The next
two articles look at two special issues – the role of the environment and that of America – in bringing about the Lesser Peace.
The fifth and sixth articles fit within an international law context
and assess the role of collective security and international legal
institutions such as the International Criminal Court (ICC) in promoting the Lesser Peace. The last two articles look at the
changing nature of governance that is inevitable with the onset
of the Lesser Peace.

Most of the talks that became articles for this book were

presented at the 1998 and 1999 conferences of BIPOLIG that focused on the Lesser Peace. These articles were submitted to the editors of this volume over 1999 and 2000. However, three additional points regarding the Lesser Peace have come to light since the end of 2000.[1] First, the 20th century ended in a relatively peaceful manner. Some Bahá'ís had anticipated earth-shattering events before the end of the 20th century leading to some kind of official establishment of the Lesser Peace. This interpretation has clearly not unfolded. What has happened is the continuation of incremental developments on many fronts that are challenging and transforming our interstate system to the global one envisioned by Bahá'u'lláh. The signs of this transition have sometimes been subtle and at other times turbulent, as evidenced by the tragic events of 11 September 2001 in New York and Washington DC and their repercussions throughout the world.

Second, it is now clear that the unity of nations and the Lesser Peace are distinct concepts. Previously, it was common for discussions and talks on the Lesser Peace by individuals presenting their own interpretations to describe these terms and ideas behind them as synonymous. In its response to an individual believer on 19 April 2001, The Universal House of Justice clarified this point, stating:

> You should take note of the distinction between the unity of nations and the Lesser Peace . . . the Lesser Peace will initially be a political unity arrived at by decision of various governments of the world. The unity of nations can be taken as that unity which arises from a recognition among the peoples of various nations, that they are members of a common human family.

According to the accompanying memorandum from the Research Department, however, the terms are related, as the unity of nations is a highly significant step in the evolutionary Lesser Peace process.

Third, and perhaps most significant, is the confirmation that the unity of nations has been established in the 20th century.

According to the Universal House of Justice, 'The twentieth century has been distinguished by the emergence of the unity of nations . . . there can be no doubt that the promise of 'Abdu'l-Bahá has been fulfilled, and the unity of nations securely established in the century now concluded.' The unity of nations was the fifth candle of unity described by 'Abdu'l-Bahá in a letter written in 1906 to Mrs Jane Elizabeth Whyte of Scotland and subsequently published as 'The Seven Candles of Unity'. The 19 April 2001 letter of the Universal House of Justice is the first authoritative confirmation that this prophecy of 'Abdu'l-Bahá, made 95 years earlier, has indeed been met. Furthermore, the document *Century of Light* refers to this same achievement and explains that the 'Century of Light', the 20th century, is luminous because of the recognition of the oneness of mankind by the peoples of the world.[2]

Review of Articles

Bahá'í Proposals for the Reformation of World Order is a detailed review of selected Bahá'í proposals on the reforming of the world order. Collectively, these proposals, many of which have been presented as documents, form what might be called 'a Bahá'í world view'. Documents reviewed include Bahá'u'lláh's Tablets to heads of State, 'Abdu'l-Bahá's 'Tablet to the Hague', the 1955 Bahá'í International Community (BIC) Proposal for UN Charter Revision and the 1995 proposals for UN institutional reform in a document entitled *Turning Point for All Nations*. The article also looks at US foreign policy and its role in shaping world order during the 20th century and the Bahá'í External Affairs Strategy and its role in promoting world peace.

The Establishment of the Lesser Peace delves into the Bahá'í writings that specifically refer to the Lesser Peace, reviewing the relevant contributions of Bahá'u'lláh, 'Abdu'l-Bahá, Shoghi Effendi and the Universal House of Justice. In so doing, the article tries to organize the various components and ideas directly and indirectly linked to the Lesser Peace into a coherent pattern. It also attempts to correlate these writings to recent theoretical work amongst leading International Relations thinkers. It puts forward the thesis that the Lesser Peace has two elements – a condition and outward manifestation that are part of the same process, with the latter trailing the former.

The Environment and the Lesser Peace provides a unique perspective on the Lesser Peace. It argues that the environmental issue is a positive stimulus to peace by demonstrating the systemic unity of the world, promoting international political cooperation through multilateral problem-solving around environmental issues and providing common interests to disparate groups with traditionally conflicting interests. It also puts forward the possibility that a global environmental crisis may be a precipitating cause for the final steps towards peace and provides some scenarios by which this may happen.

The Spiritual Destiny of America and the Achievement of World Peace assesses the unique role of the United States in bringing about peace. While recognizing its shortcomings, the article suggests that the United States has a special role in promoting world peace owing to its unique sense of destiny and material and moral leadership. This is because it has had a distinctive history of pioneering ethnic assimilation, political democracy and religious diversity. America is also significant because it has played a leading role in the creation of global institutions. However, much more is required before America can fulfil its mission of leading the world to the Lesser and Most Great Peace.

Collective Security as a Means for Ensuring Peace Among the Nations: The Contribution of the Bahá'í Faith provides a detailed assessment of collective security, a key component of the Lesser Peace that was first put forward by Bahá'u'lláh in His Tablet to Queen Victoria. In this paper, collective security is defined, its historic development under the League of Nations and United Nations is reviewed, its current operation under UN auspices is described and proposals for its reform from Bahá'í scriptures are outlined.

In *An International Legal Order* a review of the current and emerging international judicial bodies such as the International Court of Justice (ICJ) and the International Criminal Court (ICC) is conducted. Throughout the study analysis is provided on the historic developments of these institutions, their operation in practice today and how they relate to the institutional aspects of the future Bahá'í world order. It is concluded that while there is still a long way to go to the Bahá'í vision of a supreme tribunal whose judgement is binding, a positive direction can nonetheless be traced owing to a redefining of state sovereignty. Furthermore, the international judiciaries that stand today will endure as one of the most important legacies of the 20th century.

Global Governance: Has a Paradigm Shift in World Government Theory Brought the Lesser Peace Closer? examines the concept of global governance and reviews how it is different from the idea of world government. This comparison will be beneficial to Bahá'ís who have traditionally promoted the principles of world government and who may be uncertain of the relationship between these two concepts. The paper begins by examining selective texts from the post-war literature on world government and then expands the discussion by reviewing some of its critiques. It also investigates how the emergence of global governance is helping to bring about the Lesser Peace.

In *'Everything That Rises Must Converge': Global Governance and the Emergence of the Lesser Peace* recent statements of the Bahá'í International Community which collectively present a 'Bahá'í vision of global governance' are reviewed. It is suggested that globalization has put global governance on everybody's agenda. However, if global governance is to be successful, from a Bahá'í perspective, it cannot rely solely on new interests and institutions but also needs an infusion of new values such as unity, justice and consultation.

Bibliography

The Universal House of Justice. *Century of Light.* Thornhill, ON: Bahá'í Canada Publications, 2001.

References

1. While the first point is based on general observation, the second and third points are based on two new documents. The first of these is *Century of Light*, published Naw-Rúz 158 BE (2001) and prepared under the supervision of the Universal House of Justice. The second is a letter dated 19 April 2001 by the Department of the Secretariat of the Universal House of Justice to an individual believer and its accompanying memorandum by the Research Department of the Universal House of Justice.
2. The Universal House of Justice, *Century of Light*, p. 127.

Bahá'í Proposals for the Reformation of World Order

Jeffrey Huffines

In the canon of Bahá'í scripture and authorized texts, there are a number of fundamental principles and concepts that define a Bahá'í world view and identify future trends which forecast the development of human society and of the Bahá'í community within it. This world view is shaped by a teleological belief in the oneness of humanity that is at once a cardinal principle and an assertion of the ultimate goal of human existence on the planet.[1]

Bahá'í theology presupposes a linear flow of history that is defined by vast religious cycles[2], ages[3] and epochs[4] of which the contemporary global development plans[5] launched periodically by the Bahá'í World Centre give practical application. The Bahá'í writings embrace the language of a apocalyptic eschatology that anticipates not the end of time but the end of cycles, ages and epochs marked by distinct historic events and achievements. The metaphor of the human body is used to illustrate both the organic unity of the body politic and humanity's societal development as an organic process.[6] The life-cycle of childhood, adolescence and adulthood finds its parallel in humanity's successive establishment of the unity of family, of tribe, of city-state, of nation and, ultimately, of the world.[7]

The Prophet-Founders of the world's religions give to humanity teachings essential for the continued advance of civilization and the spiritual capacity to achieve it. Humanity is thus compelled to embrace ever higher stages of unity through a dialectical process of integration and disintegration, of divine retribution and redemption, of crisis and victory. The achievement of world unity, identified as the 'supreme mission' of the Revelation of Bahá'u'lláh, is considered to be the *sine qua non* of humanity's 'coming of age', whose ultimate outcome over the course of centuries will be the efflorescence of a world civilization.[8] Such overarching concepts as the 'Lesser and Most Great Peace'[9] and the 'Major and Minor Plans of God'[10] define the various stages and processes to be accomplished by humanity in the fulfilment of its destiny.

Integral to the fulfilment of this vision is the methodology to which these ends are to be achieved, namely the administrative principles and procedures upon which the processes of Bahá'í governance are based. These principles include strict adherence to the rule of law and to a rigid non-partisanship 'entirely dissociated from nationalistic ambitions, pursuits, and purposes' that prohibits members from either joining political parties or campaigning for public office; and the practice of a social activism that is non-violent and respectful of governmental authority.[11] Group unity and cohesion is maintained and strengthened through the practice of consultation, a form of non-adversarial decision-making that promotes consensus in the investigation of truth and in the discovery of solutions to problems, and by the regular election by secret ballot of local, national and international governing councils performed without nominations or campaigning.

The Bahá'í world view and its prophetic expectations of world unity both filter and mediate the believer's understanding of world events, shape the goals of the Bahá'í community adopted by its governing institutions and give substance to the public policy positions advocated by the Bahá'í International Community at the United Nations.

Bahá'í representatives have addressed institutional reform of the international political system before various fora on several occasions during the last century. This paper will offer a historical overview of selected Bahá'í proposals on the reformation of world order issued during the ministries of Bahá'u'lláh, 'Abdu'l-Bahá, Shoghi Effendi and the Universal House of Justice with a particular focus on a review of the UN reform proposals submitted by the Bahá'í International Community in 1955 and 1995.[12] Moreover, the evolution of US foreign policy and its contribution to the shaping of world order during the course of the last century will be considered from the historic and prophetic perspectives found in the writings of 'Abdu'l-Bahá and Shoghi Effendi. In conclusion, a word will be said about the evolving role of Bahá'í external affairs work in the engagement of those forces leading humanity to world peace.

Collective Security Proposals by Bahá'u'lláh and 'Abdu'l-Bahá

In 1867–8 Bahá'u'lláh wrote to various Heads of State, including Queen Victoria, to whom he enunciated the concepts of disarmament and collective security as being essential first steps to establishing world peace. He stated:

> O Kings of the earth! We see you increasing every year your expenditures, and laying the burden thereof on your subjects. This, verily, is wholly and grossly unjust . . . Be reconciled among yourselves, that ye may need no more armaments save in a measure to safeguard your territories and dominions . . . Be united, O Kings of the earth, for thereby will the tempest of discord be stilled amongst you, and your people find rest, if ye be of them that comprehend. Should any one among you take up arms against another, rise ye all against him, for this is naught but manifest justice.[13]

Not unlike the diplomatic conferences of the European powers that laid the basis for the nation-state system in Westphalia in 1648 and the development of the Congress system created in 1815 after the defeat of the Emperor Napoleon, a meeting of world leaders was called for by Bahá'u'lláh at which they would consult on establishing the conditions for an enduring peace.

'The time must come when the imperative necessity for the holding of a vast, an all-embracing assemblage of men will be universally realized,' Bahá'u'lláh wrote. He called for the establishment of collective security as a means of enforcing peace among nations. 'Should any king take up arms against another, all should unitedly arise and prevent him. If this be done, the nations of the world will no longer require any armaments, except for the purpose of preserving the security of their realms and of maintaining internal order within their territories.'[14]

Moreover, Bahá'u'lláh challenged parliamentarians worldwide to look beyond the immediate needs of just their constituents with the admonition: 'O ye the elected representatives of the people in every land! Take ye counsel together, and let your concern be only for that which profiteth mankind, and bettereth the condition thereof, if ye be of them that scan heedfully.'[15]

The silence on the part of the Heads of State in response to Bahá'u'lláh's appeals was deafening.

> 'From two ranks amongst men,' is His terse and prophetic utterance, 'power hath been seized: kings and ecclesiastics.' 'If ye pay no heed', He thus warned the kings of the earth, 'unto the counsels which . . . We have revealed in this Tablet, Divine chastisement will assail you from every direction . . . On that day ye shall . . . recognize your own impotence.'[16]

Bahá'u'lláh predicted the downfall of the absolute monarchies that then dominated much of Europe with the promise that even if the world's leaders did not respond to His message, no power on earth could prevent the mass of humanity from embracing those principles essential to the establishment of an enduring peace.[17] To this end, He laid a charge on the leaders and members of society alike. He wrote,

> 'Soon will the present day Order be rolled up, and a new one spread out in its stead . . . Now that ye have refused the Most Great Peace,' He, admonishing the kings and rulers of the earth, has written, 'hold ye fast unto this the Lesser Peace, that haply ye may in some degree better your own condition and that of your dependents.'[18]

Significantly, Bahá'u'lláh praised Queen Victoria for the abolition of slavery throughout her dominions and subsequently
praised 'the system of government which the British people have
adopted in London' because it is 'adorned with the light of both
kingship and of the consultation of the people'.[19]

At the age of 31, 'Abdu'l-Bahá applied His father's teachings
to address the abject social, economic and political conditions
then existing in Persia by publishing anonymously in 1875 a trea-
tise now known as *The Secret of Divine Civilization*. It outlined the
principles of sound governance required for the advancement of
civilization and specified those 'attributes of perfection' to be
possessed by ministers of state and elected representatives, considered by 'Abdu'l-Bahá to be second in rank in society only to
the Prophets of God themselves. Of these spiritual, inner qualities, 'Abdu'l-Bahá wrote, 'The spiritually learned must be
characterized by both inward and outward perfections; they must
possess a good character, an enlightened nature, a pure intent, as
well as intellectual power, brilliance and discernment, intuition,
discretion and foresight, temperance, reverence, and a heartfelt
fear of God'.[20]

'Abdu'l-Bahá amplified upon His father's call for a global convocation declaring that 'a certain number of distinguished and
high-minded sovereigns . . . shall . . . establish the Cause of
Universal Peace' by negotiating a 'binding treaty' to establish 'a
Union of the nations of the world'. 'Abdu'l-Bahá also endorsed
the enforcement of collective security adding that 'the limits and
frontiers of each and every nation should be clearly fixed, the
principles underlying the relations of governments towards one
another definitely laid down, and all international agreements
and obligations ascertained'.[21]

The International Peace Conference at the Hague

John Huddleston, in his books *Achieving Peace by the Year 2000* and
The Search for a Just Society, has summarized cogently the contri-
butions to the development of international law made by Hugo
Grotius, Jeremy Bentham, Immanuel Kant and others in the 18th

century and the subsequent emergence of the international peace movement that parallelled the diplomatic developments of the Congress system and of the Hague Convention during the 19th century.[22]

As foreshadowed by Bahá'u'lláh and 'Abdu'l-Bahá, the dawn of the approaching millennium at the end of the 19th century spurred the nations of the world to commence the first International Peace Conference held in 1899 at the Hague, convened by Czar Nicholas II of Russia and Queen Wilhelmina of the Netherlands. The conference resulted in the 1899 Hague Conventions and Declarations on the three themes of disarmament, the rules of war and the peaceful settlement of disputes between nations, including the establishment of a permanent Court of Arbitration. Huddleston observed that the Court 'was gravely hampered in practice because it had no compulsory authority and could only intervene in a dispute when invited to do so by the participants'.[23]

The Second Hague Peace Conference held in 1907 was largely initiated by citizen peace groups. Huddleston summarized, it 'had on its agenda rules of war on land and at sea, disarmament matters, some aspects of the procedures for investigating international disputes and, most interesting, a major effort on the part of the US government to strengthen the Court of Arbitration and to make its use compulsory'.[24] These conferences made historic advances in the development of international law, founded the Permanent Court of Arbitration and made seminal contributions to the establishment of the League of Nations and the Permanent Court of International Justice, both resident at the Hague. A Third Hague Peace Conference was proposed to convene in 1915 but never took place owing to the outbreak of the First World War.

'Abdu'l-Bahá's Travels to the West

During His travels throughout Europe and North America in 1911–12, 'Abdu'l-Bahá spoke and wrote extensively about the prerequisites for establishing world peace, the brilliant promise of the 20th century and of the destiny of nations endowed by Divinity to lead humanity to such a promised goal. In one widely circulated letter, 'Abdu'l-Bahá identified seven 'candles of unity' destined 'to come to pass' in the political realm, in world undertakings, in freedom, in religion, of nations, of races, and of language 'inasmuch as the power of the Kingdom of God will aid and assist in their realization'.[25] Significantly, 'Abdu'l-Bahá wrote, 'The fifth candle is the unity of nations – a unity which in this century will be securely established, causing all the peoples of the world to regard themselves as citizens of one common fatherland'.[26]

'Abdu'l-Bahá clearly viewed the United States to be uniquely capable of leading the world to embrace universal peace and, indeed, considered its leadership to be essential in the achievement of this goal. He also saw in the American form of federal government a model for world government. During His travels, 'Abdu'l-Bahá stated,

> May this American democracy be the first nation to establish the foundation of international agreement. May it be the first nation to proclaim the unity of mankind. May it be the first to unfurl the standard of the 'Most Great Peace' . . . The American continent gives signs and evidences of very great advancement. Its future is even more promising, for its influence and illumination are far-reaching. It will lead all nations spiritually.[27]

When a high federal official asked 'Abdu'l-Bahá as to the best manner in which he could promote the interests of his government and people, He responded, 'You can best serve your country if you strive, in your capacity as a citizen of the world, to assist in the eventual application of the principle of federalism, underlying the government of your own country, to the relationships now existing between the peoples and nations of the world.'[28]

While delivering a talk in New York, 'Abdu'l-Bahá was asked the question: 'Is it not a fact that universal peace cannot be accomplished until there is political democracy in all the countries of the world?' 'Abdu'l-Bahá answered,

It is very evident that in the future there shall be no centralization in the countries of the world, be they constitutional in government, republican or democratic in form. The United States may be held up as the example of future government – that is to say, each province will be independent in itself, but there will be federal union protecting the interests of the various independent states. It may not be a republican or democratic form. To cast aside centralization which promotes despotism is the exigency of the time. This will be productive of international peace. Another fact of equal importance in bringing about international peace is woman's suffrage.[29]

When 'Abdu'l-Bahá was in Montreal, a reporter from the *Montreal Star* asked Him, 'Are there any signs that the permanent peace of the world will be established in anything like a reasonable period?' 'Abdu'l-Bahá's answer was, as published in the *Montreal Star*, 'It will be established in this century. It will be universal in the twentieth century. All nations will be forced into it'.[30]

President Wilson's Fourteen Points Signalize the Dawn of the 'Most Great Peace'

It would seem that 'Abdu'l-Bahá's appeals for peace fell on deaf ears with the outbreak of World War I in 1914. Initially, the United States refused to take sides in what it considered a European war caused by the machinations of old world military alliances. However, 'Abdu'l-Bahá's words of 1912 appeared to have been prophetic a short five years later when President Wilson excited the world with his call for the establishment of a 'League for Peace' as an essential condition for US engagement in the war then raging in Europe.

In an address before the United States Senate in January 1917, President Wilson asserted that 'there must be, not a balance of power, but a community of power; not organized rivalries, but an organized common peace'. He concluded,

I am proposing . . . that the nations should with one accord adopt the doctrine of President Monroe as the doctrine of the world: that no nation should seek to extend its polity over any other nation or people, but that every people should be free to determine its own polity, its own way of development, unhindered, unthreatened, unafraid, the little along with the great and powerful. I am proposing that all nations henceforth avoid entangling alliances which would draw them into competitions of power; catch them in a net of intrigue and selfish rivalry, and disturb their own affairs with influences intruded from without. There is no entangling alliance in a concert of power. When all unite to act in the same sense and with the same purpose all act in the common interest and are free to live their own lives under a common protection.[31]

In his book *Diplomacy*, Henry Kissinger summarized:

Wilson asserted that the establishment of equal rights among states would provide the precondition for maintaining peace through collective security regardless of the power each nation represented. Wilson was proposing a world order in which resistance to aggression would be based on moral rather than on geopolitical judgements. Nations would ask themselves whether an act was unjust rather than whether it was threatening.[32]

The following year, in January 1918, President Wilson presented to the US Congress his plan for the post-war world, known as the Fourteen Points, that he wished to include in the Treaty of Versailles. Wilson argued for self-determination of liberated colonies, open diplomatic negotiations among all countries, and, most important, a League of Nations which would enforce liberal ideals and protect the peace.

'Abdu'l-Bahá wrote at the time, 'As to President Wilson, the fourteen principles which he hath enunciated are mostly found in the teachings of Bahá'u'lláh and I therefore hope that he will be confirmed and assisted'.[33]

The impact of Wilson's proposal on the imagination of the peoples of the world was immediate and electric. He was the star of the Peace Conference that convened in Paris between January and June 1919. H.G. Wells, in *The Shape of Things to Come*, wrote:

For a brief interval Wilson stood alone for mankind. Or at least he seemed to stand for mankind. And in that brief interval there was a very extraordinary and significant wave of response to him throughout the earth. So eager was the situation that humanity leapt to

9

accept and glorify Wilson – for a phrase, for a gesture. It seized upon him as its symbol. He was transfigured in the eyes of men. He ceased to be a common statesman; he became a Messiah. Millions believed him as the bringer of untold blessings; thousands would gladly have died for him. That response was one of the most illuminating events in the early twentieth century. Manifestly the World-State had been conceived then, and now it stirred in the womb. It was alive . . . And then for some anxious decades it ceased to stir.[34]

Shoghi Effendi reported that following the termination of the war, 'Abdu'l-Bahá 'stressed the cruel deception which [the Treaty of Versailles] held in store for an unrepented humanity. Peace, Peace, how often we heard Him remark, the lips of potentates and peoples unceasingly proclaim, whereas the fire of unquenched hatreds still smoulders in their hearts'.[35]

The tragic circumstances of President Wilson's failure to obtain the advice and consent of the US Senate is well known. Not only did the isolationist Senate refuse to allow the United States to join the League of Nations, it also denied ratification of the Treaty of Versailles, necessitating a separate peace with Germany. Despite this setback, Shoghi Effendi commented:

> To her President, the immortal Woodrow Wilson, must be ascribed the unique honour, among the statesmen of any nation, whether of the East or of the West, of having voiced sentiments so akin to the principles animating the Cause of Bahá'u'lláh, and of having more than any other world leader, contributed to the creation of the League of Nations – achievements which the pen of the Centre of God's Covenant acclaimed as signalizing the dawn of the Most Great Peace, whose sun, according to that same pen, must needs arise as the direct consequence of the enforcement of the laws of the Dispensation of Bahá'u'lláh.[36]

Tablet to the Hague

'Abdu'l-Bahá's letter of 17 December 1919 addressed to the Central Organization for a Durable Peace at the Hague provided Him an opportunity to comment upon the urgent matter of 'universal peace' following the immediate aftermath of World War I.

'Abdu'l-Bahá asserted that a 'Supreme Tribunal must be established, representative of all governments and peoples' to which 'questions both national and international' would be referred for final arbitration.[37] Moreover, 'Abdu'l-Bahá expounded upon the various teachings of Bahá'u'lláh that 'supplemented and supported' the establishment of universal peace, including the independent investigation of truth; the oneness of the world of humanity; religion as a cause of fellowship and love; the conformity of religion with science and reason; the elimination of religious, racial, political, economic and patriotic prejudices; the establishment of a universal language; the equality of women and men; the voluntary sharing of wealth; freedom from the struggle for existence; the advancement of divine civilization through religion and the promotion of universal education.

Regarding the League of Nations, 'Abdu'l-Bahá wrote: 'although the League of Nations has been brought into existence, yet it is incapable of establishing Universal Peace. But the Supreme Tribunal which His Holiness Bahá'u'lláh has described will fulfil this sacred task with the utmost might and power.' 'Abdu'l-Bahá then went on to describe how this Supreme Tribunal could be elected and confirmed by the parliaments and executives of the world with the decisions of the Tribunal enforced through a collective security pact.[38]

Manifest Destiny Reconsidered

Shoghi Effendi, the Guardian of the Bahá'í Faith from 1921 to 1957, wrote volumes of letters to the nascent Bahá'í communities during his 36-year ministry that elaborated considerably upon the Bahá'í vision of world unity.[39]

In those letters, Shoghi Effendi addressed the spiritual destiny of nations as well as of the world. In a letter dated 5 June 1947, and subsequently published under the title 'The Challenging Requirements of the Present Hour', Shoghi Effendi described the 'workings of two simultaneous processes . . . each clearly defined, each distinctly separate, yet closely related and destined to culminate, in the fullness of time, in a single glorious consummation'. He further elaborated:

One of these processes is associated with the mission of the American Bahá'í Community, the other with the destiny of the American nation.

The one serves directly the interests of the Administrative Order of the Faith of Bahá'u'lláh, the other promotes indirectly the institutions that are to be associated with the establishment of His World Order.[40]

Shoghi Effendi elaborated upon America's destiny by identifying a number of key events shaped by US foreign policy decisions that provided the impetus for the development of those international institutions and political alliances that now define the world's political order. These events included the outbreak of World War I and the formulation of President Wilson's Fourteen Points, the subsequent refusal by the US Senate to join the League of Nations, US engagement in World War II, the signing of the Atlantic Charter by the United States and Great Britain, the birth of the United Nations in San Francisco followed by its establishment in New York, the declaration of the Truman doctrine, and the submission to the UN General Assembly of the 'problem of the Holy Land' related to the establishment of the State of Israel.

Following the conclusion of World War II, the foundations were thus laid for the establishment of the United Nations, the North Atlantic Treaty Organization and the European Union. The Atlantic Charter, signed by President Franklin Roosevelt and Prime Minister Winston Churchill in August 1941, called for collective security, disarmament, self-determination, economic cooperation and freedom of the seas. Its principles were legally enforced through the establishment of the United Nations Charter in 1945. The declaration made by President Truman on 12 March 1947 before a joint session of Congress, that offered economic aid to Greece and Turkey in support of their nascent democratic institutions against the Communist insurgency, which came to be known as the Truman doctrine, paved the way for the establishment of the North Atlantic Treaty Organization in April 1949, the first permanent military alliance in the nation's history.

Another US foreign policy initiative announced by Secretary of State George Marshall in June 1947, passed by Congress ten months later as the European Recovery Act, offered unprecedented American economic and military assistance to the European countries that helped finance the economic and political integration of Europe. Together with the Bretton Woods agreements of July 1944, which established the International Monetary Fund to supervise and maintain global financial relations and the International Bank for Reconstruction and Development, popularly called the World Bank, to offer large-scale capital loans, the Marshall Plan provided over $12 billion in US aid to participating countries from 1948 to 1952.[41]

Together with his trenchant analysis of past and current events related to the destiny of America, Shoghi Effendi audaciously predicted the future course of events for both the United States and the world. For the United States, he stated that

> the great republic of the West, government and people alike, is itself, through experiment and trial, slowly, painfully, unwittingly and irresistibly advancing towards the goal destined for it by both Bahá'u'lláh and 'Abdu'l-Bahá.[42]

He concluded,

> Many and divers are the setbacks and reverses which this nation, extolled so highly by 'Abdu'l-Bahá, and occupying at present so unique a position among its fellow nations, must, alas, suffer. The road leading it to its destiny is long, thorny and tortuous. The impact of various forces upon the structure and polity of that nation will be tremendous. Tribulations, on a scale unprecedented in its history, and calculated to purge its institutions, to purify the hearts of its people, to fuse its constituent elements, and to weld it into one entity with its sister nations in both hemispheres, are inevitable.[43]

Moreover, Shoghi Effendi linked the ultimate destiny of America with nothing less than

> the political unification of the Eastern and Western Hemispheres, to the emergence of a world government and the establishment of the Lesser Peace, as foretold by Bahá'u'lláh and foreshadowed by the Prophet Isaiah. It must, in the end, culminate in the unfurling of the banner of the Most Great Peace, in the Golden Age of the Dispensation of Bahá'u'lláh.[44]

With the passing of Shoghi Effendi in 1957, the Bahá'í world community was abruptly deprived of the guiding hand of its beloved Guardian. His prescient analysis of past and current events and of future trends was infused with the authority given to him by virtue his appointment as Guardian. The Universal House of Justice, first elected in 1963, succeeded the Guardian as the head of the Bahá'í Faith in its role as the international legislative body authorized by Bahá'u'lláh to legislate on 'matters not expressly revealed' in the Bahá'í writings.[45] In a letter to an individual Bahá'í, the Universal House of Justice explained that 'beyond its function as the enactor of legislation, [it] has been invested with the more general functions of protecting and administering the Cause, solving obscure questions and deciding deciding upon matters that have caused difference'.[46]

Hence, the Bahá'í world community now looks to the elucidations[47] of the Universal House of Justice for guidance in understanding world affairs within a Bahá'í context. Although not invested with the function of immutable interpretation like that of the Guardian, the House of Justice has offered its commentary on current events with increasing frequency since its inception in 1963.

Following the UN action taken against Iraq after its invasion of Kuwait in August 1990, the Universal House of Justice wrote, 'The forces which united the remedial reactions of so many nations to the sudden crisis in this region demonstrated beyond any doubt the necessity of the principle of collective security prescribed by Bahá'u'lláh more than a century ago as a means of resolving conflict.' Liberated from the paralysis of the Cold War, the Security Council acted immediately to condemn unanimously the invasion of Kuwait and to demand an unconditional and immediate withdrawal of Iraqi forces. A total of 12 resolutions were passed by the Security Council from August to November 1990 that enforced an economic embargo and ultimately authorized UN members to 'use all necessary means' to bring about an Iraqi withdrawal after 15 January 1991. The following day forces from a 28-nation coalition launched bombing attacks in Iraq and Kuwait which met with remarkable success.

Despite questions about the intentions of the United States and the other permanent members of the Security Council being motivated primarily to counter the Iraqi threat to protect continued access to vital oil reserves, the Universal House of Justice was unequivocal in expressing what it considered to be the profound spiritual import of the action thus taken by the Member States of the UN. It asserted, 'While the international arrangement envisioned by Him for the full application of this principle is far from having been adopted by the rulers of mankind, a long step towards the behaviour outlined for the nations by the Lord of the Age has thus been taken.'[48]

Of the leadership role taken by the United States to enforce the UN Security Council resolutions, the House of Justice declared,

> In the call for a new world order, which has issued like a refrain from the statements of political leaders and influential thinkers, even when they themselves were incapable of defining their own meaning, can be discerned the slow awakening of humanity to the principal purpose of His Revelation. That such a call should have come so insistently from the head of that republic which is destined, in 'Abdu'l-Bahá's words, to be 'the first nation to establish the foundation of international agreement' and to 'lead all nations spiritually', is an indication of the efficacy and the acceleration of two simultaneous processes, one operating outside and one inside the Cause, which Shoghi Effendi tells us are destined to culminate 'in a single glorious consummation'.[49]

On every diplomatic front, whether it be in US payment of UN arrears; NATO expansion into Eastern Europe; the implementation by NATO of the Dayton Peace Accords in Bosnia; US mediation of the Middle East peace process; the US response to the Iraq crisis; the extension of NAFTA to the entire Western hemisphere by 2005; or the support of the IMF to assist in the alleviation of the South East Asian economic crisis, one may discern in the current course of events the 'slow, painful, unwitting and irresistible advance' of that process so perceptively elucidated by Shoghi Effendi.[50]

The Bahá'í International Community at the United Nations

The United Nations is the single most significant intergovernmental organization devoted to international peace and security, development and human rights. With 185 Member States, the UN comprises six main organs: the General Assembly, the Security Council, the Economic and Social Council (ECOSOC), the Trusteeship Council, the International Court of Justice and the Secretariat. These organs have various auxiliary bodies and numerous specialized agencies.

In the spring of 1947 the National Spiritual Assembly of the Bahá'ís of the United States and Canada was accredited to the United Nations as a national NGO qualified to be represented at United Nations conferences through an observer. A year later the eight NSAs then existing were recognized collectively as an inter-national NGO under the title of 'The Bahá'í International Community'.

On 9 May 1947 Shoghi Effendi, explained why he was encouraging Bahá'í association with the United Nations:

> He feels that the friends should bear in mind that the primary reason that he is encouraging Bahá'í association with the United Nations is to give the Cause due publicity as an agency working for and firmly believing in the unification of the human family and permanent peace, and not because he believes that we are at present in a position to shape or influence directly the course of human affairs! Also, he believes this association will afford the believers an opportunity of contacting prominent and progressive-minded people from different countries and calling the Faith and its principles to their attention. We should associate ourselves in every way with all movements of UN which are in accordance with our principles and objectives; but we should not seek to take the initiative or . . . focus a glare of publicity and public attention on a very wide scale upon ourselves which might prove very detrimental to our own interests.[51]

The work of the Bahá'í International Community (BIC) has grown steadily over the decades. The BIC encompasses and represents the membership of the Bahá'í Faith worldwide and has its headquarters in Haifa, Israel. Representing only eight National

Spiritual Assemblies in 1947, the BIC now represents 178 National Spiritual Assemblies with a grassroots membership numbering over five million. For the first two decades of its existence, the BIC was represented at selected UN conferences by part-time representatives who served in a volunteer capacity. Today, the United Nations Office, under the guidance of the Universal House of Justice, manages Bahá'í relations with the UN, primarily through its consultative relationship with ECOSOC obtained in 1970. The United Nations Office includes the Office of the Environment and the Office for the Advancement of Women. The BIC maintains UN Offices in New York and Geneva, where the UN Commission on Human Rights resides, and representations to UN regional commissions in Addis Ababa, Bangkok and Santiago, and to UN agencies in Nairobi, Rome and Vienna. Many national Bahá'í communities have developed relationships with UN agencies and other UN bodies in their countries, and these communities sometimes take part in international UN conferences and meetings.[52]

Bahá'í External Affairs Strategy

In 1994 the Universal House of Justice announced to the Bahá'í world an official external affairs strategy centring on the themes of human rights, global prosperity, the advancement of women and moral development. The House of Justice explained that the major channels for the execution of this strategy were National Spiritual Assemblies, with the BIC's United Nations Office in New York and Office of Public Information in Haifa to both coordinate and guide the work of the National Spiritual Assemblies. In particular, the United Nations Office was to coordinate the diplomatic work involving the management of relations with the UN and with governments and the Office of Public Information was to coordinate the management of relations with the public in general.

The memorandum on the external affairs strategy explained:

> The Lesser Peace anticipated by Bahá'u'lláh will, of course, be established by the nations themselves. It seems clear that two entities

will push for its realization: the governments of the world, and the peoples of the world through the instrumentality of the organizations of civil society. But to lend spiritual impetus to the momentum which that grand attainment will generate, the need for a Bahá'í strategy is evident. One of its expressions should be the exertion of a kind of leadership, principally a moral leadership, by coherently, comprehensively and continually imparting our ideas for the advancement of civilization, and this through a unified voice that because of the diverse composition of our community could come to be regarded as representative of the aspirations of the peoples of the world.[53]

Subsequently, the Bahá'í International Community's Office of Public Information released *The Prosperity of Humankind* in January 1995 for distribution at the World Summit for Social Development which took place in Copenhagen in March 1995. In August 1995 the United Nations Office released its statement *Turning Point for All Nations* on the occasion of the 50th anniversary of the United Nations.

In August 1997 the House of Justice announced to the National Spiritual Assemblies of the world the launching of its first coordinated programme of diplomatic work, the Human Rights Education Initiative, to coincide with the 50th Anniversary of the Universal Declaration of Human Rights in 1998. The House specified that

> The emphasis of the [BIC] United Nations Office . . . will be on the plans to be executed by your [National] Assemblies towards building effective relations with your governments and influencing official attitudes and policies on matters of global, rather than of strictly national importance . . . your concentration will be on promoting the interests of society as a whole . . .[54]

1955 BIC Proposal for UN Charter Revision

In 1955, during the first decade review of the UN Charter, and again in 1995, upon the 50th anniversary of the UN, the BIC submitted to the UN comprehensive recommendations for UN reform.[55] In May 1955 the BIC submitted to UN Secretary-General

Dag Hammarskjöld the 'Bahá'í Proposals to the United Nations for Charter Revision'. In somewhat apocalyptic terms, the BIC argued that 'no minor and legalistic adjustment of the Charter . . . can restore the supremacy of moral law in the conduct of human affairs nor seize control of events from the chaos which engulfs mankind'.[56]

The Bahá'í proposal of 1955 is notable for both its brevity and degree of specificity. It is essentially a legal brief offering specific language to amend nine of the 111 articles of the UN Charter with a call for the adoption of a UN Bill of Rights. In summary, the proposed Charter amendments give legal definition to the enforcement of collective security measures by authorizing the use of force to compel violator Member States to 'abide by the principles of the Charter' in the place of expulsion. Moreover, the proposed amendments would change the one member, one vote principle of the General Assembly into 'some form of proportionate representation' and would make that body more of an equal partner with the Security Council in the settlement of international disputes. Significantly, the permanent member status conferred upon five members of the Security Council would be eliminated with its attendant privileges, including permanent membership on the Military Staff Committee and, by implication, the veto power. Finally, the International Court of Justice would be given compulsory jurisdiction in all legal disputes between nations.[57]

These measures, by courageously tackling the politically sensitive issues of sovereignty, democratic representation and equal rights among nations and peoples, would transform the UN into a more effective international governing body.

1995 BIC Proposal for UN Institutional Reform

The 1995 submission, entitled *Turning Point for All Nations*, offers specific reforms for strengthening the legislative, executive and judicial functions of the UN. Moreover, the statement identifies four themes essential for the advancement of the individual and society and hence to be emphasized as part of the UN agenda, which include the promotion of economic development, the protection of human rights, the advancement of the status of women and the development of curricula for moral education in schools.

In the overview, the BIC reflects on the 'trend toward ever-increasing interdependence and integration of humanity' that has gained momentum over the last one hundred years, a 'trend observable in wide-ranging phenomena' in both its 'constructive and destructive expressions'. 'The trend is reflected, too, in steady efforts by the nations of the world to forge a world political system' as defined by the League of Nations and later by the United Nations. While acknowledging that the 'United Nations has blazed a bold path toward a future without war', the BIC recognizes that the UN has not lived up to its ideals and offers its proposals to strengthen the United Nations system. Moreover, the BIC commends the report of the Commission on Global Governance, entitled *Our Global Neighbourhood*, 'which argues for the widespread adoption of new values, as well as structural reforms in the United Nations system'.[58]

The Bahá'í International Community offered three initial propositions upon which its views were premised.

I. *The United Nations within the Broader Objective of the International Order*

First, discussions about the future of the United Nations need to take place within the broad context of the evolution of the international order and its direction. The United Nations has co-evolved with other great institutions of the late twentieth century. It is in the aggregate that these institutions will define – and themselves be shaped by – the evolution of the international order. Therefore, the mission, role, operating principles and even activities of the United Nations should be examined only in the light of how they fit within the broader objective of the international order.[59]

The establishment of the United Nations was premised on a State-centric model of governance. Today, the organization of regional groupings such as the European Union, the actions of multinational corporations and international trade, and the emergence of non-governmental organizations at the UN and on the international scene have transformed the international order since the establishment of the United Nations in 1945. Jessica T. Matthews, in her article 'Power Shift', 'describes a shift away from the state power – up, down, and sideways – to supra-state, sub-state, and above all, nonstate actors'.[60] Yet another mode of international governance, 'intergovernmentalism', has been identified recently by Anne-Marie Slaughter. According to this model,

> The state is not disappearing, it is disaggregating into its separate, functionally distinct parts. These parts – courts, regulatory agencies, executives, and even legislatures – are networking with their counterparts abroad, creating a dense web of relations that constitutes a new, transgovernmental order. Today's international problems – terrorism, organized crime, environmental degradation, money laundering, bank failure, and securities fraud – created and sustain these relations.[61]

These additional actors on the international scene are a major force compelling the United Nations to reform its institutions to meet the demands of a changing world.

2. *The Moral Foundation of the Universal Declaration of Human Rights*

> Second, since the body of humankind is one and indivisible, each member of the human race is born into the world as a trust of the whole. This relationship between the individual and the collective constitutes the moral foundation of most of the human rights which the instruments of the United Nations are attempting to define. It also serves to define an overriding purpose for the international order in establishing and preserving the rights of the individual.[62]

The adoption of the Universal Declaration of Human Rights (UDHR) by the UN General Assembly in 1948 was a watershed event in human history. The Declaration, taken together with the International Covenant on Civil and Political Rights and the Covenant on Social, Economic and Cultural Rights, form what is commonly known as the International Bill of Rights.

The worldwide Bahá'í community has historically been a strong supporter of UN human rights programmes and activities. As early as 1947, a major statement, 'A Bahá'í Declaration of Human Obligations and Rights', was presented to the UN Human Rights Commission.

In 1959 the BIC also endorsed officially the Convention on the Prevention and Punishment of the Crime of Genocide. When the UN established 10 December as Human Rights Day, national and local Bahá'í communities began planning commemorations and were often the only organizations observing the day. Over the years, the Bahá'ís have circulated the UDHR widely and have even assisted with the translating of the Declaration into a number of languages.[63]

In the *Bahá'í World 1996–97*, Matthew Weinberg writes,

> In a very real sense the international human rights regime is the fruit of an ongoing process of moral dialogue among diverse nations and peoples. More than establishing normative standards, the human rights discourse provides a mechanism for people of divergent convictions to learn about each other, resolve particular disagreements, and arrive at new understandings of what is possible for human beings. This cross-cultural enterprise, as evidenced by the increasing interaction among governments and organizations of civil society, has gradually given rise to a new ethos of human solidarity and collective responsibility. It has led to the adoption of new legal instruments that explicitly address the rights of women, children, and racial and religious minorities.[64]

The recently launched Human Rights Education Initiative by the BIC UN Office encourages National Spiritual Assemblies worldwide to 'become more actively involved in external affairs work and to strengthen their diplomatic skills by promoting human rights education during the United Nations Decade for Human Rights Education, 1995–2004'. The 50th anniversary of the adoption by the General Assembly of the UDHR was observed throughout 1998, culminating on UN Human Rights Day, 10 December 1998.

The ratification of the UN human rights covenants and conventions, the emergence of regional and global associations and intergovernmental bodies, and more recently the adoption of the UN Plans of Actions negotiated and agreed upon by participating nations at the UN world conferences have laid the legal foundations and institutional framework for a global society. A major task of the 21st century will be to strengthen and establish national and international institutions capable of implementing and enforcing these agreements.

3. *Universal Participation and World Citizenship*

> Third, the discussions about the future of the international order must involve and excite the generality of humankind. This discussion is so important that it cannot be confined to leaders – be they in government, business, the academic community, religion, or organizations of civil society. On the contrary, this conversation must engage women and men at the grass-roots level. Broad participation will make the process self-reinforcing by raising awareness of world citizenship and increase support for an expanded international order.[65]

In a very real sense, this has been the greatest accomplishment of the Bahá'í world community to date. The Bahá'í International Community represents over five million people who have embraced at the grassroots level a sense of world citizenship that empowers them to work cooperatively with others at every level of society with the faith and assurance that the forces of globalization can be harnessed for the betterment of society.

The 1990s witnessed a remarkable cycle of world conferences convened by the United Nations. Drawing on the best efforts of thousands of leaders and experts in many fields, the conferences – in New York, Rio de Janeiro, Vienna, Copenhagen, Cairo, Beijing, Istanbul and other venues – enabled governments to address some of the major developmental, economic, social and environmental problems of our time. At each conference, Member States demonstrated the political will to reach agreement on a series of landmark declarations and plans of action that established not only a basis for future work but also a standard by which the implementation of the commitments can be monitored and reviewed. These historic conferences achieved consensus on issues related to environment and development, human rights, population and development, social development, the advancement of women, on human settlements, and on the right to food.[66]

The UN system and governments at all levels are increasingly recognizing the critical role that NGOs play and the even larger role they could play in the affairs of society. At the international level, this recognition is reflected in the UN global plans of action. Since the Earth Summit, these plans have increasingly called for and further enlarged the notions of 'participation', 'involvement' and 'enlargement' of the general population in the development of society.

The participation of NGOs at the UN conferences, represented by tens of thousands of ordinary citizens throughout the world, signalizes a tectonic shift in the architecture of the international community. The Bahá'í International Community United Nations Office coordinated the participation of hundreds of Bahá'ís for each of these conferences. Moreover, the repeated gathering of Heads of State and foreign ministers reflects a unity of thought in world undertakings as foreseen by 'Abdu'l-Bahá at the turn of the century. In a letter written on 23 January 1995, the House of Justice commented,

> These events are as capstones to the myriad activities taking place in different parts of the world involving a wide range of non-governmental organizations and networks in an urgent search for values, ideas and practical measures that can advance prospects for the peaceful development of all peoples. In this endeavour can be discerned the gathering momentum of an emerging unity of thought in world undertakings, the realization of which our sacred scriptures describe as one of the lights of unity that will illumine the path to peace.[67]

Commenting on the participation of 250 friends from more than 40 countries at the World Summit for Social Development in Copenhagen in 1995, the House of Justice wrote,

> We applaud with heartfelt gratitude the Bahá'í institutions, agencies and individuals who produced this spate of action before, during and after the Summit, for surely it evinced both the further advance of our world community in influencing the processes towards the Lesser Peace and a multiplication of opportunities for a wider diffusion of the reformative Message of Bahá'u'lláh. As such world events take place with greater frequency and the Bahá'í community pursues its

goals with increased intensity, we can see more clearly the drawing closer together of the parallel processes about which Shoghi Effendi wrote several decades ago: the one leading to the political union of nations, the other to the ultimate union of hearts in one common faith.[68]

Specific Proposals for UN Legislative, Executive and Judicial Reform

Proposals for institutional reform of the UN system are offered that would strengthen its legislative, executive and judicial functions. The legislative proposals focus on the resuscitation of the General Assembly with five measures that include 1) enforcing minimum standards of conduct by governments as defined by the International Bill of Human Rights with unspecified consequences for Member States that violate these standards; 2) appointment of a special International Commission that would make recommendations for the resolution of all outstanding border disputes as a means of developing an early warning system to facilitate preventative diplomacy; 3) appointment of an expert Task Force to search for new financial arrangements to fund the UN, recognizing that 'voluntary payments from member states will never be a reliable approach to finance an international institution';[69] 4) appointment of a high-level Commission 'to begin careful study on the matter of an international auxiliary language and the adoption of a common script'[70] which will save the UN money from the costs of using six official languages and promote unity; 5) appointment of a Commission that will 'begin immediate exploration into the economic benefits and the political costs of a single currency and to hypothesize about an effective implementation approach'.[71]

Four measures are given to strengthen the executive functions of the UN Security Council and the Secretariat. 1) The BIC affirms its 1955 proposal to eliminate eventually permanent membership status and veto power exercised within the Security Council as confidence in the Council builds, with the recommendation that for now measures be introduced to curb the exercise of the veto power to reflect the original intention of the Charter, i.e. 'prevent the Security Council from authorizing military actions against a Permanent Member or requiring the use of its forces against its will'. 2) Creation of an International Force to support peace-keeping operations and to add credibility to resolutions of the Security Council that would reside with the Secretary-General under the authority of the Security Council and financed by the General Assembly. By doing so, an 'outright ban on all weapons of mass destruction'[72] could be made possible. 3) Apply the notion of collective security to other problems of the global commons including but 'not limited to international drug trafficking, food security, and the emergence of new global pandemics'.[73] 4) Retain successful UN institutions with independent executive functions, including UNICEF, the World Health Organization, the International Labour Organization, the International Civil Aviation Organization, the Universal Postal Union and the International Telegraph and Communications Union.

The proposals for strengthening the judicial function of the UN are focused on reform of the principal judicial organ of the United Nations, the International Court of Justice. For the long-term, the BIC affirms its 1955 proposal that 'the decisions of the World Court . . . become binding and enforceable upon all states'.[74] In the short-term, it is recommended that in addition to Member States, other organs of the UN should be given the right to bring cases before the Court and that the World Court act as an 'umbrella for existing and new thematic courts, that arbitrate and adjudicate international cases within specific thematic domains'[75] on such matters as commerce and transportation, international terrorism and drug trafficking, and in the proposals for such bodies as an International Criminal Court and a Chamber for Environmental Matters.

Recommendations for UN Programmatic Agenda

Another component of the 1995 report focused on defining various initiatives the United Nations could adopt to 'release the power of the individual' by promoting economic development, protecting fundamental human rights, advancing the status of women and emphasizing moral development. Under the theme of economic development, the BIC proposes the implementation of Agenda 21, the plan of action formulated at the Earth Summit, through the Bretton Woods institutions on a scale and level of commitment comparable to the Marshall Plan. The BIC calls for the strengthening of the machinery of the UN for monitoring and implementing human rights, beginning with the dramatic increase of resources assigned to the Centre for Human Rights; the universal ratification of international human rights treaties; and the prohibition of human rights violators from membership on the Commission on Human Rights and other monitoring agencies. Practical steps to advance the status of women include increasing the participation of women in Member State delegations; encouraging universal ratification of the conventions that protect women's rights and improve their status; and creating a monitoring system to prepare status reports on the implementation of the Beijing Platform for Action to be presented annually to the General Assembly, 'highlighting the top twenty and bottom twenty member states in terms of compliance'.[76] The BIC advocates a campaign to promote the development of curricula for moral education in schools worldwide.

To conclude, the BIC asserts that the 'formulation of a world government is at once the ultimate safeguard and the inevitable destiny of humankind'[77] and affirms that 'we have reached a turning point in the progress of nations',[78] with particular reference to its 1955 definition of world order based on the concept of a 'world Super-State' which will include an International Executive, a World Parliament and a Supreme Tribunal. The BIC echoes the call made by Bahá'u'lláh, 'Abdu'l-Bahá and more recently by the Universal House of Justice in its peace statement of 1985, by urging

> leaders at all levels to take a deliberate role in supporting a convocation of world leaders before the turn of this century to consider how the international order might be redefined and restructured to meet the challenges facing the world.[79]

The Hague Appeal for Peace and the UN Millennium Summit and General Assembly

Following the UN world conferences that took place from 1992 to 1996, many Member States were reluctant to authorize more international conferences. Some called it 'conference fatigue' while others viewed it as a conservative reaction against the increased influence of NGOs at the international and national levels. The UN General Assembly decided that the five-year reviews of the Plans of Action agreed upon at the world conferences would take place at special sessions of the General Assembly in either New York or Geneva with NGO participation necessarily limited by the venues of each location.

Two commemorative occasions, however, demanded an international response. These were the centennial of the first International Peace Conference held at the Hague in 1899 and the onset of the new millennium. In October 1997 the General Assembly approved a programme of action for the celebration of the centennial of the first International Peace Conference held at the Hague in 1899, as proposed by the Russian Federation and the Netherlands, which 'could be regarded as a third international peace conference' following the Hague peace conferences that took place in 1899 and 1907, respectively.[80] Moreover, in July 1997 UN Secretary-General Kofi Annan had recommended that a 'Millennium General Assembly' take place in the year 2000 to be accompanied by a companion 'People's assembly' for the purpose of articulating an animating vision for the UN in the 21st century.[81] In December 1998, the UN General Assembly adopted a resolution by which it decided to designate the 55th session of the General Assembly to be opened on 5 September 2000 as 'Millennium Assembly of the United Nations' and to convene a 'Millennium Summit of the United Nations' of Heads of State on 6 September 2000.

In contrast to the UN world conferences, governments were not being asked to negotiate legally-binding agreements nor were NGO forums officially incorporated into the proposed UN proceedings. The NGO community was determined, however, to use these occasions to maintain the momentum it had acquired to both influence and guide the policies and behaviour of governments through the UN.

In response to an appeal launched by the International Peace Bureau (IPB), the International Physicians for the Prevention of Nuclear War (IPPNW), the International Association of Lawyers Against Nuclear Arms (IALANA) and the World Federalist Movement (WFM), a broad coalition of NGOs organized the 'Hague Appeal for Peace' highlighted by a major international citizens' peace conference held 11–16 May 1999 in the Congress Centre at the Hague. This conference preceded the un-sponsored celebrations that took place 17–19 May, which were hosted by Her Majesty Queen Beatrix of the Netherlands, granddaughter of Queen Wilhelmina who hosted the 1899 conference, followed by a second centennial conference in the summer that took place at St Petersburg.

The news reports of war and civil strife in Kosovo, Kashmir and Sierra Leone overshadowed the centennial celebrations of the Hague Appeal for Peace that went largely unnoticed by the press. Over 10,000 participants from 100 countries representing different elements of civil society drafted and endorsed 'The Hague Agenda for Peace and Justice in the 21st Century', a set of 50 specific goals related to the four strands of the Hague Appeal. The goals of the Hague Appeal include strengthening international humanitarian and human rights laws and institutions; advancing the prevention, peaceful resolution and transformation of violent conflict; developing and linking disarmament efforts, including nuclear abolition; and identifying the root causes of war, and developing a culture of peace.[82] The Hague Appeal for Peace is an ongoing initiative that supports a number of other campaigns to promote peace education; to stop the use of child soldiers; to establish an International Criminal Court; to tackle the proliferation and misuse of small arms; to ban nuclear weapons; to ban landmines; to promote economic justice; to support women in peace building; to end genocide; to eliminate depleted uranium weapons; to oppose militarism and globalization; and to promote global action to prevent war.[83]

The UN centennial conferences at the Hague and at St

Petersburg featured expert papers and discussions on the themes of disarmament and arms control; humanitarian law and laws of war; and peaceful settlement of disputes. Participating legal experts agreed that faithful adherence to present international law rather than codification of new ones would yield the best results. A report from the Netherlands and Russia on the UN centennial proceedings and a letter from Bangladesh on the Hague Appeal for Peace agenda were adopted at the 54th session of the General Assembly in New York where the UN Decade for International Law closed in 1999.[84]

On 3 April 2000 Secretary-General Kofi Annan submitted to the UN General Assembly a report entitled 'We the Peoples: the Role of the United Nations in the 21st Century' in preparation for the Millennium Summit of world leaders at the UN in September 2000. The report outlined the main challenges facing the UN under three main headings: freedom from want, freedom from fear, and freedom of future generations to sustain lives on this planet. On a practical level, the report urges nations to cut in half by 2015 the proportion of people living in extreme poverty; ensuring that by 2015 all children complete primary education; reducing HIV infection rates for persons 15 to 24 years old by 25 per cent within ten years; and cancelling all official debts of the heavily indebted countries in return for those countries making demonstrable commitments to poverty reduction.[85]

The Bahá'í International Community played a leading role in helping to organize the Millennium Forum, a meeting that took place 22–6 May 2000 at UN Headquarters. About 1,350 NGO representatives from 106 countries participated in the gathering. On the final day of the Forum a statement entitled 'We the Peoples Millennium Forum Declaration and Agenda for Action' that spelled out a vision for a UN of the 21st century was adopted.[86] The Millennium Forum's work proceeded along six main themes: peace, security and disarmament; eradication of poverty; human rights; sustainable development and the environment; globalization; and the strengthening and democratization of the UN. Described as an action-oriented document, the Declaration calls for a UN

Global Poverty Eradication Fund to ensure that poor people have access to credit; the creation of a corps of at least 50 professionally-trained mediators for conflict prevention; the establishment of an international standing peace force; the creation of a Humanitarian Commission to assess humanitarian needs and recommend protective measures for civilian populations in times of armed conflict; and a second commission to devise ways to stop the technological development of new and more advanced weapons. The Declaration urges the UN to introduce binding codes of conduct for transnational corporations. Moreover, governments are urged to initiate a worldwide freeze on armed forces and a 25 per cent cut in production and export of major weapons and small arms, and to this end adopt an international code of conduct on arms exports. The NGOs also sought the creation and funding of a Global Civil Society Forum which would meet every two or three years.[87]

In the Millennium World Peace Summit of Religious and Spiritual Leaders held in August 2000, some one thousand religious leaders representing every major world religion gathered together for the first time at the UN to issue a declaration that called for peace, tolerance, equality and religious freedom. One week later, some 150 heads of state and government met in their largest gathering ever at the Millennium Summit to consult upon the theme 'The Role of the United Nations in the Twenty-First Century'. The proceedings included a special session of the UN Security Council that promised to strengthen peacemaking and peacekeeping, as well as four off-the-record roundtable discussions designed to allow world leaders in gatherings of 30 to 50 to exchange views freely.

The UN General Assembly adopted a values-based Millennium Declaration that affirmed its resounding support for the United Nations and its principles. The declaration emphasized certain fundamental values as 'essential to international relations in the twenty-first century', specifically freedom, equality, solidarity, tolerance, respect for nature and shared responsibility. The world leaders also adopted eight concrete goals to be achieved by 2015 in the promotion of universal primary education, gender equality, environmental sustainability, maternal health and development, and in the reduction of extreme poverty, child mortality, maternal health, HIV/AIDs, malaria and other diseases.[88]

A representative of the Bahá'í International Community, in his capacity as co-chair of the Millennium Forum, addressed the Summit on behalf of civil society at large where he presented the Millennium Forum Declaration and Agenda for Action. He emphasized the important role civil society has played in promoting positive social change, including support for the International Criminal Court, the movement for debt cancellation, and in the international campaign to ban landmines. He stated, 'We in civil society stand ready to work with you and your governments, side by side, in a strong new partnership to create this new world. At the same time, civil society stands ready to hold you to your commitments if you do not deliver on your words.'[89]

A major task of the world community in the 21st century will be to strengthen and augment national and international institutions capable of implementing and enforcing the international standards and norms developed by the UN. However, governments appear paralysed and unable to act on major institutional reforms. Moreover, far-reaching institutional change of the UN system will be difficult because it requires the broad support of Member States. Unfortunately, the record of the 20th century demonstrates that the establishment of new international institutions has occurred only after sudden and catastrophic events.

The proposals developed by the Hague Appeal for Peace and the Millennium Forum are necessarily addressed on the level of principle, as distinct from pure pragmatism. Despite the reluctance of governments to institute major reform on principle alone, the actions of regional intergovernmental groups, transnational business and labour, and NGOs on the international level are compelling the UN to reform itself to meet the demands of a changing world. This has been demonstrated in the development of new models of diplomacy based on the cooperation of numerous sectors of society to accomplish political objectives both inside and outside the UN system. The treaty to ban landmines, the statute creating the International Criminal Court and the World Court opinion on the illegality of nuclear weapons, together with the recent protests demanding major reforms of the World Trade Organization and Bretton Woods institutions, are examples of the 'new diplomacy' based on the growing partnership between governments and NGOs.

Bahá'í Global Plans of Action

During the last decade, the Bahá'í global plans of action have been shaped by an extraordinary prophecy written by Shoghi Effendi to the Bahá'ís of the world on 27 November 1954. He asserted that the completion of the administrative buildings of the Bahá'í World Centre would 'synchronize with two no less significant developments – the establishment of the Lesser Peace and the evolution of Bahá'í national and local institutions – the one outside and the other within the Bahá'í world'.[90] In 1987 the Universal House of Justice announced the commencement of a $200 million Arc Project to complete by 2000 the remaining buildings and decorative landscape of the Bahá'í World Centre as envisioned by 'Abdu'l-Bahá and Shoghi Effendi.[91] Despite the relative lack of financial resources and the chronic instability of the Middle East region, the conception and timing of the Arc Project was designed to coincide with the expectation of the imminent approach of the Lesser Peace anticipated by 'Abdu'l-Bahá to commence or occur by the end of the 20th century.

The Bahá'í World Centre and National Spiritual Assemblies worldwide have been engaged in intensive, systematic campaigns to expand the membership of the Bahá'í community, to improve the quality of its community life and leadership, to coordinate thematically and operationally its external relations programme and social and economic development projects, and to complete the Arc Project on Mount Carmel.

Conclusion

The response of the leadership and members of the Bahá'í community to the timing and ultimate realization of the Lesser

Peace is in itself a fascinating study beyond the scope of this paper. 'Abdu'l-Bahá's public pronouncements on world peace during His visits to Europe and North America (1911–13) have excited the hopes and fears of generations of Bahá'ís. The interpretation given to these pronouncements has in large part reflected the Zeitgeist of each generation, beginning with the rise and fall of expectations surrounding the circumstances that occurred before, during and after World Wars I and II; the dashed hopes surrounding the Cold War with its threat of nuclear holocaust; and the confusion confronting humanity at present as it enters a new millennium. One Bahá'í scholar has offered nine possible scenarios that could accelerate the change towards world unity by the end of the 20th century. These scenarios run the gambit from a visitation by extraterrestrials; the occurrence of natural disasters in the form of pandemic diseases, catastrophic breakdowns of the ecosystem, or an asteroid striking the earth; to man-made events of war or sudden enlightenment. The last scenario, that the 'Third Millennium will begin without a real peace' whose steps toward the Lesser Peace will be recognized only in retrospect by historians of the mid-21st century, reflects a realist view of contemporary events.[92]

The Bahá'í writings affirm that not only the Bahá'í community of professed believers but the entire human family and each of its constituent parts have essential roles to play in the achievement of the political and spiritual peace promised by humanity's sacred scriptures. According to the authorized interpreters of Bahá'í scripture, the establishment of political norms and structures necessary to ensure international peace will continue to be the primary responsibility of governments and other non-Bahá'í actors in society, with the Bahá'í community playing at most an ancillary advisory role. International legal norms have been largely established during the 20th century in response to the tragic loss of millions of lives in hundreds of violent conflicts great and small. Many of the fundamental social principles upheld by the Bahá'í Faith are now woven into the Charter of the United Nations, the Universal Declaration of Human Rights and numerous national constitutions and are accepted by the progressive elements of society. The task before the international community is the implementation and enforcement of those universal norms.

Regarding the emergence of the Lesser Peace, the Bahá'í community is not yet in a position to play a large role on the world scene. As the BIC and its national affiliates grow in their sophistication and ability in addressing the social problems confronting society without compromising either their moral integrity or social principles, Bahá'í communities will receive the increasing attention and solicitation of those responsible for the governance of society.

It is the adherence to moral principle in personal behaviour and in the conduct of public life that will ensure the development of a peaceful, progressive society. The Bahá'í praxis of politics shuns the pursuit of power and refuses to sacrifice principle for political expediency in the belief that the means must justify the ends if praiseworthy results are to endure. The Bahá'í principles of loyalty to government and adherence to the rule of law places a reciprocal responsibility upon rulers and citizens alike to uphold the highest standards of conduct without the distortion of partisan politics.

The Universal House of Justice offered the Bahá'í community as a 'model for study' in its 1985 peace statement. In contrast to the situational ethics practised by contemporary leaders of society who hesitate to acknowledge any direct link between public and private morality, the House of Justice asserts that the conduct of the Bahá'í electoral process 'portrays an aspect of that organic unity of the inner and outer realities of human life which is necessary to the construction of a mature society in this new Age'.[93] In a statement broadcast by satellite worldwide on the occasion of the Bahá'í World Congress in New York commemorating the hundredth anniversary of the passing of Bahá'u'lláh in 1992, the House of Justice declared,

> Let those seriously concerned about the state and fate of the world give due attention to the claims of Bahá'u'lláh. Let them realize that the storms battering at the foundations of society will not be stilled

unless and until spiritual principles are actively engaged in the search for solutions to social problems.[94]

It is within this context that the House of Justice advised the Bahá'í community of its role in the establishment of the Lesser Peace:

> Even though the establishment of the Lesser Peace is not dependent on any Bahá'í plan or action, and although it will not represent the ultimate goal humanity is destined to reach in the Golden Age, our community has a responsibility to lend spiritual impetus to the processes towards that peace . . . However short the path to peace, it will be tortuous; however promising the anticipated event that will set its course, it must mature through a long period of evolution, with its attendant tests, setbacks and conflicts, towards the moment when it will have emerged, under the direct influences of God's Faith, as the Most Great Peace. In the meantime, people everywhere will often face despair and bewilderment before arriving at an appreciation of the transition in progress. We who have been enlightened by the new Revelation have the sacred Word to assure us, a Divine Plan to guide us, a history of valour to encourage us. Let us therefore take heart not only from the Word we treasure, but also from the deeds of heroism and sacrifice which even today shine resplendent in the land in which our Cause was born.[95]

Bibliography

'Abdu'l-Bahá. *The Promulgation of Universal Peace.* Wilmette, IL: Bahá'í Publishing Trust, 1982.
— *The Secret of Divine Civilization.* Wilmette, IL: Bahá'í Publishing Trust, 1990.
— *Selections from the Writings of 'Abdu'l-Bahá.* Haifa: Bahá'í World Centre, 1978.
— 'Tablet to the Hague', in *Bahá'í Revelation, The.* London: Bahá'í Publishing Trust, 1955.
Annan, Secretary-General Kofi. *Renewing the United Nations: A Programme for Reform.* General Assembly Agenda Item 168, A/51/950, 16 July 1997.
Bahá'í International Community. *Human Rights Education [Manual]: An External Affairs Initiative.* Internal document, 1997.
— *The Prosperity of Humankind.* New York: Bahá'í International Community United Nations Office, 1995.

— *Turning Point for All Nations: A Statement of the Bahá'í International Community on the Occasion of the 50th Anniversary of the United Nations.* New York: Bahá'í International Community United Nations Office, 1995.

Bahá'í World, The. vol. 13. Haifa: The Universal House of Justice, 1970.

Bahá'í World, The. vol. 14. Haifa: The Universal House of Justice, 1974.

Bahá'u'lláh. *The Proclamation of Bahá'u'lláh.* Haifa: Bahá'í World Centre, 1967.

— *Tablets of Bahá'u'lláh revealed after the Kitáb-i-Aqdas.* Haifa: Bahá'í World Centre, 1978.

Baron, Robert C. (ed.). *Soul of America: Documenting Our Past 1492–1974,* Golden, CO: Fulrum, 1989.

Compilation of Compilations, The. Prepared by the Universal House of Justice 1963–1990. 2 vols. [Sydney]: Bahá'í Publications Australia, 1991.

Hatcher, William S., and J. Douglas Martin. *The Bahá'í Faith: The Emerging Global Religion.* San Francisco: Harper & Row, 1984.

Huddleston, John. *Achieving World Peace by the Year 2000.* Oxford: One World, 1988.

— *The Search for a Just Society.* Oxford: George Ronald, 1989.

Kissinger, Henry. *Diplomacy.* New York: Simon and Schuster, 1994.

Knock, Thomas J. *To End All Wars: Woodrow Wilson and the Quest for a New World Order.* New York: Oxford University Press, 1992.

Lee, Kathy. *Prelude to the Lesser Peace.* New Delhi: Bahá'í Publishing Trust, 1989.

'The Marshall Plan and Its Legacy', commemorative section, *Foreign Affairs,* May/June 1997, vol. 76, no. 3.

Matthews, Jessica T. 'Power Shift', *Foreign Affairs,* January/February 1997.

Ruhe, David. 'A New Evolution: Religious Bonding for World Unity', *Journal of Bahá'í Studies,* December 1994–March 1995, vol. 6, no. 4.

Shoghi Effendi. *The Advent of Divine Justice.* Wilmette, IL: Bahá'í Publishing Trust, 1990.

— *Citadel of Faith: Messages to America 1947–1957.* Wilmette, IL: Bahá'í Publishing Trust, 1965.

— *God Passes By.* Wilmette, IL: Bahá'í Publishing Trust, rev. edn. 1974.

— *Messages to the Bahá'í World.* Wilmette, IL: Bahá'í Publishing Trust, 1971.

— *World Order of Bahá'u'lláh.* Wilmette, IL: Bahá'í Publishing Trust, 1991.

Slaughter, Anne-Marie. 'The Real New World Order', *Foreign Affairs,* September/October 1997.

The Third Epoch of the Formative Age. Geoffrey Marks (comp.).Wilmette, IL: Bahá'í Publishing Trust, 1996.

UN Briefing Papers. 'The World Conferences: Developing Priorities for the 21st Century'. New York: United Nations, Department of Public Information, 1997.

The Universal House of Justice. *The Four Year Plan.* Riviera Beach, FL: Palabra Publications, 1996.

— Individual Rights and Freedoms in the World Order of Bahá'u'lláh. Wilmette IL: Bahá'í Publishing Trust, 1989.

— Letter to National Spiritual Assemblies, 10 October 1994, with attached External Affairs Strategy, 19 September 1994, prepared by an Ad Hoc Committee and approved by the Universal House of Justice. Internal document.

— Letter to National Spiritual Assemblies, 11 August 1997. Internal document.

— *Messages from the Universal House of Justice 1963–1986: The Third Epoch of the Formative Age.* Wilmette, IL: Bahá'í Publishing Trust, 1996.

— *The Promise of World Peace.* London: Bahá'í Publishing Trust, 1985.

— Riḍván 152 Message to the Bahá'ís of the World.

— Statement of the Universal House of Justice to the Bahá'ís of the World, 29 November 1992.

— *Wellspring of Guidance 1963–1968.* Wilmette, IL.: Bahá'í Publishing Trust, 1976.

Weinberg, Matthew. 'The Human Rights Discourse: A Bahá'í Perspective', *The Bahá'í World 1996–97.* Haifa, Israel: World Centre Publications, 1997.

Wilson, Woodrow. 'Address to the United States Senate', 22 January 1917, in Baron, *Soul of America: Documenting Our Past 1492–1974.* Golden, CO: Fulrum, 1989.

The World Commission on Environment and Development. *Our Common Future.* Oxford: Oxford University Press, 1987.

Zohoori, Elias, *Names and Numbers: A Bahá'í History Guide.* Jamaica: Caribbean Printers Limited, 1990.

References

1. 'The principle of the Oneness of Mankind, as proclaimed by Bahá'u'lláh, carries with it no more and no less than a solemn assertion that attainment to this final stage in this stupendous evolution is not only necessary but inevitable, that its realization is fast approaching, and that nothing short of a power that is born of God can succeed in establishing it.' Shoghi Effendi, *World Order*, p. 43.

2. 'CYCLE A unit of time comprising the Dispensations of numerous consecutive Manifestations of God. For example, the Adamic, or Prophetic, Cycle began with Adam and ended with the Dispensation of Muḥammad. The Bahá'í Cycle began with the Báb and is to last at least five hundred thousand years.' *Messages from the Universal House of Justice 1963–1986*, Glossary, p. 738.

3. 'AGES The Bahá'í Dispensation is divided into three Ages: the Heroic, Formative, and Golden Ages. The Heroic Age, also called the Apostolic or Primitive Age, began in 1844 with the Declaration of the Báb and spanned the ministries of the Báb (1844–53), Bahá'u'lláh (1852–92), and 'Abdu'l-Bahá (1892–1921) . . . The Formative Age, also known as the Age of Transition or the Iron Age, began in 1921 when Shoghi Effendi, according to instructions in 'Abdu'l-Bahá's Will and Testament, became the Guardian of the Cause of God and began to build Bahá'u'lláh's Administrative Order. The Formative Age is the second and current Age; it is to be followed by the third and final Age, the Golden Age destined to witness the proclamation of the Most Great Peace and the establishment of the Bahá'í World Commonwealth.' ibid. pp. 730–1.

4. 'EPOCHS Major units of time used to mark the unfoldment of ['Abdu'l-Bahá's] Divine Plan and the Formative Age.' ibid. p. 740.

5. 'PLANS Refers to the courses of action devised by Shoghi Effendi and, later, by the Universal House of Justice for expanding and consolidating the Bahá'í Faith within the framework of 'Abdu'l-Bahá's Divine Plan.' ibid. p. 750.

6. See Bahá'í International Community, *The Prosperity of Humankind*, p. 5.

7. 'Unification of the whole of mankind is the hall-mark of the stage which human society is now approaching. Unity of family, of tribe, of city-state and nation have been successively attempted and fully established. World unity is the goal towards which a harassed humanity is striving. Nation-building has come to an end. The anarchy inherent in state sovereignty is moving towards a climax. A world, growing to maturity, must abandon this fetish, recognize the oneness and wholeness of human relationships, and establish once for all the machinery that can best incarnate this fundamental principle of its life.' Shoghi Effendi, *World Order*, p. 202.

8. 'The Revelation of Bahá'u'lláh, whose supreme mission is none other but the achievement of this organic and spiritual unity of the whole body of nations, should, if we be faithful to its implications, be regarded as signalizing through its advent the *coming of age of the entire human race*. It should be viewed not merely as another spiritual revival in the ever-changing fortunes of mankind, not only as a

further stage in a chain of progressive Revelations, nor even as the culmination of one of a series of recurrent prophetic cycles, but rather as marking the last and highest stage in the stupendous evolution of man's collective life on this planet. The emergence of a world community, the consciousness of world citizenship, the founding of a world civilization and culture – all of which must synchronize with the initial stages in the unfoldment of the Golden Age of the Bahá'í Era – should, by their very nature, be regarded, as far as this planetary life is concerned, as the furthermost limits in the organization of human society, though man, as an individual, will, nay must indeed as a result of such a consummation, continue indefinitely to progress and develop.' Shoghi Effendi, *World Order*, p. 163.

9. 'LESSER PEACE The first of two major stages in which Bahá'ís believe peace will be established. The Lesser Peace will come about through a binding treaty among the nations for the political unification of the world.' *Messages from the Universal House of Justice 1963–1986*, Glossary, pp. 745–6.

'MOST GREAT PEACE The second of two major stages in which Bahá'ís believe peace will be established. The Most Great Peace will be the practical consequence of the spiritualization of the world and the fusion of all its races, creeds, classes, and nations. It will rest on the foundation of, and be preserved by, the ordinances of God.' ibid. p. 747.

10. 'MAJOR PLAN OF GOD God's plan for humanity that is tumultuous and mysterious in its progress. Its purpose in this cycle is to unify the human race and to establish the Kingdom of God on earth.' ibid. p. 746

'MINOR PLAN OF GOD The part of God's Plan that is revealed by Bahá'u'lláh to His followers and is laid out for them in detailed instructions and successive plans by 'Abdu'l-Bahá, Shoghi Effendi, and the Universal House of Justice. In contrast to the Major Plan of God, it proceeds in a methodical, ordered way, disseminating His teachings and raising up the structure of a united world society.' ibid. p. 747.

'We are told by Shoghi Effendi that two great processes are at work in the world: the great plan of God, tumultuous in its progress, working through mankind as a whole, tearing down barriers to world unity and forging humankind into a unified body in the fires of suffering and experience. This process will produce, in God's due time, the Lesser Peace, the political unification of the world. Mankind at that time can be likened to a body that is unified but without life. The second process, the task of breathing life into the unified body – of creating true unity and spirituality culminating in the Most Great Peace – is that of the Bahá'ís, who are labouring consciously, with detailed instructions and continuing Divine guidance, to erect the fabric of the Kingdom of God on earth, into which they call their fellowmen, thus conferring upon them eternal life.' The Universal House of Justice, *Wellspring*, pp. 133–4. See also *Messages from the Universal House of Justice*, pp. 126–7.

11. Shoghi Effendi, *World Order*, p. 198.

12. The ministries of the Báb (1844–50) and Bahá'u'lláh (1863–92), the twin Prophet-Founders of the Bahá'í Faith, were succeeded, respectively, by the ministries of the son and great-grandson of Bahá'u'lláh, 'Abdu'l-Bahá (1892–1921) and Shoghi Effendi (1921 –57). The Bahá'í community is led currently by an international council, the Universal House of Justice, which has been elected every five years since 1963. For more information, see Hatcher and Martin, *The Bahá'í Faith: The Emerging Global Religion*.

13. Bahá'u'lláh, *Proclamation of Bahá'u'lláh*, pp. 12–13.

14. ibid. p. 115.

15. ibid. p. 67.

16. Shoghi Effendi, *God Passes By*, p. 230.

17. Deposed monarchies include the Habsburg, Hohenzollern, Ottoman and Romanov dynasties. For a description of the sovereigns addressed by Bahá'u'lláh, see *Bahá'í World*, vol. 14, pp. 196–204. For a list of 23 monarchies deposed between 1870 and 1979, see Zohoori, *Names and Numbers*, p. 38.

18. Shoghi Effendi, *World Order*, pp. 161–2.

19. Bahá'u'lláh, *Tablets*, p. 93.

20. 'Abdu'l-Bahá, *Secret of Divine Civilization*, pp. 33–4.

21. ibid. pp. 64–5.

22. Huddleston, *Achieving Peace by the Year 2000*.

23. ibid. pp. 101–2.

24. ibid. p. 102.

25. 'Abdu'l-Bahá, quoted in Shoghi Effendi, *World Order*, p. 39.

26. ibid.

27. ibid. pp. 75–6.

28. 'Abdu'l-Bahá, quoted in Shoghi Effendi, *Advent of Divine Justice*, p. 88.

29. 'Abdu'l-Bahá, *Promulgation*, p. 167.

30. 'Abdu'l-Bahá, quoted in *Compilation*, vol. 2, p. 171.

31. Wilson, 'Address to the United States Senate', 22 January 1917 in *Soul of America*, p. 329.

32. Kissinger, *Diplomacy*, p. 227.

33. 'Abdu'l-Bahá, *Selections*, p. 311.

34. H.G. Wells, quoted in Knock, *To End All Wars*, p. 1.
35. 'Abdu'l-Bahá, quoted in Shoghi Effendi, *World Order*, pp. 29–30.
36. Shoghi Effendi, *Citadel*, p. 36.
37. 'Abdu'l-Bahá, *Selections*, p. 249.
38. 'Abdu'l-Bahá, 'Tablet to the Hague', in *The Bahá'í Revelation*, p. 215.
39. Lee, *Prelude to the Lesser Peace*. Ms. Lee identified through an analysis of Shoghi Effendi's letters 14 characteristics of the Lesser Peace, 20 characteristics of the Bahá'í Commonwealth, eight objectives of the Formative Age and seven stages of the development of the Bahá'í community. See pp. 89, 17, 32, 21.
40. Shoghi Effendi, *Citadel*, p. 32.
41. 'The Marshall Plan and Its Legacy', commemorative section, *Foreign Affairs*, May/June 1997, vol. 76, no.3, pp. 159–221.
42. Shoghi Effendi, *Citadel*, p. 31.
43. ibid. pp. 36–7.
44. ibid. p. 33.
45. 'From these statements it is made indubitably clear and evident that the Guardian of the Faith has been made the Interpreter of the Word and that the Universal House of Justice has been invested with the function of legislating on matters not expressly revealed in the teachings.' Shoghi Effendi, *World Order*, pp. 149–50.
46. *Messages from the Universal House of Justice 1963–1986*, p. 157.
47. The Universal House of Justice, Riḍván Message, 1991.
48. ibid.
49. ibid.
50. See Secretary of Secretary of State Madeleine K. Albright's Statement before the Senate Foreign Relations Committee, Washington DC, 10 February 1998 as released by the Office of the Spokesman, US Department of State <secretary.state.gov/www/statements/1998>.
51. *Bahá'í World*, vol. 13, pp. 785–6.
52. Bahá'í International Community, *Human Rights Education*.
53. Letter of the Universal House of Justice to National Spiritual Assemblies, 10 October 1994, with attached External Affairs Strategy, 19 September 1994, prepared by an Ad Hoc Committee and approved by the Universal House of Justice. Internal document.
54. Letter of the Universal House of Justice, 11 August 1997 to National Spiritual Assemblies. Internal document.
55. In October 1985 the Universal House of Justice addressed for the first time the 'peoples of the world' in a statement entitled *The Promise of World Peace*, as its contribution to the observance of the

United Nations 1986 International Year of Peace. The peace statement, distributed to Heads of State by National Spiritual Assemblies worldwide, presents the fundamental principles of the Bahá'í peace programme.

56. Letter of the Bahá'í International Community to Dag Hammarskjöld, Secretary-General of the United Nations, 23 May 1955, in *Bahá'í World*, vol. 13, p. 796.

57. The Bahá'í proposals of 1955 offered specific recommendations to amend Articles 6, 12, 18, 23, 27, 35, 47, 50 and 53 as well as calling for the adoption of a UN Bill of Rights. Article 6, which authorizes the General Assembly to expel violator Members from the UN upon the recommendation of the Security Council, would be amended to 'subject' violators to 'economic and other sanctions, and, in extreme cases . . . compelled by force to abide by the principles of the Charter'. Article 12, which prohibits the General Assembly from making any recommendations on disputes being considered by the Security Council, would be eliminated entirely. The one member, one vote principle of the General Assembly enshrined in Article 18(1) would be changed 'according to some form of proportionate representation'. The status of the five permanent members of the Security Council mandated in Article 23 would be eliminated and the membership of the Security Council would be reduced from 15 to 11 members. Decisions of the Security Council made by an affirmative vote of nine members as stipulated by Article 27(2) would be reduced to seven members with the additional amendment that a party to any dispute being considered by the Security Council shall abstain from voting. The membership of the Military Staff Committee established by Article 47 would no longer be confined to the five permanent members of the Security Council but would include all members of the Security Council in office at that time. All references to enemy states that reflected the circumstances of WWII would be eliminated. Article 35 of the 'Statute of the International Court of Justice' would be amended to give the Court compulsory jurisdiction in all legal disputes between states. See *Bahá'í World 1954–1963*, pp. 795–802.

58. Bahá'í International Community, *Turning Point for All Nations*, pp. 1– 3. See also The World Commission on Environment and Development, *Our Common Future*.

59. Bahá'í International Community, *Turning Point For All Nations* , p. 3.

60. Slaughter, 'The Real New World Order', *Foreign Affairs*, Sept./Oct. 1997, p. 183. See Matthews, 'Power Shift', *Foreign Affairs*, January/February 1997.

61. Slaughter, 'The Real New World Order', *Foreign Affairs*, Sept./Oct. 1997, p. 184.
62. Bahá'í International Community, *Turning Point for All Nations*, p. 4.
63. Bahá'í International Community. *Human Rights Education*.
64. Weinberg, 'The Human Rights Discourse: A Bahá'í Perspective', *Bahá'í World 1996–97*, p. 257.
65. Bahá'í International Community, *Turning Point for All Nations*, p. 4.
66. UN Briefing Papers, *The World Conferences: Developing Priorities for the 21st Century*, p. v.
67. Letter of the Universal House of Justice to National Spiritual Assemblies, 23 January 1995, accompanying *The Prosperity of Humankind*.
68. The Universal House of Justice, Riḍván Message 152 [1995].
69. Bahá'í International Community, *Turning Point for All Nations*, p. 9.
70. ibid. pp. 9–10.
71. ibid. p. 10.
72. ibid. p. 11.
73. ibid.
74. ibid. p. 13.
75. ibid.
76. ibid. p. 20.
77. ibid. p. 6.
78. ibid. p. 21.
79. ibid. p. 4.
80. The resolution notes that 'The year 1999 is a special one from the point of view of international law in general, and the Hague law in particular. It marks not only the centennial of the 1899 Hague Peace Conference and the resulting Conventions and Declarations, but also the fiftieth anniversary of the four Geneva Conventions for the protection of victims of war in 1949 and the closure of the UN Decade of International Law. The year 1999 will also see the 27th International Conference of the Red Cross and the Red Crescent.' General Assembly resolution A/C.6/52/3, 15 October 1997.
81. Secretary-General Kofi Annan, *Renewing the United Nations: A Programme for Reform*. General Assembly Agenda Item 168, A/51/950, July 16, 1997.
82. For more information on the *Hague Appeal for Peace*, see the website <www.haguepeace.org>.
83. See web sites to promote peace education <www.ipb.org>; to stop the use of child soldiers <www.child-soldiers.org>; to establish an International Criminal Court <www.iccnow.org>; to tackle the proliferation and misuse of small arms <www.iansa.org>; to ban

nuclear weapons <www.abolition2000.org>; to ban landmines <www.icbl.org>; to promote economic justice <www.libertynet.org/kwru>; to support women in peace building <www.international-alert.org/women>; to end genocide <www.endgenocide.org>; to eliminate depleted uranium weapons <mtpdu@ime.net>; to oppose militarism and globalization <sstables@canadians.org>; and to promote global action to prevent war <globalactionpw@idds.org>.

84. Report from the Netherlands and Russia on the Centennial Celebrations of the First International Peace Conference A/54/381; Letter from Bangladesh on the agenda adopted by the Hague Appeal for Peace Conference A/54/98.

85. For a copy of the Millennium Report of the UN Secretary-General see <www.un.org/millennium/sg/report/summ.htm>.

86. For a copy of the *We the Peoples Millennium Forum Declaration and Agenda for Action* see <www.millenniumforum.org>.

87. See Inter Press News Service 'Terraviva' Daily Journal, vol. 8, no. 97, 30 May 2000 at <www.millenniumforum.org>.

88. For a copy of the Millenium Declaration, see the United Nations web site at <www.un.org/millenium/declaration/ares552e.htm>.

89. For a copy of the statement to the Millenium Summit from the Co-Chair of the Millenium Forum, see the One Country web site at <www.onecountry.org/e121/MF_Speech_to_Millennium_Summit.htm>

90. Written in 2000.

91. Shoghi Effendi, 'Administrative Seats of Divinely Appointed Institutions', 27 November 1954, *Messages to the Bahá'í World*, p. 74.

92. The 19-terraced hanging gardens on the slope of Mount Carmel facing Haifa Bay and the three new administrative buildings were formally opened in May 2001. The approximate cost was $300 million.

93. Ruhe, 'A New Evolution: Religious Bonding for World Unity', *The Journal of Bahá'í Studies*, December 1994 – March 1995, vol. 6, no. 4, pp. 45–57.

94. The Universal House of Justice, *Individual Rights and Freedoms*, p. 10.

95. Statement of the Universal House of Justice to the Bahá'ís of the World, 29 November 1992.

96. The Universal House of Justice, Riḍván Message 1996.

The Establishment of the Lesser Peace

Babak Bahador

The ultimate completion of this stupendous undertaking (the building of the Arc on Mount Carmel) . . . will synchronize with two no
less significant developments – the establishment of the Lesser Peace
and the evolution of the Bahá'í national and local institutions . . .

Shoghi Effendi[1]

At the conclusion of these four eventful years, we have arrived at a
portentous convergence of ends and beginnings in measures of
Gregorian time and the Bahá'í era. In one instance, this convergence
entails the wrapping up of the twentieth century and, in the other,
opens a new stage in the unfolding of the Formative Age. The perspective from these two frames of time prompts us to reflect on a
vision of world-shaping trends that have synchronized, and to do so
in the context of the insight so graphically projected by Shoghi
Effendi at the inception of the Arc he conceived.

The Universal House of Justice[2]

To the Bahá'í world community, the Lesser Peace has been a
subject of much fascination and speculation over the last decades
of the 20th century. The fascination is due to the fact that it
promises to fuse monumental global processes with divine

prophecy. The speculation relates to the details of exactly how and when it may or has been inaugurated. There are numerous references scattered throughout the writings that refer to the overall historical process that will lead to the Most Great Peace. While many publications[3] have attempted to gather relevant quotes or explain the path to peace, there still seems to be some confusion over the matter in the wider Bahá'í community. Uncertainty exists as to which elements of the vision are part of the initiation of the Lesser Peace process,[4] which are relevant to the longer process itself and which belong within the realm of the Most Great Peace. There is also confusion over how all of the different references fit into a coherent pattern and whether a time frame can be assigned to the overall process and its component elements. Furthermore, there is confusion as to how the Lesser Peace correlates to the events and patterns of the international socio-political arena at the beginning of the 21st century.

This paper will attempt to provide some clarification on the Lesser Peace and explain how it can be understood in light of international affairs at the turn of the third millennium in the Gregorian calendar. It should be noted at the outset that this is only one individual's interpretation of the Lesser Peace. The only advantage that this paper may have over previous attempts to deal with this subject, many of which were published in the 1980s, is that of hindsight. This benefit, of course, could become a liability with time and make the interpretative aspects of this paper rapidly obsolete.[5] To limit this possibility, an attempt is made to rely as much as possible on the Bahá'í writings.[6] The Bahá'í writings, within a Bahá'í scholarly forum, are the equivalent of scientifically established facts within greater academia and the basis upon which subsequent thinking should ultimately flow. It is with this basic assumption that this paper begins.

There is another assumption that is fundamental to this paper. This is that there are two aspects to the Lesser Peace, its underlying condition and its outward manifestations. By 'condition', I mean a commonly accepted collective feeling, norm or understanding about the context. The German word *Zeitgeist*, which means the 'spirit of the time', perhaps best captures this idea.

47

By 'outward manifestations' I mean specific events or activities that may be pointed to as proof of the underlying condition. This distinction, I believe, is one tool that can assist in clearing some of the aforementioned confusion. To clarify this distinction further with examples, let us examine the conditions and outward manifestations of the second half of the 20th century in international affairs. During the period between 1945 and 1989 (the Cold War), the condition of international affairs was one of hostility between the US and USSR and their respective allies. The outward manifestations of this condition were the build-up of armaments and numerous proxy wars around the world whose belligerents were supported by these opposing sides. The decade following the Cold War, on the other hand, was marked by a condition of relatively friendly relations between these former adversaries. Its outward manifestations included a reduction in armament spending, increasing levels of cooperation and a virtual elimination of support for such proxy wars.

In conducting this study, the essay has been divided into three sections. The first sets the general context by elaborating on the assumption upon which the paper ultimately rests – that monumental historic change such as the Lesser Peace is initiated by a change in condition. The second section presents the thoughts of three leading international relations theorists on the unique condition that has emerged in world affairs in the post Cold War era. These thinkers – Fukuyama, Mandelbaum and Cooper – through their unique perspectives suggest that the international arena has entered a new and unprecedented condition. The third section links these new circumstances to the Bahá'í concept of the Lesser Peace. It also attempts to outline how the concept of the Lesser Peace has developed over the course of Bahá'í history. This is done in four subsections that organize the relevant writings of Bahá'u'lláh, 'Abdu'l-Bahá, Shoghi Effendi and the Universal House of Justice, respectively, on the Lesser Peace. In each of the subsections, the focus is largely on writings that specifically mention the term 'Lesser Peace', those that have elaborated on these specific writings and those that have subsequently been directly linked to the Lesser Peace.[7] In outlining these writings, an attempt is made, whenever possible, to distinguish the condition of the Lesser Peace from its outward manifestations.

Section 1: The Relationship between Underlying Condition and Outward Manifestations

In all societies, unwritten rules of conduct or norms exist. The legislation and enforcement of these norms in modern constitutional systems of government, it can be argued, is only the formalization of a conscious understanding that already exists and a means by which to control the minority who violate them.[8] The same case has also been argued in the context of international relations, where an international society with its own norms on state behaviour is claimed to exist.[9] While certain norms have remained constant for centuries, others have changed over time.[10] Slavery, for example, was a commonly accepted practice that lost its moral legitimacy throughout most of the world in the 19th century.[11] When a normative change is significant, there is often a interim between an understanding, which may be consciously practised, and the actual passage of that understanding into formal and enforceable law. This is particularly the case in international law, where current mechanisms for passing and enforcing laws are often cumbersome and easily susceptible to political manipulation.

Domestic and international laws are, thus, not born in a vacuum but are functions of socio-political processes and transformations that their adoption symbolizes.[12] Of course, there is also an antithesis to this argument that should be taken into account.[13] However, the point of significance in regard to the Lesser Peace is that there may often appear a conscious understanding about relations between nations that is not legislated and institutionalized for some time. This may be due to a number of reasons, such as the need to appease the domestic political concerns of major powers, fear of setting precedents that may limit future foreign policy options, or a number of other political considerations. However, it is important at the outset of this paper to be aware that not all international legal norms are formally established in binding legislation.

Section 2: The Post Cold War Condition

The post Cold War era has been unprecedented in many ways. The Westphalian international system, of which the Cold War was only the latest manifestation, is based on the assumption of conflict of interests between States. 'Allies and foes', 'good and bad', 'us and them' were part of its inherent vocabulary and logic. Within the international relations school of realism, the belief in the existence of the so-called 'national interest' stood as one of the key pillars of the orthodoxy. Yet since the end of the Cold War, many in the 'them' category seem to be coming to the 'us' category. The inability of policymakers in the West to create new enemies has baffled the assumptions upon which many based their world views and careers. It has not been for a lack of trying. With the dissolution of the Soviet Union, new enemies such as Iraq, Islam and China have all been exaggerated in the West to fit the role. Yet each has failed to have the power or ability to match the role of a true adversary. Nobody seems to want to play the old game with the old rules any more. The rules and the game, indeed, seem to be changing. Three leading thinkers who, each in his own way, describe this new condition are Francis Fukuyama, Michael Mandelbaum and Robert Cooper. The following section briefly outlines their central thesis to show how thinking in contemporary International Relations is shifting.

Francis Fukuyama

In the summer of 1989 a radical article jolted readers of *The National Interest* journal with the rather peculiar title of 'The End of History?'[14] In essence, its author, Francis Fukuyama, who was then an academic and US government advisor, was suggesting that world history had entered a new phase. By combining Kant's philosophy on progress with the historic analytical tools of Hegel and Marx, Fukuyama suggested that liberal democracy had become the triumphant final stage in human history. This, for Fukuyama, was because of liberal democracy's superior morality and closer connection to human nature versus competing ideologies such as

Communism. While there remained different civilizations in the world, their differences were increasingly being blurred by the integrating forces of economic and technological modernization. Ultimately, these forces promoted the establishment of homogenous and integrated economic and political institutions which were leading to an 'end of history', in the Hegelian-Marxist dialectic sense of the phrase.

This article and its subsequent arguments evolved into a book[15] with a similar title in 1992 and became a focal point for much debate in the 1990s. Despite its limitations, there are at least three important points that this thesis highlights which correlate with a Bahá'í view of history. The first is an acknowledgement that history is progressive. This, of course, is a hotly debated assumption amongst historians, many of whom believe history is non-linear or cyclical. The second, which builds on the first, is that human history is morally progressive. Therefore, not only does history move in a discernable pattern but also this movement is one of increasing goodness or righteousness. In other words, the world is becoming a better place. The third is the assumption that the world reached a certain point of great moral significance at the end of the 20th century. All three of these assumptions also hold true for the thesis of the Lesser Peace in particular and movement towards a new world order in general. Its greatest shortcoming from a Bahá'í perspective of history is its inability to visualize human moral development beyond a materialistic existence resting on the pillars of liberty and democracy.

Robert Cooper

The next thinker, who is considered by some to be the brightest conceptual thinker in the British diplomatic services, is Robert Cooper. In 1996 Cooper wrote a fascinating article entitled 'The Postmodern State and the World Order'. In his analysis, Cooper emphasizes the importance of 1989 and states that, in geo-political terms, the importance of this year and the shift it inaugurated in international affairs were on par in history only with 1648. While 1789, 1815 and 1919 were significant years, in that they represented dramatic changes such as revolutions, the end of empires and the reordering of alliances, they did not challenge the underlying balance of power system, which traces its roots to 1648.

The year 1648, of course, was different. It was the year of the Treaty of Westphalia that ended the Thirty Years' War. The peace that this treaty brought is widely recognized as the starting point of the modern State system and the balance of power mechanism that regulated relations between these States. At the heart of the Westphalian system, as it is often called, is the principle of national sovereignty. This means that only one power, the State, has the exclusive right to make and enforce rules on a given and defined territory.

The year 1989, for Cooper, represents a monumental change in which this system is clearly no longer applicable for the first time in some parts of the world. While the new system, which Cooper calls post-modern, has emerged in Europe, it can be reasonably assumed that this system, like the Westphalian, will also spread and become universal over time. Signs of the demise of the old system and characteristics of the new include alliances that survive in war and peace, interference in the domestic affairs of one another and acceptance of jurisdiction from external courts. Security, in the post-modern system is based on transparency, mutual openness, interdependence and mutual vulnerability.

Two events drove this change. The first, which represented an interesting *déjà vu* twist of history, was the second Thirty Years' War, which began in 1914 but really did not end until 1945. This war brought destruction to Europe on a scale not seen since the first Thirty Years' War, 300 years before. The second was the Cold War, which brought the possibility of devastation on a scale that had hitherto been unprecedented in history. The price of the status quo balance of power system had just become too high to pay. It is interesting how both Bahá'u'lláh and 'Abdu'l-Bahá, when referring to the reason why the Lesser Peace would come, emphasized the unbearable level of expenditure that the war-based system incorporated. It would be fair to assume that this expenditure involved more than the obvious cost of armaments but, more importantly, involved those associated with risk and lost opportunity.

Michael Mandelbaum

The third thinker to describe this new condition is Michael Mandelbaum, a professor of International Affairs at Johns Hopkins University. Like Fukuyama and Cooper, Mandelbaum also wrote a provocative article,[16] this one in the Winter 1998 issue of *Survival*, which claimed a monumental historic change in international relations had occurred. In this article, entitled 'Is Major War Obsolete?', Mandelbaum argued that major war, as has been known over the past 200 years, is obsolete, as it no longer serves the purpose for which it was designed. While it has not been outlawed in a binding manner, it has gone out of fashion by recent trends and developments that are not under the control of any particular agency or authority. What has made major war increasingly unacceptable are the rising costs of war and their declining gains. The shift in these two factors has led to a subsequent reversal over the past 100 years in the social status of war. According to Mandelbaum, 'while 100 years ago acts of war were considered legitimate, necessary, even heroic, war has now come to be widely regarded as something approaching a criminal enterprise'.[17]

The contributions of Fukuyama, Cooper and Mandelbaum all demonstrate that an important intellectual shift is taking place in international relations academia that reflects a changing reality in international politics. In relation to this paper's theme, I believe that all these writers are pointing to the condition of the Lesser Peace.

Section 3: Bahá'í Writings on the Lesser Peace

The Concept of the Lesser Peace, 1863–92

Bahá'u'lláh specifically refers to the Lesser Peace in only a limited number of Tablets, relative to His vast outpouring of revelation. Two Tablets in particular provide much of the specific detail on the Lesser Peace. The first is His Tablet to Queen Victoria and the second is *Epistle to the Son of the Wolf*. In the Tablet to Queen Victoria, which was addressed to all the rulers of the earth,[18] Bahá'u'lláh states, 'Now that ye have refused the Most Great Peace, hold ye fast unto this, the Lesser Peace, that haply ye may in some degree better your own condition and that of your dependents'.[19] He alludes to the nature of this peace by stating: 'Be united, O kings of the earth, for thereby will the tempest of discord be stilled amongst you, and your people find rest, if ye be of them that comprehend'.[20] This peace was distinct from the Most Great Peace, which was a future spiritual union of the world's people into 'one universal Cause, one common Faith' that could only be reached through the power of the Most Great Name.[21]

Before examining the condition of the Lesser Peace, let us first discern which outward manifestations Bahá'u'lláh specifically mentioned in these Tablets. These manifestations play a dual role of cause and consequence in relation to the condition of the Lesser Peace.[22] In Bahá'u'lláh's writings, there are essentially three outward manifestations that are described which we may look to for evidence: collective security, disarmament and a convocation of world leaders.

Collective security in an international relations context refers to a formal or informal system between actors (nation states) for the preservation of the system and its members. In this system, all actors agree to aid any member under attack by another State and thus deter aggression within the system through the threat of overwhelming collective force. In His letter to Queen Victoria, Bahá'u'lláh outlines such a system and writes: 'Should anyone among you take up arms against another, rise ye all against him, for this is naught but manifest justice'.[23]

In *Epistle to the Son of the Wolf*, He states, 'Should one king rise up against another, all the other kings must arise to deter him'.[24] Collective security relies on traditional balance of power formulations and is not necessarily an abandonment of the Westphalian system or its central principles.

The second outward manifestation that Bahá'u'lláh specifically mentions is disarmament. Disarmament within an international relations context is a complex term, as it usually does not refer to the elimination or ban of weapons. In most cases, it refers to the reduction, controlled expansion or nature of their usage. Bahá'u'lláh is also not calling for an outright ban but a reduction in quantity and nature of usage. In terms of quantity, Bahá'u'lláh's main reason for a reduction, aside from the obvious consequences of war, relates to the excessive financial burden that such expenditure imposes on the masses.[25] This is an unjust hardship that violates the responsibility of leadership bestowed upon the kings and rulers by God. In his letter to Queen Victoria, Bahá'u'lláh writes, 'O kings of the earth! We see you increasing every year your expenditures, and laying the burden thereof on your subjects. This, verily, is wholly and grossly unjust. Fear the sighs and tears of this Wronged One, and lay not excessive burdens on your peoples'.[26]

On the issue of the nature of usage, Bahá'u'lláh clearly states that arms are not to be used in a context of unilateral foreign policy. Their usage is strictly reserved for domestic policing. In this regard, Bahá'u'lláh states, 'O rulers of the earth! Be reconciled amongst yourselves, that ye may need no more armaments save in a measure to safeguard your territories and dominions'.[27] And again in *Epistle to the Son of the Wolf*, He writes, 'Arms and armaments will, then, be no more needed beyond that which is necessary to insure the internal security of their respective countries'.[28] Again, the maintenance of internal security suggests some acknowledgement of the key Westphalian principle of state sovereignty, possibly suggesting a gradual shift from this system.

Considered together with the concept of collective security, it can be assumed that there is an avenue for external usage of armaments to enforce the provisions of that security. In light of Bahá'u'lláh's references for kings to rise up against an aggressor State, it seems like collective security may initially be through a confederal[29] arrangement in which weapons are controlled by their respective States and troops and personnel are pooled and trained between them for assignment on a needs basis. This may be the initial step towards the eventual federalization of security through binding international legislation and ultimate institutionalization via a world army operating through an executive command structure. The initial steps towards the federalization of security issues takes us to the third outward manifestation of the Lesser Peace, a convocation of world leaders.

Collective security and disarmament are two key outcomes that are to emerge from a universal conference which the rulers of the world or their representatives are to attend. This can be considered the third outward manifestation of the Lesser Peace that Bahá'u'lláh specifically outlines. Bahá'u'lláh describes this event, its participants[30] and its purpose:

> The time must come when the imperative necessity for the holding of a vast, all-embracing assemblage of men will be universally realized. The rulers and kings of the earth must needs attend it, and, participating in its deliberations, must consider such ways and means as will lay the foundations of the world's Great Peace amongst men.[31]

It is interesting to note the terminology used in this verse. Bahá'u'lláh mentions that a time will come when the 'imperative necessity' for holding this manifestation will be 'universally realized'. Therefore, the actual meeting(s) and its related agreements on arms and security are a function of an underlying realization, which must be based on a new reality of global circumstances. What is key to the need for this meeting in particular, and the Lesser Peace in general, therefore, is a new underlying global condition. The subsequent events, which have been termed in this paper as outward manifestations, are only the delayed outcome or implementation. It should not be surprising, therefore, if there is a timelag between the new reality and its practical consequences on the international arena.

It is interesting to note that Bahá'u'lláh called on the future House of Justice to promote the Lesser Peace for the sake of reducing the burden of arms expenditure of the peoples of the world.[32] One can reasonably assume that such promotion was meant to reduce the gap between reality and action, or underlying condition and outward manifestation. In other words, promoting the Lesser Peace is a means to limit suffering owing to this gap.[33]

Let us now turn our attention to the condition of the Lesser Peace. The Lesser Peace is a condition in which the rulers of the world are united. At a basic level, unity means a joining together or combining for a common purpose or cause.[34] This unity, however, can be considered a lower-nature unity or unity at a material level, as it is one that only 'stills the tempest of discord'. It is one that leads to the finding of rest for a State's population and achieving a condition better than that brought by warfare. It is essentially a passive condition that relaxes destructive passions and activities. This can be contrasted to the condition of the Most Great Peace, which is essentially an active higher-nature unity or unity at the spiritual level.

In *Epistle to the Son of the Wolf*, Bahá'u'lláh asks for God's assistance in aiding the rulers of the world to establish the Lesser Peace, which 'is the greatest means for ensuring the tranquillity of the nations [and] . . . the chief instrument for the protection of all mankind'.[35] If this is attained, Bahá'u'lláh states that 'the people of each nation will pursue, with tranquillity and contentment, their own occupations, and the groaning and lamentations of most men would be silenced'.[36] In terms of the relations of nations, therefore, the Lesser Peace will achieve tranquillity – a condition of calmness and serenity. Domestically, people will feel a certain contentment and pursue their own occupations and self-betterment as a result. They will feel a new sense of protection unknown in wartime or times of interstate hostility and will not have to worry about these dangers.[37]

The elimination of external threat coupled with the domestic protection of property rights, of course, are widely considered to be the two key preconditions for sustained macroeconomic growth. In such a state, each individual's ability to pursue his or her economic interests without interference is claimed to lead to the most efficient transactions at a microeconomic level. This depiction evokes images of the 'end of history', which describes the emerging order after the Cold War world as one dominated by liberal democracies in a global economy.[38] This, for the author, brings the development of world history in the Hegelian sense of the word to a culminating finality of sorts. Again, this is a condition that can be described as a lower-nature optimality or perfection. This perfection is one in which people are free to pursue self-interests on the basis of domestic rule of law and external stability. This condition, while not based on a spiritual paradigm, should not be looked down upon. Bahá'u'lláh Himself refers to it as a blessing in *Epistle to the Son of the Wolf*, and it certainly is, compared to what the world has known hitherto.

The Concept of the Lesser Peace, 1892–1921

In 1892, with the passing of Bahá'u'lláh, 'Abdu'l-Bahá became the authoritative head of the Bahá'í Faith. It is interesting that 'Abdu'l-Bahá usually does not appear to distinguish between the Lesser and the Most Great Peace.[39] Instead, He usually speaks of peace in general. One reason for this may have been because many of His statements were made to public audiences which might not have comprehended the complexity of the distinction. Shoghi Effendi and the Universal House of Justice, however, have subsequently linked many of these writings and utterances to the Lesser Peace. The following section begins by reviewing 'Abdu'l-Bahá's elaborations on Bahá'u'lláh's specific references to the Lesser Peace. It then looks at the additional new insights that 'Abdu'l-Bahá introduced to the concept.

'Abdu'l-Bahá's Elaborations on Bahá'u'lláh's References to the Lesser Peace

In *The Secret of Divine Civilization*, 'Abdu'l-Bahá provides additional details on the convocation of world leaders,[40] stating that it will be led by a number of distinguished and high-minded sovereigns. It will initially involve consultations that will evolve into a binding treaty and a covenant. The covenant, after its establishment, will then be institutionalized into a 'Union of nations of the world'.[41]

Besides collective security and disarmament provisions, this covenant is also meant to incorporate a wider range of factors relevant to general peace-building including the permanent fixing of borders and the establishment of principles of international relations.[42] On the issue of collective security, 'Abdu'l-Bahá expands on Bahá'u'lláh's proposal to stop aggressors by stating that efforts should be made to destroy the violating government that breaks the arrangement.[43] On one level, 'Abdu'l-Bahá's description may be seen as a further elaboration of Bahá'u'lláh's original statements on this subject. Alternatively, the elaboration may refer to different stages in the Lesser Peace process. Perhaps in an earlier stage, which Bahá'u'lláh outlines, stopping aggression is sufficient, while at later stages aggression may be considered so abhorrent that stronger responses are necessary. The fact that 'Abdu'l-Bahá's description of collective security is within a future post-covenant institutional setting,[44] whereas Bahá'u'lláh's call to the rulers of the world is largely directed towards the ad hoc 'Congress of Europe'[45] of the late 19th century also suggests references to different stages in history.

With regard to disarmament, 'Abdu'l-Bahá provides contextual elaboration on Bahá'u'lláh's call by describing the 'security dilemma'[46] that results from unilateral arms expansion. According to 'Abdu'l-Bahá, 'if the preparation for war and the military forces of any nation should be allowed to increase, they will arouse the suspicion of others'.[47] In answers to questions published in *Star of the West*,[48] He expands on this theme and calls the end result of the security dilemma 'crazed competition'. For disarmament to be effective, 'Abdu'l-Bahá explains that it must be engaged in simultaneously through a binding treaty or 'covenant of eternal friendship'. Outside such an atmosphere, unilateral disarmament would be folly and an invitation for aggression. In an atmosphere of friendship and trust, the underlying security concerns that initially led to national arms build-up may be adequately addressed, prevented and subside. Again, the underlying condition precedes the outward manifestation.

Related to state-level disarmament is the idea of an international police force, which 'Abdu'l-Bahá introduces as a means for maintaining peaceful international relations. The existence of such a force would seem to represent a stage further along the Lesser Peace path than a collective security arrangement, which rests on a state-centric and more primitive international political architecture.[49] Therefore, based on the writings of Bahá'u'lláh and 'Abdu'l-Bahá, there seem to be at least two stages of collective security that can be associated with the Lesser Peace process. In the first, armaments are under the control of their respective nation states which agree to use them to stop an aggressor. In the second stage, which is post-covenant as outlined by 'Abdu'l-Bahá, armaments are still under the control of States but aggressor governments are not only stopped but also destroyed. This, of course, represents a much greater level of intervention. With the destruction of the government, it must be assumed that provisions in the treaty obligations of the covenant also address the steps needed to restore a new government. The new government, if it is to avoid the folly of its predecessor, will likely be one that accepts the principles of the international covenant. Nation-building, based on evidence from the Second World War with Germany and Japan and more recent examples in places like Bosnia and East Timor, is a complex and expensive affair. This is why it is often avoided.

As well as expanding on Bahá'u'lláh's provisions for the Lesser Peace, 'Abdu'l-Bahá also added further substantive insights on the Lesser Peace. The following section outlines some of the most significant references that have subsequently been linked to the Lesser Peace.

'Abdu'l-Bahá's Additional Insights on the Lesser Peace

The Tablet known as 'The Seven Candles of Unity' and 'Abdu'l-Bahá's answers to a *Montreal Star* newspaper reporter add some of the most important insights to our understanding of the Lesser Peace. 'The Seven Candles of Unity' is a letter 'Abdu'l-Bahá wrote in 1906 to Mrs Whyte of Edinburgh. In this Tablet two significant points are outlined regarding the Lesser Peace. The first relates to its qualitative characteristics while the second relates to its timing. Let us begin by assessing its qualitative characteristics.

In 'The Seven Candles[50] of Unity' 'Abdu'l-Bahá outlines seven types of unity that the world will eventually embrace. These are referred to here as 'types' and not 'stages' as Shoghi Effendi has clarified that they do not necessarily appear in any particular order.[51] These types of unity are in the political realm, in thought in world undertakings, in freedom, in religion, among nations, among races and in language. For the purposes of assessing the Lesser Peace, the first and fifth candles are of the greatest significance. Unity in the political realm, 'the early glimmerings of which' 'Abdu'l-Bahá asserts, 'can now be discerned', is a unity which politically independent and sovereign States realize amongst themselves. Unity of nations, however, seems to suggest a different level of achievement, 'causing all the peoples of the world to regard themselves citizens of a common fatherland'. According to Shoghi Effendi, the first unity amongst States involves political homogeneity, while the second refers to both political and national homogeneity.[52]

Unity in the political realm seems quite clear. There are about 200 States in the world today. Political peace, therefore, means peace among these entities. The idea of unity of nations, however, is less clear. In assessing this unity, there are essentially two approaches to consider. The first approach to the term 'nations' is a micro approach, which seeks to differentiate based on more subtle differences. According to nationalist scholars, such as Eric Hobsbawm, there are about 800 groups in the world today that claim to be independent nations. Russia by itself claims to have over 100 nationalities. Achieving unity amongst so many groups would be a difficult, if not impossible, feat. Furthermore, not all these groups have political representation or organization. Therefore, they would not even be in a position to negotiate towards any union in the foreseeable future. The fact that many of them have claims to the same territory, in a world that simply does not have the land for everyone's vision of their greater homeland, also makes this task seem like a 'non-starter', in practical political terms.

From a macro approach, however, there is the idea of pan-nationalism such as the European, Arab or African nation. This approach, which is taken up in the re-emergent civilizations dialogue, suggests that there are about ten different nations in the world today. This type of classification involves looking at larger cultural and historical commonalities in regional settings. The emergence of regional political arrangements such as the European Union representing the 'European nation', the Arab League representing the 'Arab nation' and the Organization for African Unity representing the 'African nation' put in place political representation for these pan-nations. The macro approach to nation also seems to be in line with Shoghi Effendi's reference to race and 'Abdu'l-Bahá's reference to peoples, when writing about the unity of nations, as most pan-nationalisms are based on a belief in a trans-state common ethnicity.

In comparing unity in the political realm with that amongst nations, it seems like the former is more of an outward manifestation of peace involving States, politicians, diplomats and legal mechanisms. Unity amongst nations in the macro sense, on the other hand, is more of an underlying condition. This is particularly evident when we re-examine 'Abdu'l-Bahá's original description as a feeling amongst the world's people that they regard themselves as citizens of a common fatherland. If this assessment is accurate, it also seems to suggest that the unity of nations will precede unity in the political realm, as the condition underlying the outward manifestation that will take place on the political level.

The second important contribution of this Tablet regarding our understanding of the Lesser Peace is the issue of timing. As was outlined in the introduction, one of the most confusing issues regarding the Lesser Peace relates to the details of exactly when it will unfold. 'The Seven Candles of Unity', for the first time, provides a reference to a defined time period. Specifically, when describing the fifth candle of unity, 'Abdu'l-Bahá states that such a unity 'in this Century will be securely established'.[53] This temporal element appears to have been confirmed in an interview of 'Abdu'l-Bahá in the *Montreal Star*. A reporter asked, 'Are there any signs that the permanent peace of the world will be established in anything like a reasonable period?' 'Abdu'l-Bahá's answer to this was, 'It will be established in this century. It will be universal in the twentieth century. All nations will be forced into it.'[54] In the final years of the 20th century, a good case could certainly be made that this condition, the underlying condition of the Lesser Peace in the unity of nations, had been reached.

We have already outlined how the covenant of the future institutional framework that 'Abdu'l-Bahá foresees is one of 'eternal friendship' and the unity of nations is a collective feeling of 'a common fatherland' by the peoples of the world. At the heart of these testaments is the postulate that war is against the very fibre of human nature. The condition of the Lesser Peace, therefore, is a realignment of the internal world of human nature with the external world of international politics. In describing this misalignment, 'Abdu'l-Bahá describes the weapons of war as the 'testimonials of greed and bloodthirstiness, so inconsistent with the gift of life'.[55] In striking similarity to Mandelbaum's description of the post Cold War era, 'Abdu'l-Bahá outlines that a time will come when 'The apparatus of conflict will, as preparations go on at their present rate, reach the point where war will become something intolerable to mankind.'[56]

While the writings and elaborations of Bahá'u'lláh and 'Abdu'l-Bahá on the Lesser Peace are the building blocks of our understanding, our comprehension of the Lesser Peace and its larger contextual settings could not have reached its current depth without the interpretations of Shoghi Effendi.

The Concept of the Lesser Peace, 1921–63

Through the vast collection of his writings spanning over three decades, Shoghi Effendi made numerous references to the Lesser Peace. The majority of these were in answer to questions posed to clarify the subject. Shoghi Effendi's writings provided greatly needed authoritative interpretation on a number of issues related to the Lesser Peace. One of the most important interpretive contributions of Shoghi Effendi on the subject of future world order was to elaborate on Bahá'u'lláh's distinction between the Lesser and the Most Great Peace. The first important point was that the

Lesser Peace would be achieved without Bahá'í intervention. This did not, however, divorce the Bahá'í Faith from the process. On the one hand, it was the Bahá'í Revelation that created the original spiritual impetus for the condition of the Lesser Peace to emerge. According to the Báb, this new Revelation is 'vibrating in the innermost realities of all created things'.[57] As Bahá'u'lláh stated, His Revelation has 'lent a fresh impulse and set a new direction'.[58] On the other hand, Bahá'ís are encouraged to promote the Lesser Peace while recognizing it will come about through actions independent of any Bahá'í plan or effort.[59]

The Lesser Peace and its establishment, of course, are significantly different from the Most Great Peace. According to the Guardian, 'No machinery falling short of the standard inculcated by the Bahá'í Revelation . . . can ever hope to achieve anything above and beyond that "Lesser Peace".' In the Most Great Peace, the Bahá'ís and the administrative order built up by them play the central role as the nucleus and pattern of world order.[60] This stage, according to the Guardian, 'must inevitably follow as the practical consequence of the spiritualization of the world and the fusion of its races, creeds, classes and nations'. The Most Great Peace can only thus be realized through the 'divinely appointed ordinances' of Bahá'u'lláh's world order.[61]

A second associated and even more significant interpretive contribution that Shoghi Effendi provides on the Lesser Peace relates to its placement within the historical development leading to the Bahá'í vision of world order. This path involves two distinct processes that synchronize at the Lesser Peace and merge at the Most Great Peace. The first process, referred to as the Minor Plan of God, involves the Bahá'í community and dates back to the Heroic Age of the Faith. This process is confined within the Bahá'í administrative order and relates to its evolution and maturation. This is a conscious effort based on detailed instruction and continuing divine guidance.

The second process, referred to as the Major Plan of God, involves the non-Bahá'í world and can be traced to the outbreak of the First World War.[62] This process is volatile and involves the movement of a materialistic world towards a limited degree of unity at the political level (the Lesser Peace). Some of the events that moved this process forward, as identified by the Guardian, include:[63]

- The formulation of US President Woodrow Wilson's Fourteen Points
- The outbreak of the Second World War
- The Atlantic Charter
- The birth of the United Nations
- The choice of New York as the seat of the UN

This transition is not based on any normative agenda but is largely driven by the collective instinct of humanity for self-preservation. The path of the Major Plan is not smooth or clearly linear and involves setbacks and temporary reversals, as humanity continually attempts to cling onto outdated patterns of behaviour. When the Major Plan of God reaches the Lesser Peace and political unity, it can be likened to a unified body that is lacking life.[64]

According to the writings of Shoghi Effendi, these two processes will converge at the Most Great Peace, when the Major Plan embraces the Minor Plan, as the Bahá'í administrative order and the Universal House of Justice are recognized as the last refuge of a tottering civilization.[65] This process has been described as a breathing of life and spirit into the unified and previously lifeless body. Before this consummation, however, an earlier synchronization is outlined. This earlier concurrence is particularly important in the context of this paper as it provides what seems to be a specific reference to events and processes. In this reference, the Guardian writes, 'The ultimate completion of this stupendous undertaking (the building of the Arc on Mount Carmel) . . . will synchronize with two no less significant developments – the establishment of the Lesser Peace and the evolution of the Bahá'í national and local institutions . . .'[66] In this statement, Shoghi Effendi provides a temporal link between the Major Plan (the Lesser Peace) and the Minor Plan (the completion of the buildings housing the international Bahá'í institutions, commonly referred to as the Arc, and the evolution of Bahá'í institutions). This statement on the completion of the Arc on Mount Carmel suggests a temporal connection between the Lesser Peace process and the turn of the millennium.[67]

In terms of the underlying conditions of the Lesser Peace, Shoghi Effendi provides much elaboration covering a number of spheres of human activity. In *The Promised Day is Come*, Shoghi Effendi writes, 'The interdependence of the peoples of the nations of the earth . . . is already an accomplished fact. Its unity in the economic sphere is now understood and recognized. The welfare of the part means the welfare of the whole, and the distress of the part brings distress to the whole.'[68] This echoes the circumstances that Bahá'u'lláh outlined when describing the general conditions of the Lesser Peace.

Furthermore, in *The World Order of Bahá'u'lláh*, the Guardian explains that the principle of the oneness of mankind, the 'pivot round which all the teachings of Bahá'u'lláh revolve',[69] is being consciously exerted by Bahá'ís and unconsciously applied by humankind. This is due to the 'gradual diffusion of the spirit of world solidarity which is spontaneously arising out of the welter of a disorganized society'.[70] While the Guardian acknowledges that there have been setbacks in attempts by people of noble ideas and foresight for greater unification, he is encouraged by the mere fact that these attempts are taking place, asking, 'are we not justified in deriving fresh encouragement when we observe that the very consideration of such proposals is in itself an evidence of their steady growth in the minds and hearts of men?'[71]

The Concept of the Lesser Peace, 1963–2000

Like Shoghi Effendi, the institution of the Universal House of Justice has written a vast array of texts and correspondence since its establishment in 1963. The Universal House of Justice's references to the Lesser Peace, like Shoghi Effendi's, are both statements and responses to inquiries. The Universal House of Justice's observations on the subject, while derived from the writings of Bahá'u'lláh, 'Abdu'l-Bahá and Shoghi Effendi, make at least two important contributions to our understanding. First, the House of Justice explains the Lesser Peace, more clearly than before, within a larger context of other Bahá'í principles and global social change. Second, it explains how the Lesser Peace is a process and not an event.

The Lesser Peace in a Larger Context

The most elaborate statement thus far on the Lesser Peace by the Universal House of Justice is the 1985 document *The Promise of World Peace*. As this document was written for the general public, it does not employ the terms 'Lesser Peace' and 'Most Great Peace'. *The Promise of World Peace* is an important explanatory extension on previous Bahá'í statements on peace, outlining in greater detail than ever before what stands in the path to peace and explaining how peace cannot be achieved without tackling the barriers first. These hindrances include racism, disparity between rich and poor, unbridled nationalism, religious strife, sexism, a lack of access to education and limitations in communication.[72] Overcoming these barriers essentially involves the acceptance of principles that revolve around the central Bahá'í principle of the oneness of humankind. Two other important documents released under the auspices of the Universal House of Justice that indirectly relate to peace are *The Prosperity of Humankind* and *Turning Point for All Nations*. In the former document, the argument is made that peace cannot be achieved until the underlying economic injustices that limit human potential and development are tackled. In the latter document, suggestions are made regarding reform of the United Nations that link peace to the overcoming of limitations inherent in the current UN system.

The Lesser Peace as a Historical Process

A second important explanation by the Universal House of Justice was to outline the Lesser Peace more clearly as a historic process. This was an important clarifying point for many that had previously expected the Lesser Peace to be a specific event or set of events. This is not because the Lesser Peace was not outlined as a process before. 'Abdu'l-Bahá clearly said that peace would come gradually[73] and Shoghi Effendi had often written of the Lesser Peace as part of larger historical processes. The Universal House of Justice, however, more clearly and emphatically than ever before, clarified this point. Amongst other sources, the 1999 statement *Peace Among the Nations* makes this point by stating 'The attainment of peace in the political realm is discernable through the workings of a process'; 'the process of political unification is gaining'; and again, 'the process towards peace is far advanced and can hardly be denied'.[74]

To understand the terminology more clearly, it is important to define three words and their relationship to each other. These words are 'process', 'establish' and 'event'. A 'process' is a course of action that usually involves a series of stages. To 'establish' is to set something up (a business, system, etc.) on a self-sustaining basis. An 'event' is a single occurrence that is limited in duration. A historical process has a beginning or point of establishment and an end point and is marked by incremental events of varying significance in connecting these two points. In historical processes, these points of demarcation are not always clear until well after the key event or set of events has passed. The era of state sovereignty, for example, which is one of the key parameters of the international system of the 20th century, is now widely believed to have begun with the 1648 Treaty of Westphalia. The rise of modernity and modern nationalism is now often said to have been initiated by the French Revolution. The magnitude of these events was certainly not clear at the time that they were taking place. They took decades, if not centuries, to become known as events of monumental historical change.

The same is true of the Lesser Peace. There will likely be many events in the late 20th century that may one day be looked back upon and marked as significant points in the process of the Lesser Peace. The Universal House of Justice has even identified a number of such potential landmarks, such as the 1995 gathering of world leaders at the 50th anniversary of the United Nations[75] and the 2000 Millennium Conferences.[76]

In the future, we will likely be able to identify the magnitude of these events more clearly. But we are too close to these events at the beginning of the Millennium to recognize their importance and relevance. It is a commonly accepted principle amongst historians that true historical analysis cannot begin until 50 years have passed from the events under question and all the living players have passed away. Therefore, any attempt to try and understand the events of the late 20th century in the context of the Lesser Peace, notwithstanding guidance of the Universal House of Justice, is speculative at best.

The Universal House of Justice, in releasing *The Promise of World Peace*, clearly emphasized that the conditions were ripe for world peace. It is significant that the Universal House of Justice gives the last few decades of the 20th century special emphasis, in this regard, by declaring that this condition 'is now at long last' here. This is outlined in the first paragraph: 'The Great Peace towards which people of good will throughout the centuries have inclined their hearts, of which seers and poets for countless generations have expressed their vision, and for which from age to age the sacred scriptures of mankind have constantly held the promise, is now at long last within the reach of the nations.'[77] In addition, this statement, while outlining many of the obstacles that are hindering humanity from reaching peace, suggests that there is a new urge towards unity that is struggling to express itself through these barriers. This urge, according to the statement, is the real source behind many of the movements in the late 20th century that are challenging previous antagonisms and divisions amongst humanity.

A similar sentiment marking the unique condition of the era is presented in the statement released under the auspices of the Universal House of Justice called *Who is Writing the Future?* This special document, which provides a unique overview of the accomplishments of the 20th century, acknowledges that it is now obvious that a new condition in the world has arrived. According to the statement, 'It no longer requires prophetic insight to appreciate that the opening years of the new century will see the release of energies and aspirations infinitely more potent than the accumulated routines, falsities, and addictions that have so long blocked their expression.'[78]

It is interesting to consider the timing of these two statements and the condition in world affairs over the 14 years that separate them. In 1985 the idea of world peace seemed to be a distant hope to outside observers. The world was in a period of high geopolitical tensions and overcoming such apparently impregnable differences seemed visionary at best. Yet a decade and half later, the conditions of peace seem very much at hand and 'no longer require prophetic insight'. This condition and the mounting evidence for its emergence in the latter 20th century seem to suggest that the conditions of the Lesser Peace are at last with us in a clearly identifiable manner.

Conclusion

In thinking about the Lesser Peace, it is important to look beyond the outward manifestations that mark the Lesser Peace and its maturation over time if we are to truly understand it. The events, while important in their own right, are a function of a new condition in world affairs. At the same time, history shows that there is often a time lag between the appearance of a new condition and its outward manifestations through concrete implementation. Today, a new condition is not only clear to Bahá'ís but has now become clear to many prominent academics and policymakers such as the Fukuyamas, Coopers and Mandelbaums of the world. As the statement *Peace Among the Nations* confirms, the Lesser Peace 'implies the achievement of a relationship among them [States] that will enable them to resolve questions of international import through consultation rather than war'.[79] It is the condition, therefore, that we should watch out for when assessing whether we have entered the era of the Lesser Peace, not any single event.

To conclude, let us briefly look at the cause of this new condition. The cause, essentially, can be described from both spiritual and secular accounts of history, although both are essentially part of the same thesis. From the spiritual view of history, the new condition is clearly an outcome of God's latest revelation to man, which has 'deranged the equilibrium of the world'[80] and is 'vibrating in the innermost realities of all created things'.[81] From a secular perspective, the new condition is driven by the emergence of the world's first truly global civilization.

Bibliography

'Abdu'l-Bahá. *The Secret of Divine Civilization*. Wilmette, IL: Bahá'í Publishing Trust, 1990.

— *Selections from the Writings of 'Abdu'l-Bahá*. Haifa: Bahá'í World Centre, 1978.

'Abdu'l-Bahá in London. London: Bahá'í Publishing Trust, 1987.

Bahá'í International Community Office of Public Information. *Peace Among the Nations*. Statement in response to a question about the Lesser Peace and the catastrophic events of the end of the Twentieth Century, 20 March 1999. Haifa: Bahá'í International Community Office of Public Information, 1999.

— *The Prosperity of Humankind*. New York: Bahá'í International Community United Nations Office, 1995.

— *Turning Point for All Nations: A Statement of the Bahá'í International Community on the Occasion of the 50th Anniversary of the United Nations*. New York: Bahá'í International Community United Nations Office, 1995.

— *Who is Writing the Future? Reflections on the Twentieth Century*. New York: Office of Public Information, February 1999.

Bahá'u'lláh. *Gleanings from the Writings of Bahá'u'lláh*. Wilmette, IL: Bahá'í Publishing Trust, 1983.

— *Tablets of Bahá'u'lláh revealed after the Kitáb-i-Aqdas*. Haifa: Bahá'í World Centre, 1978.

Bull, H. *The Anarchical Society: A Study of Order in World Politics*. London: Macmillan, 2nd edn. 1985.

Compilation of Compilations, The. Prepared by the Universal House of Justice 1963–1990. 2 vols. [Sydney]: Bahá'í Publications Australia, 1991.

Cooper, Robert. *The Postmodern State and the World Order*. London: Demos, 1996.

Fukuyama, Francis. 'The End of History?' *The National Interest*. Summer 1989.

— *The End of History and the Last Man*. New York: Free Press, 1992.

Hainsworth, Philip. *Bahá'í Focus on Peace*. London: Bahá'í Publishing Trust, 1986.

Huddleston, John. *Achieving World Peace by the Year 2000*. Oxford: One World, 1988.

Lee, A.A. (ed.), *Circle of Peace: Reflections on the Bahá'í Teachings*. Los Angeles: Kalimát Press, 1985.

Lee, Kathy. *Prelude to the Lesser Peace*. New Delhi: Bahá'í Publishing Trust, 1989.

Lerche, Charles. *Emergence: Dimensions of a New World Order*. London: Bahá'í Publishing Trust, 1991.

Mandelbaum, Michael. 'Is Major War Obsolete?' *Survival*, Winter 1998/99.

McDougal, M.S. and Associates. *Studies in World Order*. New Haven, CN: Yale University Press, 1960.

Oxford Dictionary of Current English. Oxford: Oxford University Press, 2nd edn. 1992.

Peace. A compilation of the Universal House of Justice. London: Bahá'í Publishing Trust, 1985.

Peace: More Than an End to War. Selections from the Writings of Bahá'u'lláh, the Báb, 'Abdu'l-Bahá, Shoghi Effendi and the Universal House of Justice. Wilmette, IL: Bahá'í Publishing Trust, 1986.

Shoghi Effendi. *Call to the Nations*. Haifa: Universal House of Justice, 1977.

— *Citadel of Faith: Messages to America 1947–1957*. Wilmette, IL: Bahá'í Publishing Trust, 1965.

— *Messages to the Bahá'í World*. Wilmette, IL: Bahá'í Publishing Trust, 1971.

— *The Promised Day is Come*. Wilmette, IL: Bahá'í Publishing Trust, rev. edn. 1980.

— *The World Order of Bahá'u'lláh*. Wilmette, IL: Bahá'í Publishing Trust, 1991.

Tyson, J. *World Peace and World Government: A Bahá'í Approach*. Oxford: George Ronald, 1986.

The Universal House of Justice. *The Promise of World Peace*. London: Bahá'í Publishing Trust, 1985.

— *Wellspring of Guidance*. Wilmette, IL: Bahá'í Publishing Trust, 1976.

Waging Peace: Selections from the Bahá'í Writings on Universal Peace. Los Angeles: Kalimát Press, 1984.

References

1. Letter of Shoghi Effendi, 27 November 1954, in Shoghi Effendi, *Messages to the Bahá'í World*, p. 74.
2. Universal House of Justice, Riḍván Message 2000.
3. Three sources that gather a wide range of relevant quotes are *Peace*; *Peace: More Than an End to War*; and Lee, *Prelude to the Lesser Peace*.

Other books that have dealt with issues relating to the path towards world peace and the new world order include, amongst others: *Waging Peace: Selections from the Bahá'í Writings on Universal Peace*; Lee (ed.), *Circle of Peace: Reflections on the Bahá'í Teachings*; Hainsworth, *Bahá'í Focus on Peace*; Huddleston, *Achieving World Peace by the Year 2000*; and Lerche, *Emergence: Dimensions of a New World Order*.

4. There has been much speculation regarding the minimum criteria required for the start of the Lesser Peace process. One of the more ambitious interpretations suggests: 'Its initiation would seem to require, as a bare minimum, the establishment of a true world legislature, or parliament, a binding world tribunal or court, a world executive and an effective international force, together with universal disarmament – both nuclear and conventional – the creation of a code of the rights of individuals and nations, and some form of international taxation' (Tyson, *World Peace and World Government*, pp. 59–60). In *Peace: More Than an End to War*, the glossary defines the Lesser Peace as: 'The first of two major stages in which Bahá'ís believe peace will be established. The Lesser Peace will come about through a binding treaty among the nations for the political unification of the world. It will involve the boundaries of every nation's [sic] being clearly fixed, the size of their armaments strictly limited, the principles underlying the relations of governments toward one another definitely laid down, and all international agreements and obligations ascertained' (p. 276).

5. We should always look at the example of Shoghi Effendi who, despite his authoritative position, was conservative in his approach towards outlining the world order of Bahá'u'lláh, stating: 'All we can reasonably venture to attempt is to strive to obtain a glimpse of the first streaks of the promised Dawn that must, in the fullness of time, chase away the gloom that has encircled humanity. All we can do is to point out, in their broadest outlines, what appear to us to be the guiding principles underlying the World Order of Bahá'u'lláh . . .' In this passage, the Guardian puts seven qualifiers in his description of the process towards the World Order. He also states that it would be presumptuous and premature for the believers of the Faith to make claims that they have fully grasped this order and its related processes. Shoghi Effendi, *World Order*, p. 35.

6. Bahá'ís believe these to contain divine truths which will guide humanity at least until the appearance of the next Manifestation of God, which will not be for at least a thousand years after Bahá'u'lláh's Revelation.

7. For the sake of brevity and focus, the institutional aspects of the

Lesser Peace are not dealt with in this paper. Some of the other papers in this book address these issues at much greater depth.

8. In domestic (or civil) societies, for example, the vast majority of people do not commit murder or theft because they believe such acts to be morally deplorable, not because they are against the law.

9. Bull, *The Anarchical Society*, pp. 23–38, 122–55.

10. From a spiritual historical viewpoint, this may be accounted for by progressive revelation, the concept which posits that spiritual truths stay constant, while social laws change with the maturity of humankind.

11. Significantly, a wide range of major societal normative changes in Western societies began in the early to mid 19th century. While secular accounts link this to the enlightenment and the implications of the revolutionary movements in France and America, a Bahá'í account of history sees these profound changes as part of a spiritual infusion that divine revelation dispenses into the world. As 'Abdu'l-Bahá explains, 'The Call of God, when raised, breathed a new life into the body of mankind, and infused a new spirit into the whole creation' (quoted in Shoghi Effendi, *World Order*, p. 169).

12. There is a large literature on this thesis. For example, see McDougal and Associates, *Studies in World Order*.

13. The other side of the argument, usually promoted by advocates of public international law, suggests that laws can exist that are not commonly popular at the time of passage but over time begin to have an impact on politics by their very existence. For example, war as an instrument of foreign policy has been banned for many years (as enshrined in the League Covenant, the 1922 Kellogg-Briand Pact and the UN Charter). The very existence of these laws, it has been argued, had a major impact on the actions of potential belligerents and created the impetus for changing the general perception of war from a normal activity to a criminal one.

14. Fukuyama, 'The End of History?' *The National Interest*, Summer 1989.

15. Fukuyama, *The End of History and the Last Man*.

16. Michael Mandelbaum, 'Is Major War Obsolete?', *Survival*, Winter 1998/99.

17. ibid. p. 24.

18. Cited in Shoghi Effendi, *Promised Day is Come*, p. 26.

19. ibid. p. 27.

20. ibid.

21. Bahá'u'lláh, *Gleanings*, p. 255.

22. On the one hand, it can be argued that their emergence can assist

in creating the condition of the Lesser Peace. On the other hand, it can be claimed that their existence is an outcome or proof that the condition has been established. This dual role is not a contradiction but a sign that the Lesser Peace is a long historical process that evolves in stages marked by numerous events that are sometimes unique and repetitive at other times.

23. Cited in Shoghi Effendi, *Promised Day is Come*, p. 27.

24. Bahá'u'lláh, *Epistle to the Son of the Wolf*, p. 31.

25. 'Abdu'l-Bahá also confirms this position stating, 'the nations will be forced to come to peace and to agree to the abolition of war. The awful burdens of taxation for war purposes will get beyond human endurance . . .' in *Compilation*, vol. 2, p. 171.

26. Cited in Shoghi Effendi, *Promised Day is Come*, pp. 26–7.

27. Cited in ibid. p. 27.

28. Bahá'u'lláh, *Epistle to the Son of the Wolf*, p. 31.

29. In a confederation, legal and political power resides with the constituent units which transfer rights temporarily to a collective entity for a desired outcome. NATO or the Commonwealth of Independent States (CIS) are modern examples of confederations.

30. While in the forthcoming passage Bahá'u'lláh states that the rulers and kings must attend this meeting, in *Epistle to the Son of the Wolf*, He also states that 'ministers' of the 'Sovereigns of the world' may attend the meeting in their stead (pp. 30–1).

31. Bahá'u'lláh, *Tablets*, p. 165.

32. See ibid. p. 89.

33. The 1985 document *The Promise of World Peace*, issued by the Universal House of Justice, may be considered as a response to this exhortation of Bahá'u'lláh written at a time when the House must have felt that world conditions were ripe for such a document. This is perhaps why it begins by stating 'The Great Peace . . . is now at long last within the reach of the nations.' The Universal House of Justice, *The Promise of World Peace*, p. 1. The time of this document's release was also one of significant suffering from exorbitant arms expenditure. If one looks at the international political landscape, it was precisely in the early 1980s that Reagan significantly increased the US defence budget, causing a similar response by the USSR. The inability of the USSR to maintain the financial burdens of this new arms race, which also pushed the US into record national debt, has been widely recognized as a leading factor for the demise of the USSR and the Cold War system it helped to co-support.

34. *Oxford Dictionary of Current English*, pp. 1003–4.

35. Bahá'u'lláh, *Epistle to the Son of the Wolf*, p. 30.

36. ibid. p. 31.
37. The economic benefits of this peace, of course, are only one dimension of the bounty. Other dimensions may be social, cultural, political, psychological and spiritual.
38. See Fukuyama, *The End of History and the Last Man*.
39. This is an analysis based only on the author's limitations in terms of breadth of research and understanding of published translations in the English language.
40. 'True civilization will unfurl its banner in the midmost heart of the world whenever a certain number of its distinguished and high-minded sovereigns – the shining exemplars of devotion and determination – shall, for the good and happiness of all mankind, arise, with firm resolve and clear vision, to establish the Cause of Universal Peace. They must make the Cause of Peace the object of general consultation, and seek by every means in their power to establish a Union of the nations of the world.' 'Abdu'l-Bahá, *Secret of Divine Civilization*, p. 64.
41. ibid.
42. ibid.
43. ibid. pp. 64–5.
44. 'Abdu'l-Bahá describes collective security within the context of a future covenant between the nations of the world leading to a Union of nations. In my understanding, this suggests collective security as one element within a broader agreement.
45. The 'Congress of Europe' is a term used to describe the international political condition between the great powers of Europe for most of the 19th century. In this system, which was composed of Great Britain, France, Prussia, the Austro-Hungarian Empire and Russia, with the Ottoman Empire as an outside player, certain rules of conduct existed that created stability in the system and relative peace on the continent (which explains why the period between 1815 and 1914 is often referred to as the Hundred Years' Peace).
46. Within the academic discipline of international relations, the term 'security dilemma' refers to the contradictory result of lowering one's security by increasing defensive and armaments spending. The dilemma emerges when increased defence leads to reciprocal actions by potential adversaries who attempt to safeguard their own security by matching or exceeding these measures. The dilemma arises because security, like power, is a relative concept, not an absolute one.
47. 'Abdu'l-Bahá, *Secret of Divine Civilization*, p. 65.
48. 'Abdu'l-Bahá, in 'Universal Peace', *Star of the West*, vol. 5, no. 8 (August 1914), pp. 115–17.

49. It is assumed that this international police force is under international executive command and not subject to collective consent, as is presently the case in NATO police deployments in the former Yugoslavia.

50. There is probably great significance in the term 'candles'. However, it is beyond the scope of this paper to speculate on this.

51. Letter written on behalf of Shoghi Effendi, 19 November 1945, cited in *Prelude to the Lesser Peace*, p. 82.

52. Cited in ibid.

53. 'Abdu'l-Bahá, *Selections*, p. 32.

54. 'Abdu'l-Bahá, cited in *Compilation*, vol. 2, p. 171. It should be noted that this reference is to a newspaper article and, therefore, is a secondary source that is not authoritative.

55. 'Abdu'l-Bahá, *Secret of Divine Civilization*, p. 66.

56. ibid. p. 67.

57. The Báb, cited in Shoghi Effendi, *Call to the Nations*, p. 14.

58. Bahá'u'lláh, *Gleanings*, p. 95.

59. From a letter of Shoghi Effendi, 14 March 1939, in *Compilation*, p. 194.

60. Shoghi Effendi, *World Order*, p. 144.

61. ibid. p. 162.

62. From a letter of Shoghi Effendi, 5 June 1947 to the Bahá'ís of the West, in *Citadel of Faith*, p. 6.

63. Shoghi Effendi, *Citadel of Faith*, pp. 32–3.

64. Universal House of Justice, *Wellspring of Guidance*, pp. 131–4.

65. Shoghi Effendi, *World Order*, p. 89.

66. Shoghi Effendi, *Messages to the Bahá'í World*, p. 74.

67. It should also be noted that the Secretariat of the Universal House of Justice wrote the following response on 14 December 1987: 'The Universal House of Justice . . . knows of nothing in the writings of the Faith to indicate that the establishment of the Lesser Peace depends on the completion of the Arc on Mount Carmel.' This is because not all three of these elements are events. While the completion of the Arc had an official event associated with it in May 2001, the maturation of the Bahá'í institutions and the Lesser Peace are processes that are more gradual and beyond any single event.

68. Shoghi Effendi, *Promised Day is Come*, p. 122.

69. Shoghi Effendi, *World Order*, p. 42.

70. ibid. p. 44.

71. ibid.

72. The Universal House of Justice, *The Promise of World Peace* and *Peace: More Than an End to War*, pp. 10–15.

73. *'Abdu'l-Bahá in London*, p. 106.

74. Bahá'í International Community, *Peace Among the Nations*, paras. 3, 5.
75. The Universal House of Justice, Riḍván Message 153 BE (1996).
76. Riḍván Message 155 BE (2000). Furthermore, in a statement of 24 September 2000 composed after the Millennium Summit of World Leaders, the Universal House of Justice wrote, 'For any observer imbued with the Bahá'í vision of peace and its inherent processes, the substance and implications of these recent events, seen together with previous world conferences that during the last decade also involved leaders of nations, must be gratifying indeed to contemplate.'
77. The Universal House of Justice, *Promise of World Peace*, p. 1.
78. *Who is Writing the Future?*, pp. 9–10.
79. Bahá'í International Community, *Peace Among the Nations*, para. 3.
80. Bahá'u'lláh, cited in Shoghi Effendi, *God Passes By*, p. xi.
81. The Báb, cited in Shoghi Effendi, *Call to the Nations*, p. 14.

The Environment and the Lesser Peace

Arthur Lyon Dahl[1]

The environment refers to everything that surrounds us and particularly everything that has some influence on us. It thus includes the natural resources and life-support systems of the planet, its physical and chemical processes and biological riches. It also includes human beings, who have become the dominant species in the planetary ecosystem, and all the social and cultural conditions that influence our life.[2] The human environment that we have built for ourselves has been imposed on nature. When we think of the environment, most often we think first of all the problems caused by human activity, such as pollution and resource depletion, and the consequences they may bring including climate change, stratospheric ozone depletion, land degradation and desertification, and the loss of biodiversity. These are generally negative associations derived from the damage modern civilization has caused to the natural environment.

The environment and peace are two subjects that are not usually directly associated, the former being scientific in orientation and the latter political. If anything, environmental problems are seen as an important source of conflict, as well as a consequence of war and preparations for war. Population pressure overshooting the environmental carrying capacity of available resources was one of the causes of the genocide in Rwanda. The Gulf conflict saw environmental pollution used as a weapon of war. The Vietnamese environment has only slowly recovered from the widespread use of defoliants during the Vietnam War. The destruction caused by war inevitably produces widespread pollution. Unexploded munitions and land mines can render large areas of the environment inaccessible and unproductive. Warfare is an environmental as well as a human calamity.

One could easily see the environment as just another source of human discord but this would disregard the larger context of the evolutionary pressures on society. It is this context that gives the relationship of the environment and peace its directionality, with the environment a driving force more towards peace than conflict. Society is not simply buffeted by various random pressures. It is in the midst of a significant evolutionary transformation driven by technological developments.[3] A biological example can help to illustrate this. If islands in an archipelago are long isolated by water, their plant and animal populations will evolve distinct differences, as Charles Darwin observed in the Galapagos Islands.[4] If the sea level then dropped, joining all the islands into one land area, the different species would intermingle and compete with each other. After a period of chaos and confusion, a new ecological balance would be struck, either by some species replacing others or by competing species evolving different means of coexisting. This is precisely what has happened with human societies. The many tribes, cultures and nations of the planet evolved in relative isolation until the technological revolution of the last two centuries broke down the barriers between them and transformed the social environment. Much of today's warfare and conflict results from this recent mixing of peoples and cultures and represents part of a natural transitional process towards a larger level of unity in the human system.[5] This also allows some optimism about the natural outcome of what is really an organic process:[6] the evolution of a single world human system balancing unity and diversity. We can swim with the current and accelerate the process, or fight against it and slow things down. The result will ultimately be the same, unless we destroy the very basis of modern society in the process and force a reversion to a more primitive culture.

In this larger sense, the environment has joined technology as an important force pushing nations towards unity and peace over the last four decades of the 20th century. Governments have increasingly recognized that their own self-interest in protecting their environment requires cooperation with other States. Transfrontier problems require collaboration among neighbouring States and those sharing common river basins and airsheds. Global environmental problems necessitate global management mechanisms. Cooperation in the environmental area can often help to improve relations in other areas, as States develop habits of working together. Peace is often made of many such small steps. The significance of the environment as a force for peace in the recent past carries over as well into its potential role in a world challenged to make peace. This paper focuses on the positive contributions that the environment has made and can continue to make to the achievement of world peace.

The 'Lesser Peace', in Bahá'í terminology, refers to the political unification of the world and the achievement of peace among nations through simultaneous disarmament and arms limitation, with a universal agreement to abandon war as a way of settling conflicts and the establishment of mechanisms of collective security.[7] It therefore implies a process of political unity among States, as a step in the gradual progress towards a larger unity among the nations and peoples of the world.

There are several dimensions to the interaction between processes for peace and the environment:

- Environmental science has demonstrated the unity of the world system.
- The need for international environmental management has driven increasing political cooperation and trends in the

years to come will inevitably increase the pressure for shared efforts and common solutions.
• The environment has provided areas of common interest for disparate groups to work together.

Each of these points will be elaborated in the sections that follow.

The Force of Scientific Evidence

The growing number of international environmental problems has great significance for the political evolution of society. They communicate the interrelationships of all things with the force of scientific evidence which is politically neutral and hard to deny. The hole in the ozone layer, the headlines about dioxin contamination and declining sperm counts, and the worries about climate change all drive home the message that this Earth is a single system and we are all living in it together. Science is also building a better understanding of how the planetary system works, with satellite observations, new monitoring technologies and computer models. The El Niño Southern Oscillation, which shifts warm water masses across the tropical Pacific Ocean and has severe repercussions on weather patterns all around the world, can now be modelled and predicted with reasonable accuracy. There is a reality to these and other scientific discoveries about the linkages and interactions of the global environment that no politician can argue against. They emphasize the shared responsibility of all nations and peoples. The following examples, showing how science has leveraged global political action on emerging environmental issues, are based on summaries prepared for the UN system by Earthwatch.[8]

Ozone Depletion

The discovery of damage to the stratospheric ozone layer is a good illustration of a truly global problem. Scientific research in 1974 (which won the 1995 Nobel Prize for its authors) suggested that man-made chemicals such as the chloroflourocarbons (CFCs) might catalyze the destruction of ozone. This would increase ground level ultraviolet solar radiation, resulting in skin cancer and unpredictable damage to plants, algae, the food chain and the global ecosystem. A seasonal hole in the Antarctic ozone layer was in fact discovered in the 1980s. It has been growing larger and similar damage has now been observed in the Arctic. Scientists have obtained conclusive proof that CFCs and similar chemicals used in refrigerators, in manufacturing processes and as pesticides are the cause of ozone depletion in the stratosphere, by finding chemicals there that could come from no other source.[9] Since these chemicals are entirely man-made, the solution is for all countries to stop manufacturing and using them. However, the damage to the ozone layer continues to accelerate, thinning twice as fast as predicted, for reasons scientists cannot explain. The greenhouse effect, which causes stratospheric cooling, may be contributing to ozone hole formation and may also slow recovery even after ozone depleting substances start declining.[10]

Persistent Organic Pollutants

One of the most pressing environmental issues today is that presented by persistent organic pollutants (POPs), which take a long time to break down in the environment and cannot be contained once released. Pesticides such as DDT were considered one of the great miracles of industrial civilization in mid-century, until it was discovered that these and other persistent organic pollutants were accumulating in the environment, passing up the food chain and affecting human and animal health. Over the past few years there has been an increasing body of evidence documenting their devastating effects on wildlife, including wasting syndromes, shrinking populations, birth defects such as missing eyes and deformed reproductive organs, and behavioural disorders such as same-sex nests and loss of sex drive. POPs present serious human health risks including mimicking reproductive hormones, immune suppression, carcinogenesis, and effects on embryonic development including lowered intelligence, poor short-term memory, a shortened attention span and difficulties in learning to read.[11]

POPs are now found in a variety of food products, with millions of people potentially exposed to dangerous levels. They accumulate exponentially in fatty tissue as they move up the food chain, such that concentrations can be 70,000 times the background levels in a top predator. They thus collect in human blood and body fats, with high concentrations in breast milk.[12] We now have 300 to 500 measurable man-made chemicals in our bodies that would not have been found there 50 years ago.[13]

Furthermore, POPs are transported globally. For example, dioxin in the Great Lakes comes from as far away as Florida and California[14] and potentially damaging levels of DDT, PCBs and dioxin-like compounds have been found in wildlife on remote Pacific islands thousands of kilometres from heavily populated areas. There is a systematic transfer of these chemicals from warmer to colder areas through the process of global distillation. The pollutants evaporate from soils in warm areas such as the tropics, are transported as vapour around the globe and condense over cold areas as toxic snow or rain, causing widespread contamination of the arctic and antarctic ecosystems, with high levels found in wildlife and people. In some traditional Inuit villages, two-thirds of children have blood-PCB levels above Canadian health guidelines.[15]

Climate Change

Another example is the threat of global warming and climate change. The principal driving force is the accumulation in the atmosphere of carbon dioxide from the burning of the fossil fuels that power most of Western civilization and to a lesser extent from forest destruction and other factors. Other greenhouse gases also contribute. Everyone is responsible, even if the most industrialized countries have contributed longest and the largest share. The only possible solution is a coordinated international response and the United Nations adopted a Framework Convention on Climate Change in 1992 for this purpose.[16]

The third assessment of the Intergovernmental Panel on Climate Change (IPCC), adopted in September 2002, states that the world is now warming faster than at any time since the last ice age, with the 1990s the warmest decade and 1998 the warmest year in the instrumental record. It concludes that some of these changes are attributable to human activities.[17] The IPCC has identified an 'increased risk of hunger and famine, particularly among the poor in sub-Saharan Africa, south, east and south-east Asia, tropical areas of Latin America, as well as some Pacific Island nations'.[18] In its assessment of regional vulnerability to climate change impacts, it has shown that billions of people could be affected by exacerbated problems in drinking water supply, sanitation and drought. Food production could decrease in the tropics and subtropics, despite steady global production. Significant adverse effects on small island States and low-lying deltas such as in Bangladesh, Egypt and China could displace tens of millions of people with one metre of sea-level rise. Heat stress mortality and vector-borne diseases could increase. Most effects are negative for the most vulnerable developing countries.[19]

Much of the controversy about proving scientifically the reality of climate change is because the wrong effects are being measured. The effects should appear not as global warming, since the tropics and the poles will show little temperature change, but as global heating expressed by increased variability and shifts in the latitude of biological and climatological features in temperate regions. The tropics will grow wider and the polar regions will shrink. These effects are already being demonstrated.[20] Critics also pointed to a cooling rather than heating trend in the atmosphere as measured from satellites but this was recently shown to be an artifact of the failure to correct for the decreasing altitude of the satellites. While it still may be some years before human-induced climate change can be confirmed statistically, the scientific evidence is growing steadily stronger.

Global System

These and other global environmental problems demonstrate the interconnectedness of the Earth system.[21] Some scientists go so far as to describe the planet as a single self-regulating system comparable to an organism[22] based on the fact that the necessary conditions for life were created and are maintained by biological activity. It is true that the oxygen in the atmosphere was generated millions of years ago by biological processes and that the mechanisms that maintain the temperature of the biosphere within an acceptable range for living things appear quite sophisticated. The processes of evolution are also clearly planetary in scope. Drifting continents separating and combining species, global extinction events like the meteorite impact that probably eliminated the dinosaurs, and the evolution of humans and their migration across the face of the Earth, all demonstrate that nature knows no borders.

We are far from understanding how complex ecological systems and biogeochemical cycles work on this planet but rapid progress is being made. Each new discovery reinforces the picture of complex interrelationships, interactions and feedbacks, combining surprising resilience and worrying vulnerability. In addition, many of the large-scale systems operate with very long time lags. By the time we detect a problem, it may be far too late to do much about it, hence the importance of modelling, predictions and the application of the precautionary principle. Still, natural systems have a much longer record of success than human systems. Ecological systems can therefore provide models with many useful lessons for the design of human society.[23]

The environmental movement has built itself on this scientific demonstration of world unity. The early concern focused on widespread contamination by pesticides and on major oil spills resulting from the global trade in petroleum products. Whales, which roam all the seas of the world and were nearly driven to extinction by unregulated hunting, became a symbol of environmental concern. The slogan of the first world environmental conference in 1972 was 'Only One Earth'.

Political Cooperation on the Environment

From the time of that first United Nations Conference on the Human Environment, held in Stockholm in June 1972, the environment has been a growing force for political cooperation. That conference gave rise to the United Nations Environment Programme (UNEP), charged with catalyzing a global response to environmental problems. Many international conventions have been adopted to legislate controls on environmental problems ranging from marine pollution, trade in toxic chemicals and hazardous wastes, to biodiversity conservation, trade in endangered species, climate change and desertification. Agreements on biosafety and persistent organic pollutants have recently been concluded.

Ozone Depleting Substances

The response to the damage to the ozone layer illustrates the success of this approach. When research in 1974 first indicated that some man-made chemicals had the potential to harm the stratospheric ozone layer, UNEP called for preventive international action and finally succeeded in convincing 28 governments to adopt the Vienna Convention on the Protection of the Ozone Layer in 1985. The first evidence soon after of the ozone hole over the Antarctic pushed governments to adopt the Montreal Protocol on Substances that Deplete the Ozone Layer in 1987.[24] As scientific knowledge of the causes and effects increased, the protocol was amended in 1990, 1992 and 1997 to speed up the elimination of emissions of man-made ozone-depleting substances. One hundred eighty-four countries are now parties to the convention[25] and the substances controlled under it are now beginning to decline in the lower atmosphere.

The reduction and elimination of the production of many ozone-depleting substances in industrialized countries under the Montreal Protocol is a major international environmental accomplishment.[26] The results of the latest WMO/UNEP scientific assessment of ozone depletion confirm its effectiveness. The abundance of ozone-depleting substances in the stratosphere has probably peaked, although detecting the start of the ozone layer recovery may not be possible for some years. A full recovery of the Earth's protective ozone shield could occur by the middle of this century if the Protocol is fully implemented. However, even with the reduction in the use and release of ozone-depleting substances, the long life of chemicals already released in the atmosphere will keep the depletion going for years to come. If control measures had not been taken, the ozone decline would have been much stronger and would have continued for many more decades.[27]

Chemicals

Persistent organic pollutants are another area where governments have recognized that unified international action is needed, despite the difficulty in reconciling their concerns. They are taking action against the most threatening chemicals through legally binding conventions to ensure the protection of public health and the environment. In June 1998, 33 countries and the European Community agreed the UN/ECE Protocol on Persistent Organic Pollutants to the Convention on Long-range Transboundary Air Pollution, which bans 16 different POPs. In September 1998 in Rotterdam a legally binding convention requiring the prior informed consent of countries to international shipments of toxic chemicals was signed by 61 countries. And in 2001, over 150 countries signed the Stockholm Convention, a legally binding international agreement to reduce and/or eliminate releases of 12 of the POPs most widely implicated in damage to human health and the environment, including pesticides like DDT and dieldrin, polychlorinated biphenyls (PCBs) and dioxins.[28]

Greenhouse Gases

In the area of climate change, the scientific uncertainty is greatest, the economic forces involved the largest and the conflict of national interests the most intense. The latest work by the IPCC on climate inertia and the long life of gases shows that the full effects of past emissions will occur even if industrialized countries reduce emissions by 30 to 90 per cent, since global emissions will still reach two to three times 1990 levels. There are still large margins of error in calculating natural sources and sinks.[29] The most damaging effects will be felt in the developing countries of the tropics, while the costs of the necessary control measures will fall most heavily on industrialized countries in temperate regions. The fossil fuel technologies that produce the most greenhouse gases are the very foundation of industrial society, so there is strong resistance to any change. In addition, the long time lags before serious effects will be evident encourages decision-makers to procrastinate. Yet, given the scale of the potential consequences, failure to act would be irresponsible. The UN Framework Convention on Climate Change establishes the political mechanism to work out these conflicts, and with the Kyoto Protocol of 1997 some significant progress has been made. However, it seems unlikely at present that most industrialized countries will live up to their commitments, and the world's largest contributor to the problem has withdrawn from the protocol, seeing it as a threat to its national interests. An active interaction between science, economics and politics can be expected in this area for years to come. The fact that those interactions are now taking place within an appropriate international mechanism is already a hopeful sign, even if real progress is slow in coming.

Regional Seas

The environment has also been a force for regional cooperation despite the most daunting political obstacles. UNEP, for instance, brought countries together starting in 1974 to cooperate in the protection and management of shared Regional Seas, such as the Mediterranean, the Caribbean, the Persian/Arabian Gulf and the South Pacific. In each sea area the countries adopted a Convention and implemented a joint action plan.[30] The imperative need to manage a shared environmental resource overcame many political barriers. In the Mediterranean, countries like Greece and Turkey, Israel and Libya cooperated successfully despite their political differences. During the

Iran–Iraq war, the two warring countries continued to meet and cooperate in the Kuwait Action Plan and its Regional Organization for the Protection of the Marine Environment while the exploding bombs across the Gulf resonated in the background. In these circumstances, the environment was truly a force maintaining the collaboration between countries that is an important step toward peace.

Earth Summit

The United Nations Conference on Environment and Development in Rio de Janeiro in 1992 was another important step towards global awareness and cooperation. In what was then the largest meeting ever of Heads of State and Government, more than 100 gathered at the 'Earth Summit' and adopted a declaration and Action Plan (Agenda 21) that mapped out a wide range of cooperative activities to protect the environment and achieve sustainable development.[31] Conventions on climate change and on biodiversity were also signed. Another unique feature of the Rio Conference was the associated Global Forum where thousands of representatives of non-governmental organizations across the whole spectrum of major groups in civil society gathered to build their own cooperative networks and to encourage and reinforce the governmental efforts. The momentum started at Rio has continued in the work of the UN Commission for Sustainable Development that was established after Rio to pursue the implementation of Agenda 21 and been taken a step further at the World Summit on Sustainable Development held in Johannesburg ten years later.[32]

Other collaborative activities have spun off from the Earth Summit. The Small Island Developing States adopted their own plan of action in Barbados in 1994 and continue to explore innovative solutions to global problems.[33] A convention on desertification has been adopted,[34] as well as a global programme of action for the protection of the marine environment from land-based activities.[35]

All of this intergovernmental effort to address common environmental problems has been building habits of cooperation among governments. While it is never easy to reconcile conflicting national interests, in case after case the need for joint efforts to address problems from which everyone suffers has led to a consensus for action. If the disparate nations of the world can do this for the environment, perhaps some day they will be ready do it as well in the interests of a just and lasting peace.

Development Choices

Some issues do not stand out clearly when the environment is considered on a global basis. One of these is the very different environmental situations and perceptions of different groups of countries, particularly the highly industrialized countries on the one hand and the poor developing countries on the other. This debate has been going on since the Stockholm Conference in 1972 and has perhaps even been aggravated by the growing gap between the richest and poorest countries in recent years.

The industrialized countries have been trying to learn from their past environmental mistakes and recognize the cost and difficulty of cleaning up pollution and repairing past environmental damage. They therefore urge the poor countries to leapfrog the damaging stages of industrialization and to do as they say, not as they did. The poorest countries, however, faced with the often desperate needs of their population, say that environmental protection is a luxury they cannot afford. They ask why they should forego opportunities for their development, or adopt more expensive technologies, in order to protect the environment. In addition, much of the planetary capacity to produce raw materials and absorb wastes (such as the greenhouse gases) has been used up by the wealthy countries, leaving little possibility for the poor countries to develop without causing major damage.

This is a particularly challenging area in the efforts to achieve a just peace among nations. It has roots in the colonial past of many wealthy countries and is complicated today by the fact that much economic power and control formerly held by governments has now passed to multinational corporations, institutional investors and other elements of the private sector. Only a few facets of the problem can be touched on here.

Part of the issue is the willingness to transfer financial resources in order to pay the costs of sustainable development. Agenda 21 was costed at about $120 billion (thousand million) per year in international costs to achieve the sustainable development of the planet. This may seem high but it is only a fraction of global arms expenditures and would come out favourably in a cost-benefit analysis. However, only about $20 billion was pledged at the Rio Earth Summit and in fact global official development assistance and support to the organizations expected to implement Agenda 21 has declined considerably since 1992. Only a few countries have respected the international engagement to contribute 0.7 per cent of their GNP in development assistance. The failure to fund the commitments made at United Nations conferences has been a major area of international friction. The wealthy nations push for others to make sacrifices but are unwilling to do so themselves. This problem will probably continue until systems of international taxation are agreed that can raise revenues for international obligations without competing with national treasuries and political pressures.

There are a few exceptions that demonstrate that international solidarity is possible. Under the Montreal Protocol to phase out ozone depleting substances, a Multilateral Fund was established to finance the costs to developing countries for the necessary changes in technologies. The Global Environment Facility (GEF) was also established to help pay developing countries for the incremental costs of adopting measures in the areas of climate change, ozone depletion, biodiversity and international waters that benefit the international community but not the country itself. The GEF has become the financial mechanism for the Framework Convention on Climate Change and the Convention on Biological Diversity signed in Rio.[36]

What this issue demonstrates is that both peace and the environment require a reduction in economic and technological inequalities between countries. This will have a direct benefit on the environment, not least because much environmental damage is in fact caused by the excessive consumption of the rich and the desperate struggle for survival of the poor. There also needs to be a greater willingness to consult together in a search for the welfare of the whole planet and not just in defence of national interests. It is evident that priorities must be different at different levels of social and economic development and an evolutionary progression in environmental standards is often the only realistic option. Consultation and the application of the best scientific knowledge can help all countries to understand each others' situations and to strike an appropriate balance. Despite these differences in perspective, many developing countries have recognized the importance of sound environmental management and have made important progress in this area.

A New Partnership of Science and Religion

The environment has also become a force bringing disparate groups together in new partnerships based on a commonality of interests. For example, science and religion have often been in opposition. Yet in recent years the environment has not only brought scientists and religious leaders together but has united the religions themselves in common actions for environmental protection. While there were already discussions on this theme at the Environment Forum associated with the Stockholm Conference in 1972, it was only in 1986 that the World Wide Fund for Nature (WWF) invited the major religions to Assisi to form a network on religion and conservation. Nine years later the WWF convened a World Summit on Religions and Conservation at Windsor Castle in 1995, where leaders of the Bahá'í Faith, Buddhism, Catholic, Orthodox and Protestant Christianity, Hinduism, Islam, Jainism, Judaism, Sikhism and Taoism agreed on the common moral imperative for conserving nature and protecting the environment, and launched an Alliance of Religions and Conservation.[37]

Another sign of this convergence has been the series of Klingenthal Symposia on ecology, ethics and spirituality organized by Pax Christi in France between 1995 and 2001, where scientists and representatives of various religious and spiritual traditions met to agree on areas of common concern and action.[38] The Orthodox Church has also organized major symposia on Religion, Science and the Environment, of which the second in September 1997, on the Black Sea in Crisis, brought together nearly 200 religious leaders, leading scientists, politicians and journalists for ten days of intensive consultations on the necessary partnership of religion and science if the problems of the environment are to be solved, while visiting by ship all the countries around the Black Sea.

Trends Ahead

Despite progress in a few areas, the environmental problems of the planet are worsening.[39] The driving forces are the growing world population and the unsustainable consumption of resources in the most developed countries and by the wealthy everywhere. The pressures for global cooperation on the environment will thus inevitably increase. Many of the past environmental agreements are still far from being implemented effectively, so further effort will be required within existing mechanisms. There are also some major threats requiring further agreement on action. It is not possible to review all the trends ahead but a few examples will illustrate the environmental pressures on governments to cooperate.

Climate Change

Responding to the threat of climate change caused by the release of greenhouse gases is a major challenge, as it threatens the very foundations of the present industrial society. Imagine the economic and social impact if all technologies using fossil fuels (oil, coal, gas) had to be phased out and the related infrastructure junked or adapted to other uses. On the other hand, failure to act in time could result in sudden climate change driving whole populations to migrate as their environments become uninhabitable. The challenge that this limit to environmental capacity presents to society is immense. In many ways, the effluents and wastes of our affluent society are overwhelming the capacity of the environment to absorb and neutralize them. As Bahá'u'lláh warned over a hundred years ago: 'The civilization, so often vaunted by the learned exponents of arts and sciences, will, if allowed to overleap the bounds of moderation, bring great evil upon men.'[40]

Invasive Species

The dangers represented by invasive species introduced accidentally or intentionally from other parts of the world are now attracting increasing attention because of the ecological havoc they are causing in many ecosystems and the high economic costs of controlling them, where that is even technically possible. The full extent of the problems caused by this 'biological homogenization' of the planet can only be dimly imagined at present and is not yet fully appreciated. Another worrying trend is the overuse of pesticides and antibiotics, resulting in growing resistance in pests and diseases, which could become uncontrollable. Coupled with this is the steady erosion of natural areas and the accompanying loss of biodiversity. The rate at which productive natural ecosystems such as coral reefs are being stressed and degraded is frightening. The causes are multiple: pollution by eutrophication and siltation from adjacent land; overfishing; mining corals and sand for construction; destructive fishing methods; temperature stress from global warming; and biological imbalances and epidemic diseases; all largely of human origin or probably aggravated by human interference. Because of the long time lags between causes and effects, the significance of this biological and ecological damage and loss of diversity will only be apparent in the future.

Economic Globalization and Trade

The process of economic globalization, with the free movement of capital and increasing liberalization of trade, will bring with it increasing global pressures to exploit natural resources wherever they occur. The global trade in forest products, for instance, puts equal pressures on all the world's forests. However, trade only values the forest as a source of marketable materials, not as an ecological system with multiple benefits. If the demand for wood chips for paper pulp or for plywood can be met more cheaply from tropical rainforests than from temperate conifers, then the tropical forests will be cut regardless of their non-market values such as for biodiversity conservation, watershed protection or carbon sequestration. It is often the poorest countries that cannot afford to say no to international logging companies, even if they know their long-term interest is in more sustainable forest management for multiple uses. New mechanisms will be required to manage these global forces and to protect environmental and other interests not accounted for by the market. In the case of forest resources, for example, a global tax on trade in forest products could be used to compensate those forest owners who forego exploiting their forests because of other non-market values they represent for society.[41] Ultimately, global resource exploitation will have to be accompanied by global management of all the world's resources by a world federal system for global benefit.[42]

This globalization of the market could have dire consequences in the case of food. If the world reaches the point where the food demand of the growing population outstrips the supply, then the wealthy countries will bid up the price of grain to feed their livestock for high-priced meat and in the process take food out of the mouths of the poor who will no longer be able to afford it. There has already been some concern that the rising standard of living in China, and therefore the demand for more meat in the rice, could already have a similar effect.[43] Other estimates do not suggest a food crisis in the immediate future but the mechanism is a logical consequence of global market forces. Only a collective global response that puts other human values above the free operation of the market could prevent such a situation from arising. Whether such a situation becomes a source of conflict or a pressure for more just and peaceful relations will depend on the quality of leadership at the time.

Conflicting International Legislation

Another evident trend is the logical consequence of the current procedures for international legislation. At present each environmental problem gives rise to negotiations to conclude another multilateral environmental agreement. Each such agreement is a separate convention, signed and ratified by its own parties (government members), with its own decision-making bodies and secretariat. Even if the government members are largely the same, there is no direct connection between different agreements. Already there are overlaps and contradictions between different pieces of international legislation. The Convention on International Trade in Endangered Species, for instance, bans trade in listed endangered species[44] and the Basel Convention controls trade in hazardous wastes which industry might want to dispose of cheaply in developing countries,[45] while the World Trade Organization adopts agreements which prohibit any barriers to free international trade.[46] As more and more international legislative texts are adopted in this way, the world will move towards a kind of legislative gridlock or paralysis, since there is no mechanism to harmonize the different independent conventions or to resolve disputes between them. Ultimately the only solution will be the formation of an international legislature able to pass and modify laws across the whole spectrum of international action, as is presently done at the national level.[47] The processes of international environmental legislation are thus also a force that, through their present internal contradictions, will encourage the world to establish the structures necessary to bring peace.

Global Environmental Information

The need for global environmental management also requires reliable information on the state of the environment and its resources. International organizations and the scientific community are putting into place the necessary programmes for observing and assessing the state of and trends in the environment, including a Global Climate Observing System, a Global

Ocean Observing System and a Global Terrestrial Observing System within the framework of an Integrated Global Observing Strategy bringing together the space agencies, the UN organizations, the scientific community and major global research programmes.[48] Building a coordinated international environmental information system will also reinforce cooperation and joint action among governments.

Another difficult but necessary step will be the realization that global action requires the support of global financial mechanisms, including global taxation. Such proposals are already being increasingly aired in various quarters. From the environmental perspective, some forms of global taxes could assist in a just burden-sharing of the needs of environmental protection and resource management.

Risks of Environmental Crisis

These environmental trends will certainly help to leverage the coming of that political unification of nations referred to as the Lesser Peace. What is not so clear is the combination of processes by which governments and nations will finally take the necessary steps to bring such a peace to the world. It could be only after unimaginable horrors, or voluntarily through an act of consultative will.[49] It will probably be some combination of crisis and advancement. Unfortunately, major steps forward in human social development have generally only resulted from crises that overcame inertia and created sufficient will for action.

A major environmental crisis could be a precipitating cause for the final steps towards peace. Some possible scenarios for such a crisis might include:

- an abrupt shift in weather and climate patterns driven by changed ocean currents,

- contamination of large densely-inhabited areas by a nuclear accident, terrorist attack or the use of biological warfare agents, or

- widespread health impacts and epidemics from irretrievable chemical pollution impairing the immune system.

An environmental catastrophe could wreak ecological as well as human havoc, create floods of environmental refugees, or render large areas uninhabitable for a long period. Severe environmental impacts would almost certainly accompany any other potential crises such as a global war or economic collapse. Bahá'u'lláh warned that civilization, if carried to excess, would prove a prolific source of evil: 'The day is approaching when its flame will devour the cities.'[50]

If a major crisis in civilization causes widespread famine, disease and migration, environmental problems will certainly aggravate the consequences. For example, the populations in urban areas and developed regions are increasingly dependent on highly technological systems to deliver food, provide clean water and eliminate pollution. Any breakdown in those systems will leave them vulnerable to famines and epidemics. Agriculture is also increasingly dependent on sophisticated inputs. Just consider how much more interdependent Western society has become in the 60 years since the last major disruption of civilization during the Second World War and imagine the consequences of a similar disruption today.

Ecology and the Lesser Peace

Regardless of whether the environment contributes directly to moves to establish peace in the world, it is difficult to imagine a political peace that is not also supported by a more sustainable society. The kinds of environmental problems described in the sections above would be a continuing source of tension and conflict incompatible with establishing and maintaining peace. Thus even the Lesser Peace implies changes in society to bring it around towards environmental sustainability. The creation of international institutional mechanisms for peace will also facilitate global decision-making and resource management to resolve environmental problems. Without them, there is little hope of significant progress on the environment.[51]

There are various groups and authors developing scenarios of such possible futures.[52] These generally start by describing 'business as usual' with the simple projection of present trends based on the dominance of the Western capitalist free market approach. The tendency is for increasing material success in the wealthiest countries and among the middle classes but growing extremes of wealth and poverty and unsustainable use of resources. This is then contrasted with a scenario of social breakdown, with the industrialized countries retreating into a 'fortress world' and giving up on trying to help solve the anarchy and chaos of the poorest regions. A third scenario explores the practicality of a constructive response based on fundamental changes in direction in present society. Such positive scenarios have the merit of demonstrating that a transformed world based on solidarity and sustainability is a rational alternative if society is prepared to make the necessary changes and sacrifices. What they do not show is how to do it.

Such studies also demonstrate that the world's problems of environmental protection and sustainability cannot be addressed in isolation. Only when all the nations come together in unity and work wholeheartedly for their common benefit will much real progress be made. The establishment of the institutions of the Lesser Peace will reinforce processes of consultation and joint action at the global level. The stage will then be set for the increasing application of spiritual principles to environmental protection and management as the foundations are laid for a new world civilization.[53]

The Bahá'í writings also contain a scenario or vision of a future peaceful society that incorporates essential elements of sustainability,[54] some excerpts from which are discussed below. They set the institutional context for sustainable management of the planetary environment as a single system. In this view, the unity of the human race will be reflected in the establishment of a world commonwealth including legislative, executive and judicial powers. A world legislature will act as the trustees of the whole of humanity to 'control the entire resources of all the component nations, and will enact such laws as shall be required to regulate the life, satisfy the needs and adjust the relationships of all races and peoples . . . The economic resources of the world will be organized, its sources of raw materials will be tapped and fully utilized, its markets will be coordinated and developed, and the distribution of its products will be equitably regulated.' The establishment of peace will free enormous resources for scientific research, technological development, increases in human productivity, improvements in human health, and 'the exploitation of the unused and unsuspected resources of the planet'. The result will be a world federal system exercising its authority over the Earth's unimaginably vast resources and exploiting all the available sources of energy on the surface of the planet.[55]

Within such a framework, it will finally be possible to develop comprehensive and effective solutions to the complex challenges of sustainable development and sound environmental management on this planet. A coherent set of international environmental legislation, regulations and incentives could be evolved. The threat of climate change could be countered by reducing the increase in greenhouse gases in the atmosphere to slow the rate of change and by assisting countries and regions most affected to adapt to the consequences of inevitable change. The excessive use of threatening chemicals could be regulated and ozone depleting substances could be rapidly phased out. Development could be directed away from those areas essential to preserve biological diversity and to maintain the ecological balance of the planet. Special attention would need to be paid to the social implications of such changes. Peace will already be socially and economically traumatic, eliminating most of the armaments industry and employment possibilities in the military services. The need to respect environmental limits will impose other changes, such as in the energy and transport industries and in agriculture. Major pillars of Western economies will disappear, and while new opportunities will be created, the changes required are never easy and require a strong sense of solidarity and assistance to the millions who will be affected. The Lesser Peace will not be the end of a process of transition but only one intermediate step.

One important component of the new international machinery for peace will have to be a new approach to science. Maintaining the ecological balance of the world will require a great increase in scientific knowledge and multiple levels of environmental monitoring and management ranging from the global to the local levels. Science will have to cease being the preserve of an intellectual elite and be so organized that everyone has a basic environmental understanding and can think in terms of scientific processes. Science also needs to be combined with religion and ethical values as two complementary knowledge systems necessary to build a peaceful and prosperous society.[56] Providing a common scientific understanding of the environmental issues facing the planet will facilitate the search for just and peaceful means to resolve them and reinforce other dimensions of the peace process.

In this way, peace, science and the environment will be intertwined, with each supporting the others. The environment may well help to give birth to the Lesser Peace, which will in turn contribute to the resolution of the environmental challenges which are among the tragic legacies of the 20th century.

Bibliography

Bahá'í International Community. *International Legislation for Environment and Development*. Statement presented to the 2nd session of the Preparatory Committee of the United Nations Conference on Environment and Development (UNCED), Geneva, 5 April 1991. New York: Bahá'í International Community, 1991.
<www.bcca.org/ief/bicileg.htm>

— *The Prosperity of Humankind*. New York: Bahá'í International Community United Nations Office, 1995.

Bahá'u'lláh. *Gleanings from the Writings of Bahá'u'lláh*. Wilmette, IL: Bahá'í Publishing Trust, 1983.

Barry, James P., Chuck H. Baxter, Rafe D. Sagarin and Sarah E. Gilman. 'Climate-related, long-term faunal changes in a California rocky intertidal community'. *Science*, no. 267, 1995.

Brown, Lester R. 'Facing the prospect of food scarcity', in Brown et al., *State of the World 1997: A Worldwatch Institute Report on Progress Toward a Sustainable Society*. New York: W.W. Norton & Co., 1997.

— et al. *State of the World 1997: A Worldwatch Institute Report on Progress Toward a Sustainable Society*. New York: W.W. Norton & Co., 1997.

Colborn, Theo, Dianne Dumanoski and John Peterson Myers. *Our Stolen Future*. New York: Dutton, 1996.

Conservation of the Earth's Resources. Compilation of the Research Department of the Universal House of Justice. London: Bahá'í Publishing Trust, 1990.

Dahl, Arthur Lyon. *The Eco Principle: Ecology and Economics in Symbiosis*. Oxford: George Ronald; London: Zed Books, 1996.

— 'Global Sustainability and its Implications for Trade'. *GATT Trade and Environment Bulletin*, no. 009, 28 July 1994.

— *Unless and Until: A Bahá'í Focus on the Environment*. London: Bahá'í Publishing Trust, 1990.

Darwin, Charles. *Journal of Researches by Charles Darwin into the Natural History & Geology of the Countries Visited during the Voyage of H.M.S. Beagle under the Command of Capt. FitzRoy, R.N. 1845*. Reprint: Cambridge: The Limited Editions Club, 1956.

EEA. *Europe's Environment 1995*. European Environment Agency, Copenhagen, 1995.

Edwards, Jo and Martin Palmer (eds.). *Holy Ground: The Guide to Faith and Ecology*. Yelvertoft Manor, Northamptonshire: Pilkington Press, 1997.

ENB. Report of the Meetings of the FCCC Subsidiary Bodies 20–31 October 1997. *Earth Negotiations Bulletin*, vol. 12, no. 66, 1997. <www.iisd.ca/linkages/vol12/enb1266e.html>

Gove, P.B. (ed.). *Webster's Third New International Dictionary of the English Language, Unabridged*. Springfield, MA: G. & C. Merriam Company, 1976.

Hammond, Allen. *Which World? Scenarios for the 21st Century: Global Destinies, Regional Choices*. Washington DC: Island Press and Covelo, CA: Shearwater Books, 1998.

IPCC. *Climate Change 1995*. WMO/UNEP Intergovernmental Panel on Climate Change, Second Assessment Report. Cambridge: Cambridge University Press, 1995.

— *Climate Change 2001: Synthesis Report. Summary for Policy Makers*. <www.ipcc.ch/pub/SYRspm.pdf>

Kleiner, Kurt. 'Long-lived pollutants threaten the great Lakes'. *New Scientist*, 13 July 1996.

Lee, Kathy. *Prelude to the Lesser Peace*. New Delhi: Bahá'í Publishing Trust, 1989.

Lovelock, James E. *The Ages of Gaia: A Biography of Our Living Earth*. New York: W.W. Norton & Co., 1988.

— *Gaia: A New Look at Life on Earth*. Oxford: Oxford University Press, 1979.

Lowrie, Margaret. *CNN Environment*, 27 June 1997.

MacKenzie, Debora. 'Rich and poor split over ozone'. *New Scientist*, 9 December 1995.

Pearce, Fred. 'Big freeze digs a deeper hole in ozone layer'. *New Scientist*, 16 March 1996.

— 'Northern Exposure'. *New Scientist*, 31 May 1997.

Ribaut, Jean-Pierre and Marie-José Del Ray. *The Earth Under Care: Spiritual and Cultural Approaches to the Challenges for a Sustainable Planet*. The Klingenthal Appeal and Contributions for the October 1995 Symposium. Dossier pour un Débat 73 bis. Paris: La Librairie FPH, 1997.

Russell, James M., M.Z. Luo, R.J. Cicerone and L.E. Deaver. 'Satellite confirmation of the dominance of chloroflourocarbons in the global stratospheric chlorine budget'. *Nature*, no. 379, February 1996.

SEI/UNEP. Paul Raskin, Gilberto Gallopin, Pablo Gutman, Al Hammond and Rob Swart. *Bending the Curve: Toward Global Sustainability*. PoleStar Series Report no. 8, 1998; UNEP/DEIA/TR.98-4.

Shoghi Effendi. *The World Order of Bahá'u'lláh*. Wilmette, IL: Bahá'í Publishing Trust, 1991.

Tolba, Mostafa K., Osama A. El-Kholy. E. El-Hinnawi, M.W. Holdgate, D.F. McMichael and R.E. Munn. *The World Environment 1972–1992: Two Decades of Challenge*. UNEP and London: Chapman & Hall, 1992.

UNEP. *Global Environment Outlook 3*. London: Earthscan Publications Ltd, 2002.

United Nations. *Earth Summit. Agenda 21: The United Nations Programme of Action from Rio*. New York: United Nations, 1992.

The Universal House of Justice. *The Promise of World Peace*. Haifa: Bahá'í World Centre, 1985.

Van den Brink, N.W. 'Directed transport of volatile organochlorine pollutants to polar regions: The effect on the contamination pattern of Antarctic seabirds'. *The Science of the Total Environment*, vol. 198, no. 1, 1997.

WMO/UNEP. *Scientific Assessment of Ozone Depletion – 1998*, WMO Ozone Report no. 44. Geneva: World Meteorological Organization, 1998.

References

1. The views expressed are those of the author and do not necessarily reflect those of the United Nations Environment Programme.

2. Gove, *Webster's Third New International Dictionary of the English Language.*
3. Dahl, *The Eco Principle*, p. 133.
4. Darwin, *Journal of Researches.*
5. Dahl, *Unless and Until*, p. 23.
6. Universal House of Justice, *Promise of World Peace*, p. 3.
7. Lee, *Prelude to the Lesser Peace*, pp. 25, 75ff.
8. <www.earthwatch.unep.net>
9. Russell, Luo, Cicerone and Deaver, 'Satellite confirmation of the dominance of chloroflourocarbons in the global stratospheric chlorine budget', *Nature* no. 379, pp. 526–9.
10. MacKenzie, 'Rich and poor split over ozone', *New Scientist*, 9 December 1995; Pearce, 'Big freeze digs a deeper hole in ozone layer', *New Scientist*, 16 March 1996.
11. Colborn, Dumanoski and Myers, *Our Stolen Future*; Pearce, 'Northern Exposure', *New Scientist*, 31 May 1997, pp. 24–7.
12. Colborn et al., *Our Stolen Future.*
13. Lowrie, *CNN Environment*, 27 June 1997.
14. Kleiner, 'Long-lived pollutants threaten the Great Lakes', *New Scientist*, 13 July 1996.
15. Van den Brink, 'Directed transport of volatile organochlorine pollutants to polar regions: the effect on the contamination pattern of Antarctic seabirds', *The Science of the Total Environment*, vol. 198, no. 1, 1997, pp. 43–50; Pearce, 'Northern Exposure', *New Scientist*, 31 May 1997, pp. 24–7.
16. <www.unfccc.de>
17. IPCC, *Climate Change 2001*, p. 4. <www.ipcc.ch>
18. IPCC, *Climate Change 1995*, p. 5.
19. ENB, 'Report of the Meetings', *Earth Negotiations Bulletin*, vol. 12, no. 66. <www.iisd.ca/linkages/vol12/enb1266e.html>
20. Barry, Baxter, Sagarin and Gilman, 'Climate-related, long-term faunal changes in a California rocky intertidal community', *Science* no. 267, pp. 672–5.
21. UNEP, *Global Environment Outlook.*
22. The 'Gaia' hypothesis. Lovelock, *Gaia* and Lovelock, *The Ages of Gaia.*
23. Dahl, *The Eco Principle.*
24. Tolba, El-Kholy, El-Hinnawi, Holdgate, McMichael and Munn, *The World Environment 1972–1992*, p. 34.
25. <www.unep.org/ozone>
26. European Environment Agency, *Europe's Environment 1995.*
27. WMO/UNEP, *Scientific Assessment of Ozone Depletion – 1998*, WMO

Ozone Report no. 44.
28. <www.pops.int>
29. ENB, 'Report of the Meetings', *Earth Negotiations Bulletin*, vol. 12, no. 66. <www.iisd.ca/linkages/vol12/enb1266e.html>
30. <www.unep.ch/seas>
31. United Nations, *Earth Summit. Agenda 21*.
32. <www.un.org/esa/sustdev>; <www.johannesburgsummit.org>
33. <www.un.org/esa/sustdev/sids.htm>
34. <www.unccd.ch>
35. <www.gpa.unep.org>
36. <www.gefweb.org>
37. Edwards and Palmer, *Holy Ground*.
38. Ribaut and Del Ray, *The Earth Under Care*.
39. UNEP, *Global Environment Outlook*.
40. Bahá'u'lláh, *Gleanings*, p. 342.
41. Dahl, 'Global Sustainability and its Implications for Trade', *GATT Trade and Environment Bulletin* 009, 28 July 1994.
42. Shoghi Effendi, *World Order*, p. 204.
43. Brown, 'Facing the prospect of food scarcity', in Brown et al., *State of the World 1997*.
44. <www.cites.org>
45. <www.basel.int>
46. <www.wto.org>
47. Bahá'í International Community, 1991.
48. <www.igospartners.org>
49. The Universal House of Justice, *Promise of World Peace*.
50. Bahá'u'lláh, *Gleanings*, p. 343.
51. The Universal House of Justice, *Conservation of the Earth's Resources*, p. 16.
52. SEI/UNEP, Raskin, Gallopin, Gutman, Al Hammond and Rob Swart, *Bending the Curve: Toward Global Sustainability*; UNEP/DEIA/TR.98-4; Hammond, *Which World?*; UNEP, *Global Environment Outlook 3*.
53. See papers on this topic on the International Enviroment Forum web site <www.bcca.org/ief>
54. Shoghi Effendi, *World Order*.
55. ibid. pp. 203–4.
56. Bahá'í International Community, *The Prosperity of Humankind*.

The Spiritual Destiny of America[1] and the Achievement of World Peace

John Huddleston

Introduction

Any review of the establishment of world peace would be incomplete if it did not refer to the role of the United States. That subject is explored briefly in this essay. It begins with America's sense of destiny, the nature of world peace and the vital importance of moral leadership in achieving peace. The essay then briefly reviews three major factors in America's experience which have prepared this nation for its destiny: the melting pot, federal democracy, and religious diversity and commitment. It then reviews contributions to world peace already made by America. The essay concludes with a short comment on what now needs to be done. First, America will have to take the initiative to lead all nations further along the path to a federal world democracy, an essential permanent framework for lasting peace. Second, to be effective in such leadership, it will have to rise above present materialism to a new spiritual awakening.

America's Sense of Mission

From the days of the earliest European immigrants, Americans have had a sense of being special. This self-assessment is very different from the arrogant belief of some nations that they are superior to others, most extremely manifested in the Nazi ideology of the 'master race'. Rather it has been one of a sense of mission: setting an example of a moral society and, indeed, leading all humanity to the achievement of such a society. The general idea is captured in a book review by Jonathan Yardley[2] of *The Way of the World: From the Birth of Civilization to the American Centuries* by David Fromkin, who, it is observed, sees the latest stage in human development as

> the American Revolution with, in its aftermath, the consent of the governed, the rule of law, and the freedom of the individual – freedom of conscience, freedom to shape one's own faith, freedom of thought and inquiry . . . He believes in the essential soundness of a world dominated by the United States because the American way may prove to be the only viable one to deal with the consequences of the modernizing revolution . . . In Jacob's dream, the ladder reached to Heaven. The rungs of progress up which the United States might lead the world cannot reasonably be expected to reach that high; but at any rate they, too, point, as did Jacob's ladder, up to the sky.

In *America: A Narrative History* by George Brown Tindall and David Shi, the spirit of the American people at the time of the War of Independence is described as follows:[3]

> This sense of mission was neither limited to New England nor rooted solely in Calvinism. From the democratic rhetoric of Jefferson to the pragmatism of Washington, to heady toasts bellowed in South Carolina taverns, Americans everywhere articulated a special American leadership role in human history. The mission was now a call to lead the world toward liberty and equality.

The theme has been repeated many times since the War of Independence by statesmen such as Abraham Lincoln, Woodrow Wilson, Franklin Roosevelt and John Kennedy, as well as by ordinary people. As America grew to be one of the world's great powers, the theme increasingly was expressed not just as an ethical model but as political leadership of all nations. It was recognized that such leadership had to be more than conventional material power, economic, diplomatic and military, but would have to have a moral dimension in order to be effective. Senator William Fulbright expressed this idea clearly in a speech in 1961:

> It is not our affluence, or our plumbing, or our clogged highways that grip the imagination of others. Rather, it is the values on which our system is built. These values imply our adherence not only to liberty and individual freedom, but also to international peace, law and order, and constructive social purpose.[4]

The Dark Side of America

In recent decades there has been growing scepticism, not to say cynicism, about such a leadership role, among Americans and non-Americans alike, encouraged by the media with its focus increasingly, and almost exclusively, on negative aspects of the American experience. Clearly the war in Vietnam and the Watergate scandal were key events in this process which prompted revised assessments of the whole of American history: alliances with unsavoury dictatorships during the Cold War, the dirty tricks of the CIA, such as involvement in the overthrow of legitimate and popularly elected governments, and a long record of bullying and exploitation in Latin America. Revisionist historians have increasingly highlighted the hypocrisy of the Founding Fathers in allowing slavery to continue whilst drawing up a constitution supposedly built on the freedom of all inhabitants of the country, a failing which has been a major factor in making for a violent and brutal dark side to American culture. Others are appalled by the corruption of politics by big money, and more generally by the crass materialism of much of American culture, where the trend seems to be to slide further and further down towards the lowest common denominator, most evidently in the media and the entertainment industry. How can such a nation aspire to the political and moral leadership of the world?

Cynicism and Human Nature

All this is undoubtedly part of the historical record but it is not the whole story as the critics seem to imply. Such one-sided cynicism about America is part of a broader trend in perspective that has affected humanity, especially in the West, in the 20th century. This pessimistic viewpoint is clearly a reaction to the previous theme of optimism which had prevailed during the 19th century as a result of 1) the ideas of the European Enlightenment, with its view that man is essentially good and only becomes corrupted by authoritarian and selfish institutions[5] and 2) the growing wealth of society made possible by the new technologies of the Industrial Revolution. The reaction came with the horrific experiences of the 20th century: two World Wars, the Holocaust, the failure of the Socialist dream, etc.

Two comments should be made about the prevailing philosophy of cynicism. First, it is one of the most formidable barriers to progress and the establishment of world peace because logically it leads to the view that any effort in that direction is not worthwhile because it will never work:

> There is, however, a paralysis of will; and it is this that must be carefully examined and resolutely dealt with. This paralysis is rooted, as we have stated, in a deep-seated conviction of the inevitability of quarrelsomeness of mankind, which has led to the reluctance to entertain the possibility of subordinating national self-interest to the requirements of world order, and in an unwillingness to face courageously the far-reaching implications of establishing a united world authority. *The Universal House of Justice*[6]

Second, the pessimistic viewpoint is no more adequate as an explanation of the world than the overly optimistic perspective. The reality is that, at both the personal level and the community level alike, the human experience is a mix of the inspiring and the shameful with a great deal in the grey area in between. Much more realistic is the Bahá'í view of human nature which argues that it has two sides: the material and the spiritual.

The material is the innate physical drive, that we have in

common with all living things, to survive and to propagate the species. We struggle to acquire the necessary physical require-ments of living: food, clothing, shelter and, of course, the sex drive is one of the most powerful instincts. Clearly, the material side of our nature is essential to survival; the trouble begins when it becomes an obsession and we start to take far more than we need and in the process to dominate others. Then a human can become greedy, selfish, aggressive, cruel, violent, and the material side of our nature changes from being a life-giving force to one of destruction.

What keeps it in reasonable bounds is the development of the other side of our nature, the spiritual, which is unique to human-ity. The spiritual side is a search for the transcendental, a reaching beyond ourselves for the meaning and purpose of life. Its chief characteristic is a sense of attraction, unity, love, for God and for His Creation, including, most specifically, for our fellow human beings. When this side of our nature flourishes and keeps the material side in moderation then we start to fulfil our poten-tial as noble beings and as builders of an ever-advancing civilization. It is the purpose of religion to nourish the spiritual side of our nature.

What is true of individual human beings is also true of nations which, after all, simply consist of individuals. Thus nations like individuals have the choice to follow an exaggerated material side of their nature, the dark side, or to respond to their spiritual destiny and become examples of true civilization. This philoso-phy is surely both realistic, describing, as it does, the spiritual struggle that all face throughout life, and, at the same time, hopeful because it shows that all individuals and nations have the possibility of subduing the dark side and of becoming truly noble.

America's Spiritual Destiny

The Bahá'í view of the spiritual destiny of America is a logical development of the traditional American dream. It foresees a leadership role for America in the achievement of both the Lesser Peace and the Most Great Peace:

The American nation . . . will . . . play a preponderating role, as fore-told by 'Abdu'l-Bahá, in the hoisting of the standard of the Lesser Peace, in the unification of mankind, and in the establishment of a world federal government on this planet.   *Shoghi Effendi*[7]

The American people are indeed worthy of being the first to build the Tabernacle of the Great Peace, and proclaim the oneness of mankind . . . The American nation is equipped and empowered to accomplish that which will adorn the pages of history . . . Its future is even more promising, for its influence and illumination are far-reaching. It will lead all nations spiritually.   *'Abdu'l-Bahá*[8]

Having noted this point, it should be added that all nations have a very special and unique contribution, based on their own history, experience and culture, to the process of establishing world peace. Moral leadership such as that provided in interna-tional aid and peacekeeping operations by Canada, Costa Rica, the Netherlands and the Scandinavian countries, the contribu-tion of the United Kingdom, in the 19th century, to the abolition of the world trade in slaves, and the Gandhian philosophy of India, are all examples of valuable contributions to the process. The American role is to provide the overall leadership.

The Most Great Peace and the Lesser Peace

A word should also be added here to clarify the Bahá'í expres-sions 'the Most Great Peace' and 'the Lesser Peace'. The coming of world peace is seen as a logical continuation of history and the process of globalization which has been gradually accelerating over the last few centuries. World peace is necessary both as a simple matter of survival, in view of the immense destructive power of modern weapons of war, and as a means for the further advancement of civilization. It can be achieved as a result of dis-aster or as a result of rational and principled action:

Whether peace is to be achieved only after unimaginable horrors precipitated by humanity's stubborn clinging to old patterns of behaviour, or is to be embraced now by an act of consultative will, is the choice before all who inhabit the earth.

                    The Universal House of Justice[9]

The Lesser Peace is a long developing process which will lead eventually to the Most Great Peace. Key stages in the Lesser Peace process will be an end to war between nations and the establishment of a democratic federal world commonwealth. It will feature a world parliament, a supreme tribunal and an international executive, including a world police force to ensure compliance with the decisions of the parliament and the tribunal, a free trade economy and a single code of international law, all supported by a humanity that has a consciousness of world citizenship.[10] Such features will provide an orderly, principled and democratic framework necessary for a lasting peace among nations. In the first stages of moving towards a world democratic federation, the Bahá'í International Community[11] has proposed a 19-point programme to strengthen the present United Nations (UN) confederation model by, for instance, introducing minimum human rights standards for UN membership, curtailing the use of the veto in the Security Council, enhancing the position of the World Court, giving the UN independent sources of income, exploring possibilities for the introduction of an auxiliary world language and a single world currency, encouraging a more equal role in international affairs for women, and providing, in all countries, a basic school curriculum of global moral education.[12]

The ultimate Most Great Peace will come about when there is a deep sense of the unity of humanity and an understanding of the twin ethical purposes of life: to become noble beings in preparation for the spiritual life after completion of the physical existence and to create an ever-advancing civilization.

The Material and Spiritual Power of America

Of course, when it is said that America has a role in leading the nations of the world towards a global peace, the assumption is, almost inevitably, that this must be on account of the primacy of America as the only remaining superpower. This, indeed, is an important aspect of the situation. Clearly, America has immense influence as a result of its military, economic and political power. It is the only nation today with true global military reach. Time after time the other nations of the world look to America for leadership in international affairs, with such clear recent examples as the European expectation of the United States with regard to resolution of problems in Europe's own backyard, the Balkans.[13]

However, experience shows that material power is not enough. Material power, especially when used selfishly, begets opposition, almost as a reflex action, from other powers, and in the long run a materially powerful nation will only have real influence if that material power is underpinned by a spiritual strength or moral principle: it is respected, even loved, for what it stands for. Any State that attempts to dominate the world or its neighbours by force will be strongly opposed, and usually frustrated, as a result of a very human reaction as expressed in the diplomatic game of *realpolitik*. Certainly, the United States, when it has tried to dominate and bully other nations to obtain short-term material advantage, has been met by popular antagonism, sometimes hatred, around the world but when it has acted on the basis of moral principle, altruism, and in the general interest of humanity, it has been given enthusiastic popular support, e.g. in 1918 when President Wilson came to Europe with his plan for a League of Nations, or in 1961 when President Kennedy made his proposal to neighbouring countries in Latin America for an Alliance for Progress. It is an indicator of the special role of America that it is a country and people that the rest of the world has passionate feelings about: either hate or love, but *not* indifference. President Eisenhower caught the point when he said:

'America's leadership and prestige depend, not merely upon our unmatched material strength, but on how we use our power in the interest of world peace and human betterment' . . . He added that he hoped that . . . 'all peoples will come together in peace guaranteed by the binding force of mutual respect and love'.[14]

America's Spiritual Inheritance

There are at least three aspects of the spiritual destiny of America that, in particular, would appear to merit some discussion. First, what is it in the American experience that has prepared it for its destiny? Second, what has been achieved already by America in moving towards that destiny? Third, what needs to be done to encourage America to truly fulfil its spiritual destiny of leading the nations of the world in the establishment of a lasting global peace?

With regard to the first question, America's spiritual inheritance, it is proposed to discuss three of the most obvious factors: 1) the melting pot, 2) the politics of federal democracy and 3) the deep religious experience that has underpinned the movement towards the American dream.

The Melting Pot

DIVERSITY

Perhaps the most striking characteristic of the United States is the extraordinary diversity of origin of its citizens. There are United States citizens, in significant numbers, with family roots in all five inhabited continents. In effect, the United States is the world in embryo. There is no other nation in the world that has had such diverse population roots. The nearest might be Australia, Brazil or Canada, all, like the United States, essentially nations of immigrants, but all of these countries, in their different ways, have had a shorter and/or less broad experience.[15]

THREE EXPERIENCES

The American people may be divided into three broad groups in terms of their cultural and spiritual inheritance and experience. The largest group comprises the voluntary immigrants and their descendants (about 87 per cent of the total); the second largest group comprises the involuntary immigrants, those who came from Africa as slaves, and their descendants (about 12 per cent of the total); and, finally, there are the indigenous peoples, the original inhabitants of the country and their descendants, the Native Americans (about one per cent of the population), who were in this land long before regular contact with Europe started after the voyages of Christopher Columbus.[16] However, as the following review suggests, and as seems to be indicated by the statements of 'Abdu'l-Bahá which are quoted, these ratios are certainly not an indication of the relative importance of the contributions of the three groups to America's spiritual inheritance, as it pertains to preparation of America for its great destiny. Perhaps a more reasonable assessment would be that each group has made a contribution of approximately equal importance and value.

The Voluntary Immigrants

The voluntary immigrants came to America in a series of great waves beginning with the English, Scots-Irish and Germans in the 17th and 18th centuries. The first two-thirds of the 19th century saw the arrival of more Germans, West European Jews and, especially after the potato famines of the 1840s, large numbers of poor Irish. In the following half century there was a great wave of poor immigrants from Northern and Eastern Europe and the Mediterranean: Scandinavians, Poles, Jews, Italians, Greeks, Armenians, etc., as well as the first significant tide of Asians: Japanese, Chinese and Filipinos. After a general pause in immigration between the two World Wars, largely caused by tough new legal (and racist) immigration barriers erected in the 1920s but made more severe by the Great Depression in the 1930s, there was a revival of the flow of immigration, especially from the 1960s onwards. This time the main immigration came from Asia (Vietnam, Korea, Iran and the Indian subcontinent, etc.), from Central America (Mexico, Nicaragua, Ecuador, etc.), and from the Caribbean (Cuba, Haiti, Jamaica, Trinidad, Puerto Rico, etc.).[17] In addition, there were modest numbers coming from the Middle East and from Africa. By contrast with the mass of immigrants in the previous wave, many of these immigrants, especially those from Asia, brought with them technical skills and a culture which placed great value on education.

Freedom and opportunity. In broad terms the vast majority of immigrants came for economic reasons, fleeing poverty at home and hoping for opportunities for material advancement in the New World. A significant number came also to escape religious or political persecution, or war and civil turmoil at home, and to find freedom and security. Examples of those fleeing religious persecution include the early Puritan Protestants settling in New England and Roman Catholics in Maryland, as well as Jews coming from Russia in the late 19th-century and Nazi Germany in the 1930s. Political refugees included political radicals fleeing repressive regimes in 19th-century Germany, Armenians fleeing a brutal Ottoman regime, and Vietnamese and Cubans fleeing Communist dictatorships. These reasons for migration to America are captured in the welcoming and inspiring words carved, in the 1880s, at the base of the Statue of Liberty in New York harbour: 'Give me your tired, your poor, your huddled masses yearning to breathe free.'

Valuable qualities of character. This diverse mass of voluntary immigrants had some common general characteristics that deeply affected the evolving culture of the new nation of America in ways that would be of value in preparing it for its spiritual destiny. It might be added that behind these characteristics was the general quality and capacity of peoples who uprooted themselves from lands where they had lived for many generations and who overcame formidable physical and emotional challenges to settle in new lands, usually thousands of miles away across an ocean, lands about which they had very little knowledge beyond vague stories of wealth and opportunity for a better life. This was a course of action that only the most desperate, adventurous, capable and courageous would undertake.

The common characteristics of most of the voluntary immigrants included initiative, enterprise, generosity, and a dynamic 'can do' approach to the challenges of life, the latter being a quality that later served the world so well in the Second World War and still does today.

Indeed, the most important quality America brings to the world scene is its sheer capacity to get things done.[18]

This is the dynamic spirit that will be needed to take humanity forward from the stick-in-the-mud, obsolete and dangerous habits of the past, to a vision of the opportunity for advancement for all humanity that will come from the establishment of world peace and political unity.

Discrimination. The hardships of the voluntary immigrants included periods of discrimination, most notably for the Chinese and the Japanese in the latter half of the 19th century and the first half of the 20th century,[19] but also, though on a less intense basis, for such ethnic groups as the Irish, Italians, Poles, Hispanics and Jews. However, such discrimination and suffering paled, in terms of intensity and longevity, by comparison with what was to be endured by the other two groups of Americans: the involuntary immigrants and the indigenous people of America.

The Involuntary Immigrants

Suffering of a people. The African Americans first came to the United States under the most horrific conditions on slave ships (about one in seven died en route), and for about 200 years (1660 to 1865) the experience of the vast majority was to be a slave (during this period on average more than 90 per cent of African Americans were slaves), a cruel, brutalizing and demeaning condition in which there was very little if any opportunity for self-improvement and fulfilment.[20] When slavery was brought to an end after a civil war that for four years tore the nation apart in bloody strife, there was hope of a new beginning, a Great Jubilee. Soon, however, this hope was dashed to the ground and African Americans had to endure another hundred years of extreme political, legal, social and economic discrimination, before, at long last, they achieved something like true equality with their fellow citizens. Wonderful as has been this outcome, it has been marred by the fact that large numbers are not able to fully take advantage of it because of deep lingering scars, both material and emotional, caused by the past collective experience. And yet this collective experience of immense suffering is a major aspect of the spiritual inheritance of America because, as 'Abdu'l-Bahá said, it is through suffering that humanity grows and learns how to handle difficulties.

> The mind and spirit of man advance when he is tried by suffering. The more the ground is ploughed, the better the seed will grow, the better the harvest will be. Just as the plough furrows the earth deeply, purifying it of weeds and thistles, so suffering and tribulation free man from the petty affairs of this worldly life until he arrives at a state of complete detachment . . . Look back to the times past and you will find that the greatest men have suffered most. *'Abdu'l-Bahá*[21]

With good reason, America has been sharply criticized for its racist society over the years by non-Americans. Nevertheless, in the longer perspective, it is Americans who have learned, albeit the hard way, the beginnings of how to deal with this most pernicious of human prejudices. Collectively, they have been through the valley of tears, in a way that is not true of other countries that have homogeneous populations and that are sometimes too prone to giving lectures without having had the test themselves.[22]

Spiritual and cultural gifts. Despite overwhelming odds, which, it is reasonable to expect, would crush any community, the African Americans have come through it all with great fortitude and ability to find happiness and joy in even the most limited of circumstances. As a consequence, African Americans have contributed immensely to the richness of American culture which is so loved by the rest of the world, especially the young. They have produced some of the greatest heroes of American history: Benjamin Banneker, Frederick Douglass, Harriet Tubman, Booker T. Washington, W.E.B. Dubois, Jesse Owens, Marion Anderson, Paul Robeson, Rosa Parks, Muhammad Ali, Thurgood Marshall, Ella Fitzgerald, Dizzie Gillespie, and two winners of the Nobel Peace Prize – Ralph Bunche and Martin Luther King. Undoubtedly this inner strength, that has borne such fruits, comes, in major part, from the culture of Africa itself.

This is a culture that has great exuberance and close links with the spirit of God and His creation. In surveying the history of the African American people it can surely not be a surprise that the Bahá'í writings state that they have a very special spiritual role in America's destiny:

> Bahá'u'lláh once compared the coloured people to the black pupil of the eye surrounded by the white. In this black pupil is seen the reflection of that which is before it, and through it the light of the spirit shineth forth. *'Abdu'l-Bahá*[23]

The Indigenous Peoples

Harmony with nature. This leads to consideration of the contribution of the third group of Americans, the indigenous peoples, an immensely diverse band of nations with roots in America that go back at least 30,000 years.[24] This group of Americans is distinguished for its deep spiritual connection with the natural environment in a vast range of differing climates and land conditions over many centuries. These people, of all Americans, are the ones that remind us of the truism that we have to live in harmony with the natural environment in order to prosper, perhaps to survive, a teaching that other Americans are now beginning to appreciate, despite a habit of short-sightedness and waste with regard to nature associated with immigrant pioneers on the Western frontier. This deep sense of harmony with nature is the unique side of the Native American contribution to the spiritual inheritance of America which is of inestimable value for the well-being of the human race.

Another suffering people. Of immense importance also is the great suffering that the Native American peoples have endured, different from that of African Americans, but surely as painful. These are a people who initially greeted the European settlers with friendship. They showed the settlers how to survive in the new environment and were willing to share their vast lands with them.[25] In return, they were to be steadily driven off their lands, to be treated as inferiors in administration of American law, to be cheated over and over again, to be corrupted by alcohol, to be deprived of their freedom and way of life, to be humiliated in battle because they had less advanced weapons, to be told that their culture was worthless, to be herded into reservations on the poorest lands of the country, etc. It is no wonder that the Native American population by the end of the 19th century was in grave danger of dying out altogether (indeed this did happen to many of the several hundred original nations) and that a significant portion of the population today, especially on the reservations, is in despair and drowned in alcohol.

The noble image. And yet Native American culture is making a comeback and is treated by much of America, and, indeed, by the world as a whole, with increasing respect and affection. The words of wisdom that come down to us from leaders and others during the struggle to survive the immigrant invasion are now given great value and the popular image is no longer that of the Redskin savage but of the noble warrior, the brave sitting on his horse with his magnificent lithe body and feathered headdress.[26] 'Abdu'l-Bahá's statement of nearly 90 years ago pertaining to the special spiritual role of the Native American is increasingly easy for others to understand and accept, a remarkable tribute to the quality of the civilization of the indigenous peoples of America.

> You must attach great importance to the Indians . . . there can be no doubt that through the Divine teachings they will become so enlightened that the whole earth will be illumined. *'Abdu'l-Bahá*[27]

THE MELTING POT: GENERAL QUALITIES OF VALUE FOR A GLOBAL SOCIETY

Beyond the special contributions of each of the three broad groups of Americans to an inheritance that prepares the nation for its spiritual destiny in leading humanity to a global society, united in peace and justice, there are also some experiences of great value from the nationality melting pot that span all three groups.

Unity in diversity. The first of these is that, despite all the stresses and strains of living in proximity with peoples of very different cultures and all the prejudices this has entailed, over a period of nearly 400 years, the Americans have gradually learned to live together in relative harmony, though enduring much pain along the way and with still some way to go before it is truly realized. There is real hope of achieving one day the dream mentioned on US coins: *E pluribus unum* (from many, one). One indicator of progress is the rate of intermarriage between cultural groups. The normal experience has been that by the third generation, between 30 and 50 per cent of young people find marriage partners outside their own cultural group. The major exception to this intermarriage phenomenon has been that between African Americans and others. This is clearly a reflection of residual prejudices but in recent years even this barrier is starting to crumble.[28] This profound experience of learning toleration, mutual respect and appreciation of diversity is an inheritance of the greatest significance in preparing America for its future role.

One language. Closely related to this strength is a second experience of great value, in the context of this discussion, and that is the fact that out of the melting pot has come a unity based on one language, English. Experience of nations shows that one of the strongest cultural forces that binds a nation together is language (there are, of course, a few exceptions, such as Switzerland), and this is clearly an important factor in the evolution of a united humanity. Thus the Bahá'í Faith includes, as a basic principle, the teaching that there should be a universal auxiliary language so that all peoples can communicate clearly and efficiently with one another. Today, English has become, in effect, the informal global language owing to the economic and political power in the world of, first, Great Britain in the 19th century, and, second, the United States in the 20th. The choice of English in America arose from the fact that the early settlements were English colonies and that when later immigrants came they were largely isolated by huge distances and the slowness of communication from their homelands, so that by the second and third generations they would typically adopt the language of their new country without too much concern, simply as a matter of economic advancement. The main exception to this process has been with regard to Hispanics coming in large numbers, in a short period of time, to concentrated areas in the southern areas of the country which are contiguous to Mexico and to other nearby Spanish-speaking countries. This has sparked some degree of controversy, which has spilled over into treatment of other ethnic groups. Nevertheless, the case for a single uniting language remains as strong as ever, though clearly it is preferable to let the matter evolve naturally rather than through bullying by the law. As might be expected, it is usually poor immigrants (Haitians, Hispanics) who are the readiest to adopt English and better-off immigrants who are more resistant.

Emotional ties with other nations. A third experience that spans all three groups of Americans, which is of immense value in preparing America for its destiny is the special bonds of blood, culture and affection which link America to nearly all countries around the world. This is unique in its depth and width. Similar ties may be found in other former colonies such as Canada, Australia and New Zealand, in the British Commonwealth, and in the Spanish, Portuguese and French cultural worlds, but it is suggested that these are of a much lower order of intensity than that pertaining to America. Though most immigrant groups were physically cut off from their homelands, many long kept up an interest in them,[29] maintained cultural links and often injected their concerns into the democratic political process.

This periodically means that in American foreign policy, *realpolitik* is modified not only by ethical principle (as discussed later) but also by cultural sentiment. Some of the most obvious examples of such attachment are with the United Kingdom (Winston Churchill's 'special relationship'), Ireland, Poland, Israel, Korea, the Philippines, Japan, Liberia (a creation of Americans) and South Africa. The latter connection is of special significance because of a common struggle against racism but with the interesting difference that in America the oppressed were a minority whilst in South Africa they were the majority.[30] Such connection of sentiment is not limited to descendants of immigrants. Native Americans are also building bridges to other indigenous peoples around the world who have had similar historical experiences of oppression and harmony with nature, e.g. the Aborigines of Australia and the Maoris of New Zealand.

This phenomenon of sentimental attachment to other countries is not confined to the obvious. Thus even in relations with other countries where there is periodically an apparent antagonism, an underlying bond of affection is often not far below the surface. One such case is that of France which, though prickly about its proud culture being swamped by that of the Anglo-Saxon nations,[31] has, nevertheless, a deep connection with America from a common experience of revolution against oppression (the support of Lafayette and others in the American War of Independence), the well-known favourable analysis of American democracy by Alexis de Tocqueville in the 1830s, the gift from the French Third Republic of the Statue of Liberty on the occasion of the first Centennial of the United States, and the Anglo-American liberation of France in 1944.[32] Another example is Vietnam which is, despite a dreadful war against America that ended only a quarter of a century ago, clearly a country with which America has a growing sense of mutual affection and care. The same is true of China which has emotional bridges with America that predate present political differences. Even India, so critical of America on account of the North–South conflict and clumsy diplomatic alignments, has 1) increasing personal connection – large numbers of middle-class families have some member studying or working in America – and 2) a common interest in that they are the two largest democracies, representing the West and East of global culture.

The popular culture of America. Underpinning all this is a popular global love affair with many aspects of democratic, fun-loving American culture with its almost child-like innocence,[33] though most foreign commentators only talk about their complaints, some reasonable, some less so. The most obvious attraction is for

American music and dance, which has its roots in African American culture, from the spiritual, to ragtime, to jazz, to the blues, to rock and roll, and so on. Another attraction is the American movie (including the musical and the animated cartoon pioneered by Walt Disney, etc.) with its origins largely in the creativeness of Jewish culture and the tradition in German culture for providing fun times for the child.[34] Closely related is American television, which with the satellite has made possible the first all-world television programmes. These were pioneered by CNN, which has a well-earned reputation for a reliable news service and a concern for the environment. America has also given the world the cola soft drink, as an alternative to alcohol, and the concept of delicious fast food – evolving originally from the German-American hamburger and hot dog and Italian-American pizza and ice cream. Such development may be deplorable in some respects but it has also helped liberate women from the kitchen so that they have more opportunity to broaden their experience by working in the marketplace.

The Political Experience: Federal Democracy

The second dimension of the American experience which is of great relevance in preparation for leading the world to unity and peace is its political inheritance.

AN OVERVIEW

Long experience of freedom and democracy. The first aspect of this inheritance is that America has had one of the longest evolving experiences of a free society and democracy. Such experience has roots long preceding independence, from both the mother nation, Britain, and from its own history during the colonial period. Few other nations have such a long and deep experience of democracy – perhaps only the United Kingdom, the Netherlands and Switzerland can compare. Recent studies in Italy (with regard to good governance) confirm an instinctive common sense that long collective experience is a vital factor for the steadiness of a society in maintaining social values, especially during times of stress. Clearly this is important in preparing America for its leadership role because a future world society has to be built on the principle of freedom, as the alternative – an authoritarian world government – would result in a cure (oppression) that could be as bad as the disease (war). In any case, an authoritarian world system would simply not be acceptable to most of the nations of the world which are now maturing towards democracy and whose peoples are putting increasing value on participating in the management of their own public affairs.

The federal model. The second aspect of the political inheritance that is of relevance in this discussion is the particular structure of democracy that America has experienced: federal democracy. The American experience of federal democracy goes back over two centuries to the end of the 18th century, a length and depth of experience that cannot be matched by any other nation. Thus of the most important functioning federal democracies in the world today, those of Canada and Switzerland date back only to the mid-19th century, whilst those of Australia, Brazil, Germany, India, Russia and South Africa are 20th-century creations. It is clear from the Bahá'í writings, and from political experience, that any future world democratic government would have to be built on the federal model with emphasis on maximum 'subsidiarity', because the alternative unitary model would inevitably be unmanageable and too far removed from ordinary people and their everyday lives.[35]

English roots. The American democratic inheritance has deep roots in the history of the founding imperial power, Britain. This was a gradually evolving experience of the rule of law, applying to the State as well as all subjects equally, of representative government, and of the idea of universal civil rights, rationalized in the theory of the social contract as explicitly spelt out in the brilliant writings of John Locke. Underpinning these ideas was a society with significant numbers of independent and self-reliant subjects: the yeoman farmer, following the erosion of classic European feudalism, and the middle-class craftsman and merchant. The spirit of independence of such subjects was fanned by the Protestant Reformation. Key events in this process of evolving democracy included the Magna Carta (1215); the institution of a regular national parliament with elected representation as the result of the promptings of Simon de Montfort and King Edward I (13th century); a moderate approach to class tension that emerged from the Peasants Rebellion (1381); the Reformation and the associated need of the Tudor monarchy to have parliament on its side in its dispute with Rome (16th century); and the defeat of the Stuart monarchy's attempt to impose a continental style all-powerful authoritarian State apparatus, which provoked, first, a parliamentary republic (17th century), and, later, the Glorious Revolution of 1688 and constitutional monarchy.

Colonial roots. The culture of a free society evolved further in the North American colonies of the 17th and 18th centuries. Several broad factors were at play. The colonists were independently minded and self-reliant both as a result of the reasons why they had come in the first place and the tremendous challenges of building a new society from scratch. Those who came, no matter how poor, felt they had a chance of achieving a prosperous life and they did not easily defer to outside orders.[36] Class distinctions were always much weaker than in Europe and were much less of a barrier to advancement. Furthermore tight control by the mother country was not practical because of the huge distances and slowness of communication at the time. Most of the colonies came about as a result of private initiative rather than direct Crown investment. In all of this, the colonies differed significantly from those of the authoritarian French and Spanish imperial powers where a culture of independence and freedom was much less in evidence.

A common experience of all 13 of the colonies was election of legislative assemblies, going back to the first half of the 17th century in Virginia, Massachusetts and Maryland. In many cases such assemblies had increasing power over the executive governor and his council of government, i.e. controlling not just legislation and taxation ('no taxation without representation') but also with authority to set salary levels of the executive, sometimes even to elect the governor and occasionally to be free of veto by the governor. The lower houses were generally elected by a suffrage with a minimum property qualification which, in effect, meant near universal suffrage for white males, by far the most broad and democratic suffrage in the world of the 18th century. With regard to the third, judicial, dimension of government, the British tradition of trial by jury was soon firmly established and the Crown's attempt to bypass it with authoritarian Admiralty Courts was to be one of the main colonial grievances which eventually prompted revolt. The spirit of religious toleration was also well-established in many of the colonies, usually, it is true, restricted to Christians who accepted the Trinity, but on occasion, as in Pennsylvania and the Carolinas, extending to Unitarians, Jews and even non-believers.

Underpinning the formal institutions of elected government was a strong tradition of voluntary organizations which, over time, formed a web of connection between the colonies, starting with the committees of correspondence to resist the Tea Tax (1765) and eventually leading to the first (1774) and second (1775–6) Continental Congresses. It was the second of these Congresses which, after vain attempts to compromise with the British Crown in a peaceful way, spelt out, in the second paragraph of the Declaration of Independence (4 July 1776), the basis of the American idea of liberty:

> We hold these truths to be self-evident, that all men are created equal, that they are endowed by their Creator with certain unalienable Rights, that among these are Life, Liberty, and the pursuit of Happiness. – That to secure these rights, Governments are instituted among Men, deriving their just powers from the consent of the governed, – That whenever any Form of Government becomes destructive of these ends, it is the Right of the People to alter or to abolish it, and to institute new Government, laying its foundation on such principles and organizing its powers in such form, as to them shall seem most likely to effect their Safety and Happiness.

Americans saw themselves as citizens, not as subjects.

THE FEDERAL CONSTITUTION

The informal wartime alliance of the 13 colonies under the Continental Congress led logically to a permanent Confederation when peace came in 1781. However, it was soon found that the Confederation, which was essentially limited to cooperation on external affairs, was totally inadequate to meet the common needs of the newly independent states. It did not even have taxing powers or a formal Head of State. The spirit of frontier initiative and independence, together with the immense challenge of defeating one of the most powerful States in the world produced a generation of truly remarkable political and intellectual leaders[37] who were able to devise a more practical federal constitution to replace the Confederation. To a large degree they were able to balance normal short-term petty political considerations with grand and noble philosophy to produce an ideal, but realistic, written constitution. This took account not only of the traditions of the English parliamentary system but also of the experience of Ancient Greece and Rome and even, it is said, of the 17th-century Iroquois Confederation, as well as ideas from the French Enlightenment, such as the separation of powers theories of Montesquieu. There were at least three aspects of the resulting Federal Constitution of 1787/88 which are of significance from the point of view of planning for a future global society.

Union–States balance. The first was the division of responsibility between the federal government and the constituent states, with the principle that all powers should remain at the state level except those specifically delegated to the federal government. A balance was struck between democracy at the new national level, on the one hand, and protection of the rights of smaller states *vis-à-vis* the larger ones, on the other hand, by having a bicameral federal legislature with a lower assembly, the House of Representatives, elected on the basis of population[38] and an upper house, the Senate, made up of equal representation for every state (two senators), regardless of the relative size of each state. Frequent accountability was balanced by the need for continuity in government by having the lower house elected once every two years whilst senators were to have office for six years, with election of one third of the Senate every two years. Amendments to the Constitution would require not only two-thirds majorities in each house but also ratification by the legislatures of two-thirds of the states (Article 5 of the Constitution).

Branches of government. The second important feature of the Constitution was a formal separation of powers among the three branches of government: the legislative, the executive and the judicial (addressed in the first three Articles) to prevent authoritarian and arbitrary government. By contrast with the English parliamentary system, the executive, the President, was to be elected directly by the people and not indirectly through Congress, whilst the judiciary (the Supreme Court) would be nominated by the executive and confirmed by the legislature (the Senate) for life-time appointment so that its members would be independent of crude political pressure. To protect the principles of the Constitution against the sometimes short-sighted passions of a democratic majority, the judicial branch was given authority to declare unconstitutional and, therefore void, unsound actions of either the executive or the legislature. Other elements in the division and balance of power included requirements that all foreign treaties negotiated by the executive be ratified by the Senate and that Congress have the power to remove the President or other office-holders if found guilty of a serious offence against the Constitution.[39]

Bill of Rights. The third vital dimension to the Constitution was the addition of a Bill of Rights (an important precursor of the 1948 Universal Declaration of Human Rights of the United Nations), which consists of the first ten Amendments to the Constitution. Some of the most important principles of the Bill of Rights are trial by jury, banning of cruel and unusual punishment, separation of church and state, i.e. freedom of religious conscience, and freedom of speech. The latter is the basis of protection for an independent media, which, in a real sense, is an informal fourth branch of government, with the function of holding the formal branches up for review and audit by the people. The egalitarian spirit of the new Constitution was expressed in such matters as the banning of aristocratic titles and the precedent of a low-key presidential style set by the first President, George Washington: the antithesis of traditional pomp of royal and imperial government.

REMOVAL OF THE MORAL CONTRADICTION IN THE CONSTITUTION

Testing by fire I. Though an extraordinary advance in the history of government, the federal Constitution of 1787/88 was deeply flawed because, as a political compromise, it permitted the hypocrisy, not to say absurdity, of the continuation of the institution of slavery whilst claiming that the fundamental principle of the new Constitution was liberty. This moral contradiction was to haunt the nation for 70 years. A series of further compromises in the hope that slavery would eventually die by attrition[40] only postponed the problem which eventually came to a bloody conclusion in the Civil War of 1861–5, which cost America more lives than any other war in its history.[41] However, the Civil War, by ending slavery whilst preserving the Union, was a vital step of the onward march of democracy in the world, at a time when the vast majority of independent States still had authoritarian governments. This was clearly understood by one of the greatest of American Presidents, Abraham Lincoln, 'Honest Abe', the all-American model of wisdom and virtue:

> . . . that this nation, under God, shall have a new birth of freedom; and that government of the people, by the people, for the people, shall not perish from the earth.[42]

Testing by fire II. Though African Americans became legal citizens of the United States as a result of the 13th, 14th and 15th Amendments,[43] they were to be denied the reality of citizenship for another hundred years as a result of the crude racism that had infected American society, partly because this was the character of much of Western culture[44] and partly because it was so deeply ingrained and reinforced by 200 years of slavery based on race. What is important about this tragic story is that eventually America had to confront the contradiction in its own being and in the 1960s took the steps, as a result of moral pressure of the Civil Rights movement, to finally eliminate legal support for social and political discrimination.[45] However, as already noted, problems arising from the terrible psychological wounds, inflicted on all of society by 300 years of racism, still remain to be finally healed.

The spark that illumined the world. That heroic experience of the Civil Rights movement had wide repercussions beyond the immediate condition of African Americans. Thus it eventually benefited Native Americans who had also suffered tremendous discrimination[46] and led to improvement in the status of American women. America had been in the forefront of the battle for the emancipation of women in the 19th century[47] owing to the spirit of liberty that inspired American society and to the vital and equal role that women had taken in developing this new country. Bahá'ís are, of course, very conscious of the critical importance of equal participation of women in the management of society, not only as a matter of equity and justice, but because of their particular perspective on the need for peaceful processes, as so frequently enunciated by 'Abdu'l-Bahá during His travels in the West. America was one of the first nations in the world to fully enfranchise women in 1919 (19th Amendment to the Constitution) and was undoubtedly in the lead of the march of the Civil Rights movement in subsequent decades to bring about economic and social as well as political emancipation.[48] But the American Civil Rights movement had an even wider impact than this because it soon crossed national frontiers to be a major inspiration for the spread and strengthening of civil rights around the world. In short, beyond the model of the US Constitution is an inheritance in the American political experience of an immense struggle to implement its true spirit through application of a systematic approach to human rights – an experience that is surely not matched in intensity by any other nation.

GOOD GOVERNANCE, REGULATION OF THE ECONOMY AND PROTECTION OF THE ENVIRONMENT

Good governance. This brief overview of America's political inheritance would not be complete unless it made reference to three additional aspects of significance for this discussion. First has been leadership, going back to the post Civil War period, in recognizing the importance of 'clean government', what today is called 'good governance', to making a free society work effectively. American experience of a raw frontier society, sale of government office, bribery in elections and corruption of government decisions, e.g. in the Teapot Dome scandal of the 1920s, combined with the ideals of democracy and a free media, have led to constant concern and action to address this critical question.[49] It is a question that is of vital importance in, for instance, renewing the United Nations today in preparation for a much more prominent role in the 21st century and for the stabilization of new democracies around the world.

Free markets. The second subject of importance is the role of government in monitoring and regulating the free-market economy to see that it functions efficiently for the benefit of the whole people, an experience that goes back to one of the basic functions of the US federal government: the regulation of interstate commerce. This was later to extend into such important activities as regulation of monopoly, safeguarding of public safety with regard to food production and distribution, working conditions in factories, mines, etc., countering unemployment and inflation with fiscal and monetary policies, and provision of social safety nets, most obviously shown in the New Deal and the welfare state.[50]

Harmony with nature. Closely related has been the third activity: the role of government in protecting the natural environment and managing the economy so that it is broadly in harmony with nature. America has a patchy record, to say the least, in carrying out this responsibility, but at least it has been a public issue for a long time, going back to the establishment of the world's first national parks in Yosemite and Yellowstone in the last half of the 19th century. America has pioneered legislation in recent decades to ensure cleaner air and water, to protect endangered species and to eliminate toxic-waste sites. Much of the impetus forcing action on these issues has come from voluntary organizations, a constant and strong feature of American democracy with roots, as mentioned earlier, in the colonial period.

The Religious Experience

This leads to consideration of the third of the major themes of the American inheritance which is the inspiration for much of the voluntary activity of American democracy: the spiritual or religious dimension.

DIVERSITY

The first aspect of the American religious experience which is most evident has been its diversity, depth and importance since the founding of the European colonies and before, through to the present day.

> In fact, it could be argued that the very premise for the American nation arose out of a Christian experiment, and one in which the notion of building a spiritual utopia was central to its creation . . . A land anointed by the Lord. One nation under God.   *Garry Wills*[51]

Religion with a special connection to nature was always a central aspect of Native American culture in all its diversity. When the Europeans came, religion was to play a major role in the foundation of many of the colonies of New England as well as Pennsylvania and Maryland. The early experience of the 17th and 18th centuries was mainly Protestant Christianity: Episcopalian, Congregational, Presbyterian, Baptist, Methodist and Quaker (Society of Friends), though from the earliest times there was also a small minority of Roman Catholics and Jews.[52]

In the 1730s a new religious movement, called the Great Awakening, spread across the country, especially in frontier areas: evangelical Baptist and Methodist preachers responding to a popular need for a more passionate and less intellectual spirit than that prevailing in the more established churches. Later, in the second half of the 18th century, Deism arising from the European Enlightenment arrived and had followers among the Revolutionary leadership, including Thomas Jefferson, Benjamin Franklin and Thomas Paine.

With the mass immigrations of the 19th century, there came a large number of Lutherans (Germans and Scandinavians), Roman Catholics (Irish, Italian and Polish) and Jews (first from Germany then from Poland and Russia), with smaller numbers of Orthodox Christians, Armenians and other Christian denominations, as well as Buddhists, Shintoists and Confucianists from Asia. At the same time new religious movements, originating in America, came into being: the Church of the Latter-Day Saints (Mormons), Seventh Day Adventists, Jehovah's Witnesses and Christian Scientists, as well as frontier versions of established religions, e.g. the charismatics and Pentecostals. Of particular significance were the breakaway churches meeting the special needs of African Americans, which, to survive, had to be largely secretive and underground during the time of slavery. An important aspect of these developments was the so-called 'Second Great Awakening', which was inspired, in part, by the Transcendental idea of an intuitive relationship with God and the Adventist prophecy of the imminent Second Coming of Christ.[53]

The 20th century saw even more diversity with the arrival of significant numbers of Muslims and Hindus, a strengthening and diversification of the Catholic Church, associated with the arrival of large numbers of Hispanic immigrants, and the addition of a range of new local groups ranging from the Black Muslims to the New Age movement, not to speak of marginal doomsday cults that are sometimes paranoid, disruptive of family relations and a threat to public safety.

Of particular significance in connection with the present theme was the emergence of the Bahá'í Faith with its strong moral principles, rational teachings on the relationship of religion and science and vision of a future world civilization, to the development of which America would be destined to contribute so much.

COMMITMENT

With regard to the importance of religion in the life of the nation today, statistical surveys have consistently shown that Americans have a much greater commitment to belief in God and to the regular attendance of religious events than do other Western and industrialized countries.

> Religion is more important in America than in most industrial countries. Americans display a greater level of commitment and a greater level of diversity. *Barry Kosmin*[54]

Recent surveys have shown that about 85 per cent of the American population believe in God compared with about 60 to 70 per cent in Western Europe and 40 per cent in Japan and Russia. Some of the most widely watched programmes on TV are those of televangelists and nearly every newspaper has a religious section at least once per week. Americans acknowledge its importance in such symbolic statements as 'one nation, under God' (incorporated into the Pledge of Allegiance which is recited on many public occasions and each day at state schools), 'in God we trust' (on all US coins) and, of course, the final words of the Declaration of Independence: 'with a firm reliance on the protection of divine Providence'.

CHRISTIANITY AND OTHER WORLD RELIGIONS

In terms of diversity, the *World Christian Encyclopedia*[55] states that there were more than 2,000 denominations in the United States in 1980. However, it should be added that this diversity, from a global perspective, is somewhat different from the diversity of ethnic peoples in America. Thus Christians, in the broadest sense, account for nearly 90 per cent of the population and the other great world religions (Judaism, Islam, Buddhism, Hinduism,

Zoroastrianism and the Bahá'í Faith) only account for about five per cent.[56] Having said this, it should be further added that since the 1960s there has been a trend for this Christian preponderance to become slightly less. In any case, such figures do not necessarily reflect the actual balance in terms of significance of the contribution of each world religion to the spiritual inheritance of America.

NEGATIVE AND POSITIVE ASPECTS OF THE RELIGIOUS EXPERIENCE

Many have a very sceptical view of religion in America, associating it with 1) paranoid pseudo-Christian sects such as those involved in the Jonestown suicides, the Waco siege and others that deliberately alienate children from their families; 2) extremist Jewish sects; 3) the anti-Semitic diatribes of Black Muslims; 4) televangelists who con the poor and lonely and get caught out in silly sexual and monetary scandals; and 5) ranting right-wing Christian fundamentalists turning Jesus' message of love into hatred. These are the stories that the daily media puts in the headlines but an objective assessment of religion in America must surely show that the negative has been vastly outweighed by the positive. Indeed religion has been a great civilizing factor in a society that has had much of the rawness of the frontier in its development and, undoubtedly, this has been a major factor in preparing America for its destiny.

> The new American republic, in other words, would endure as long as the majority of the people were virtuous and willingly placed the good of society above the self interest of individuals.[57]

There are at least three important aspects to this civilizing role, i.e. making society more law-abiding, peaceful, refined and caring for the disadvantaged and the natural environment.

Toleration of Diversity

The first is that the very diversity of the religious experience has forced society to adopt religious tolerance as a basic social value simply as a matter of necessity for the public peace. Some religious groups such as the Quakers and the Bahá'ís specifically teach religious tolerance as a spiritual principle. The earliest religious communities came to America to escape persecution and, though sometimes they themselves were for a time intolerant, the logic of the situation prevailed. As noted earlier, many of the charters/constitutions of the original colonies included religious toleration clauses and this process came to a systematic conclusion with the federal Constitution and its provision for separation of church and state (not by chance addressed in the opening phrase of the First Amendment). It should be added that the Founding Fathers, nearly all religious men, took this action not to crush religion but rather to ensure that no one religion was in a position of state-backed dominance as had been the case in England and most other States of Europe. It is questionable as to whether they would have approved the present practice of rigidly excluding religious and spiritual teachings from state schools.[58] Though religious prejudice has certainly played a role in American history, on the whole the country, initially largely Protestant Christian, became open to Catholic Christianity, even if the reception for many decades was less than enthusiastic,[59] and Jews coming from Europe certainly found far more acceptance than they had ever experienced back home. Later, when other religions were to come from the Middle East and Asia there was comparatively little opposition. Today, the United States perhaps more than any other country has a strong commitment to religious tolerance, based not on indifference but on acknowledgement of the vital role of religion in breathing the spirit of life into society and its institutions.

Reinforcing Social Solidarity

The second positive impact of religion in the American experience has been its place as a refuge and support during times of extreme stress for particular segments of the population. The most obvious example has been the central role of religion in holding together the African American community through two centuries of slavery and one century of intense discrimination. Initially this role was played by religious tradition brought from Africa and then by Christianity, especially after the community established its own independent branches of Baptism, Methodism, Pentacostalism, etc. Most recently, the Black Muslim movement has made useful contributions to the revival of a sense of pride and self-worth in the community, especially among young men. Though the case of the African Americans is the most striking, it should be remembered that religion was also vital for the early survival and development of other groups too, e.g. the Catholic Church in support of poor Irish immigrants, the Lutheran Church in support of the Scandinavians and Germans, and the various branches of Judaism and the Jewish community. In all these cases the religious institutions played a central role in mutual economic, political and social support. Indeed, in the African American community the church was virtually the only institution where they were truly in charge of their own affairs and not under the tutelage of European Americans. It is no coincidence that even today the political power base of the African American community remains in the church and that many leading African American politicians have been clergymen.

Force for Progress and a Humane Society

The third positive aspect of religion in American history is that generally, despite the aberrations mentioned earlier, religion has always been in the forefront of progressive movements to make for a more humane society. Indeed, religious inspiration has been at the heart of the public service voluntary organization which has been one of the great strengths and distinctive features of American democracy and, in turn, it was the American experience which prompted the worldwide movement of non-government organizations (NGOs) that are now recognized as a key feature in the evolution of a global civil society. This voluntary sector, inspired by religion, has produced, *inter alia* most of the 18 Americans who have won the Nobel Peace prize.[60] The voluntary sector has been supported financially by a remarkable amount of voluntary giving, which is another important nuance of American public life. Of special significance were the contributions of so-called 'robber barons' at the end of the 19th century, led by Andrew Carnegie, who gave generously to non-profit organizations devoted to promotion of the public welfare – a precedent that continues to the present day, e.g. the recent donation of a $1 billion to the UN by Ted Turner.

Examples abound of religion being at the forefront of progressive movements in America. The Quakers of Pennsylvania were known for the honourable way they dealt with their Native American population, setting a precedent that would be followed throughout the history of the frontier of religious bodies showing the most empathy for the condition of the Indian nations. Religious groups were the driving force in the anti-slavery movement (including notably the Quakers, Congregationalists and the Methodists) and a hundred years later in the Civil Rights movement, whose great leader, Martin Luther King was, indeed, a clergyman, as were many of his colleagues. Religious inspiration was also behind the abstinence and later prohibition movements as well as efforts to ameliorate the lot of the poor in the new immigrant cities. Later still, religion would be a factor in the peace movement, including inspiration for the League of Nations, the Kellogg-Briand Pact to make war illegal and the Cold War anti-nuclear campaign.[61] Most recently religious bodies and individuals inspired by religion have been active leaders in the environment movement.[62] Bringing the various progressive ideas into one comprehensive and all-encompassing vision for the future has been the work of the Bahá'í community, with its special emphasis on the spiritual dimension to human rights, conscious abolition of prejudice, combatting of racism with love, the equality of men and women, a new economic model based on spiritual principle and the establishment of world peace. As noted in this article, of particular significance has been the Bahá'í vision of a very special spiritual destiny for America in leading humanity towards a lasting world peace based on justice.

America's Destiny: Achievements to Date

Having discussed some of the factors in the American experience that have prepared it for its spiritual destiny, there remain for discussion the two other questions mentioned near the beginning of this article that seem to be relevant: 1) what America has already achieved in moving towards its destiny and 2) what action needs to be taken to carry forward the process.

America's Relations with Other Nations: The Ugly Side

MANIFEST DESTINY

In its relations with other sovereign States it is certainly true that there has been an ugly aspect, that is when America has followed conventional Machiavellian or *realpolitik* policies. Thus in the 19th and early 20th centuries, America would sometimes act like a conventional European imperialist power, especially in the Americas and in the Pacific, prompted in part by the free-booting style of the Western frontier with its sometimes casual approach to the rule of law. For a time, the spiritual destiny of America was corrupted by the idea of 'Manifest Destiny', which, as first promulgated in 1845, was 'to over spread the continent allocated by Providence for the free development of our multiplying millions'.[63] This affected not only Native Americans but Mexico, which was also blocking the way in the West. Though the causes of the US–Mexican War of 1846–8 were not all one-sided and after it was over the United States did compensate Mexico quite generously for the territory it annexed,[64] nevertheless the war, as Tindall and Shi put it, 'was increasingly seen as a war of conquest provoked by a president (Polk) bent on expansion'.[65] As a result, perhaps out of shame, the event has 'somehow never become entrenched in the nation's legends'.[66]

During this period the United States also gradually fell into the habit of interfering, sometimes with military force, in the affairs of Central America and the Caribbean, and often with overtones of racism. Such behaviour has created a deep suspicion of the United States which lasts to this day in Latin America – a feeling captured in use of the term 'gringo' to describe a European American. Some of the most blatant such episodes included the separation of Panama from Colombia (1903) so that America could more easily control the subsequently built Panama Canal, as well as a long military occupation of Haiti (1915–34). An extension of 'Manifest Destiny' was the 1898 war with Spain, 'the splendid little war', which *inter alia* resulted in the annexation of Puerto Rico in the Caribbean and the Philippines in the Pacific. That episode occurred at about the same time as the engineering of a *coup d'état* in Hawaii and that island's subsequent annexation.

THE COLD WAR: ENDS JUSTIFY MEANS

This ugly side of American foreign policy became manifest a second time during the period of the Cold War when it was considered necessary to ally with any anti-Communist regime around the world, including some of the most unsavoury and oppressive right-wing military dictatorships. This ruthless war of ideology so corrupted America that this bastion of democracy and freedom sank into the hysteria of McCarthyism at home while abroad it made use of secret intelligence agencies to conduct covert and not so covert operations (*coup d'états*, assassinations, etc.) against other governments, including, on occasion, those that had democratic legitimacy. Some of the crudest incidents of this sort were in connection with Iran, Guatemala, Chile and Cuba. The worst example of poor judgement was when America allowed itself to become sucked into the civil war in Vietnam, an incident that cost millions of lives and for a time did untold damage to the cause of democracy around the world. However, there was a silver lining to that war in that it forced a complete reassessment of American attitudes and of the underlying approach to the management of foreign policy.

America's Relations with Other Nations: The Face of Civility

REGIONAL POWER

This leads logically to acknowledgement that the 'ugly American' is only one aspect of American foreign policy and that indeed there has always been a tendency towards expression in foreign policy of the fundamental aspirations of the democratic ideal and its linkage with America's destiny. The beginnings of such a dimension can be traced to the very first principles of the new federal republic with the emphasis on not being entangled in foreign alliances and the *realpolitik* of European authoritarian monarchies. Thomas Jefferson, as Secretary of State, spoke of 'honest friendship with all nations but entangling alliances with none'. It was further expressed in the Monroe Doctrine in which the United States made clear its strong objection to the European powers interfering in the New World, a policy combining selfish consideration with protection of the independence of the new republics of South America. To the north, following an initial period of tension after the War of Independence, the United States concluded an agreement with Canada which established the longest and most lasting demilitarized frontier in the world.

WORLD POWER

In the first decades of the 20th century, as America became a power of the first rank, this tendency in foreign policy acquired more complex expression. The administration of Theodore Roosevelt took the initiative to help bring to an end the Russian–Japanese War of 1905 at the Treaty of Portsmouth (New Hampshire) and to advocate a strengthened world court at the second Hague Conference in 1907. In addition, there was an enlightened side to the follow-up to the Spanish war and the annexation of Hawaii: contrary to European practice of the time, America supported independence for Cuba and commonwealth status for Puerto Rico and the Philippines, and eventually agreed to statehood for Hawaii (1959). The culmination of this enlightened aspect of American foreign policy was the action of the administration of President Wilson in converting the objectives of the allies in the First World War into democratic principle through promulgation of the 'Fourteen Points'. One result of this approach was national self-determination for

Eastern Europe.[67] A second result, even more significant, was the establishment of the League of Nations, a truly historical advance along the path towards world peace. The full benefit of such advance, however, was greatly reduced by the subsequent failure of the United States to join the new organization because the Senate did not ratify the agreement.[68] This was a tragedy of major proportion because if America had joined the League it is possible that the Second World War, which, worldwide, cost some 60 million lives, might never have happened.

GLOBAL LEADERSHIP

This side of American foreign policy, after a period of silence in the 1920s, was to be given strong voice again beginning in the 1930s with Franklin Roosevelt's call for a policy of 'good neighbours' with Latin America (a policy later taken up by President Kennedy with his Alliance for Progress) and the rallying of democracy against the fascist dictators in the Second World War (initially America was the 'arsenal of democracy' but by 1943 it was the leading fighting democracy as well). The United States again took the lead in insisting that the World War should be concluded with strengthened international organizations for peace: a new United Nations to replace the discredited League, along with specialized agencies with the mission of reducing world poverty, a major cause of conflict.

The United States gave generously, through the Marshall Plan, to help with reconstruction in war-devastated regions and through such international aid organizations as the World Bank, to relieve poverty in less developed countries. In recent years it has been, despite occasional faltering, a forceful advocate of world free trade, in the long run one of the most effective means for reducing world poverty and for creating a peaceful global society.[69] Under the leadership of Eleanor Roosevelt, the Universal Declaration of Human Rights was drawn up and approved by the UN General Assembly in 1948. Though initially dismissed as empty rhetoric, this statement has gradually become a powerful tool for enforcing civilized behaviour by all governments around the world, especially with the increased credibility of America since the civil rights advances of the sixties and seventies and the end of the Cold War.[70] This is clearly a major step forward along the road to world peace.

Pax Americana. Since the end of the Cold War, America, as the only remaining superpower, has several times taken the lead role in resisting aggressor nations, in peacekeeping operations, and in helping to facilitate peace agreements between nations in conflict, sometimes when America had an obvious material self-interest but also when such interest was less important than the general welfare of the international community. Thus America expended much effort in rolling back the invasion of Kuwait in 1991 (just as it had earlier in Korea) and took part, along with others, in peacekeeping operations in Somalia, Haiti, Bosnia and Kosovo. In several instances, the US government felt obliged to intervene in the general interest in response to domestic popular pressure to stop human suffering: in short, an example of democracy functioning according to moral principle. America has taken a leading role in negotiating peace in Northern Ireland, the Middle East and Korea as well is in several conflicts in the Americas and Africa that were left over from the Cold War. By contrast with traditional great power behaviour, America, warned by the Vietnam disaster, has been careful when committing its armed forces to have in place an 'exit strategy', which is reassuring not only for the American public but also for other countries concerned about the imperial ambitions of powerful nations. America has taken a leading role, also, in 1) the critical task of preventing the spread of weapons of mass destruction, 2) the suppression of international crime, particularly that spawned by drug trafficking, and 3) supporting the spread of good governance and democratic institutions, most notably in establishing democracy in the defeated Axis powers – Germany, Italy and Japan – after the Second World War.[71]

Limits to Pax Americana. Though *Pax Americana* has been of much benefit to the world community (this was also true earlier of certain aspects of *Pax Britannica*, which supervised the abolition of the international slave trade in the 19th century and also of *Pax Romana* in ancient times), it is clearly not an arrangement that can lead to a permanent world peace. This is because other nations, especially those that are relatively powerful, will tend to resist, always suspicious of American motives (sometimes with good reason) and often concerned about their own selfish interests anyway. Furthermore, even if America were to be trusted, it has shown that it cannot always be relied upon to do the right thing. In the democratic political context there is always an audience for those asking, 'Why should our boys be killed in other peoples' wars?' and, in America's case, there is the seductive tradition of isolationism and the 'America first' philosophy: 'We can live in peace and comfort in our vast and rich land without having to get mixed up in the affairs of a lot of difficult foreigners'. In other words, commitment to the general good can be decidedly erratic. These two considerations are well illustrated in the disgraceful bullying of the UN with regard to refusal to pay legally obligated financial contributions and periodic snubbing of the World Court, as in the case of US mining off the Nicaraguan coast in the 1980s.

What Needs to be Done Now?

The Power of Positive Thinking

This leads to the remaining topic of this paper: how to motivate America and protect it from its own dark side, which, as noted at the beginning of this essay, can so divert America from its true self when there is lack of attention by the public and government. Experience surely confirms that focusing on the negative, as is the knee-jerk response of America's critics around the world, who often have questionable agendas of their own, is not a practical answer. On the contrary, it inevitably provokes an unthinking nationalist response in America against perceived external 'enemies' and internal 'traitors'. Anyone knows this who has raised a child or observed the way of politics of their own country. Wisdom is surely to follow the advice of 'Abdu'l-Bahá:

> To look always at the good and not at the bad. If a man has ten good qualities and one bad one, to look at the ten and forget the one; and if a man has ten bad qualities and one good one, to look at the one and forget the ten.[72]

Following this line of thinking, focusing on America's spiritual destiny as described in the Bahá'í writings is clearly a first step. When this theme is linked to the familiar concept of the special nature of America, it is the experience of this writer that Americans of all backgrounds, almost without exception, react positively and with enthusiasm. Such a positive view of America which contrasts so sharply with the usual negative images that are generated every day by the media is an immense boost to morale and self-esteem. This is not a matter of prompting excessive pride and arrogance but rather of responsibility and an associated sense of humility, generosity and prayfulness. But in addition to the dream, there is a need to provide reinforcement and reassurance by addressing also some of the practical issues: typical fears and the specific benefits that America would gain from following its spiritual destiny.

'The only thing we have to fear is fear itself'[73]

One fear that has been common in America in recent decades, whenever there has been talk of strengthening international institutions, has been that this will inevitably lead to world dictatorship. In its most extreme form this is expressed in paranoid stories in Western states about sightings of black helicopters and UN troops coming to occupy the United States. Another variation is the theme of extreme religious fundamentalists that world government will signal the coming of the antichrist. How can such fears be addressed? First, it should be pointed out that today, by contrast with even 30 years ago, the majority of nations are democratic and will therefore insist that any world federal commonwealth also be democratic.[74] In any case, the United States as the only remaining superpower will clearly have immense influence in the design of the constitution of a world commonwealth, an influence which clearly would prevail when combined with that of America's long-time democratic allies.[75] The self-appointed gurus, who with amazing lack of self-doubt, monopolize the media with their scorn for any thought of world federal democracy should be challenged to spell out the consequences of their boring, myopic and backward-looking philosophy. As for the purveyors of paranoia, everyone of goodwill should take every opportunity to demand that they produce real, verifiable evidence or to shut up. The only way to deal with lies is to force them into the bright light of public discussion. Similarly, fundamentalists should be asked to say why their particular interpretation of the Bible with regard to the coming of the antichrist is to be preferred to that of the vast majority of religious scholars and leaders, today and in the past.

Benefits of World Federal Democracy for America

With regard to America's interests, it has to be pointed out that a democratic federal world government would have the following advantages. First, it would immensely increase America's military security over the long run. Second, it would eliminate the expense of the less reliable role of playing the world's policeman (today America still spends a significantly higher percentage of its GNP on defence than other wealthy countries[76]). Third, it would offer much increased protection overseas for American citizens and commerce. Fourth, it would create an environment conducive to the further growth of democracy and the decline of authoritarian-style governments with their built-in penchant for the use of force to get their way.[77] Another important consideration, which gives the matter some urgency, is that America needs to act while it, indeed, does have unchallenged leadership of the world, a position it may not always have, so that it is able to ensure that world democracy and the rule of law become the permanent governing principles of global society.[78]

What America Should Do Now to Help Establish World Peace

Beyond addressing the inspiration of America's glorious destiny and the practical aspect of present fears and immediate American advantage that flow from following its destiny, there is a need to draw attention to what corrective actions should be made in the immediate future in the conduct of America's external relations. Most important is to build on past precedent and aspiration to make moral principle the guiding force in external affairs. Within this broad objective, there is a particular need to start seriously responding to some of the ideas regarding plans for the world in the 21st century that were presented by the Commission on Global Governance and others (including the Bahá'í International Community) in connection with the 50th anniversary of the United Nations. The approach should be one of courage and vision, as shown by America at the end of the First and Second World Wars, rather than nitpicking and carping for petty national advantage and counting of pennies.

> A serious new effort imbued by a spirit similar to that of Bretton Woods or the San Francisco U.N. conference must be made and soon. It's in the interests of all nations to redefine and shore up the international institutions that are rapidly becoming obsolete.
>
> *Jim Hoagland*[79]

In particular, careful consideration should be given to the highly democratic idea of calling for a world constituent assembly ('a mighty convocation'), elected by the peoples of the world, which would have as its mandate the drawing up of a world federal constitution. In the meantime, America should be adjusting its policies 1) to give strong support for the new International Criminal Court, by abandoning overly cautious, not to say unreasonable, demands for an exclusive position above the law,[80] 2) to promptly pay its arrears in dues to the United Nations as an example to all nations of responsible behaviour and 3) to sharpen the focus of sanctions against rogue States so that they punish the real guilty parties, i.e. those in power, rather than innocent citizens who are under the heel of authoritarian regimes and who have, therefore, little or no say in the actions of their governments. Failure to act on this point simply means loss of the moral high ground and of global support, and thereby the frustration of justice.

ELIMINATING THE DEAD WEIGHT OF MATERIALISM

Beyond all these considerations is the most fundamental issue that America is not going to be able to fully realize its spiritual destiny until it gets its gross materialism under control, i.e. as discussed earlier, there is a balance between the material and the spiritual. It is one of the paradoxes of America that it is simultaneously one of the more religious countries in the world whilst at the same time one of the most consumed with material indulgence. This is a clear example, at the national level, of the constant struggle in life between the two sides of human nature, described in the Bahá'í teachings, as mentioned earlier. Whilst America is obsessed with materialism it will not have the will or capacity to be true to its spiritual destiny. Moreover, it is the material crassness of American civilization that arouses deep anger and opposition in other nations, fearful that such American materialism will undermine all that they value in their own cultures. Thus Shoghi Effendi spoke of the need for a thorough purging in America of:

> ... the accumulated dross which ingrained racial prejudice, rampant materialism, widespread ungodliness and moral laxity have combined, in the course of succeeding generations, to produce, and which have prevented her thus far from assuming the role of world spiritual leadership forecast by 'Abdu'l-Bahá's unerring pen – a role which she is bound to fulfil through travail and sorrow.[81]

When this statement was made just before the Second World War, few understood its true significance. The continuing decline in religion since that time and of associated public morality has made it far more obvious as shown, for instance, in the recent views attributed to Zbigniew Brzezinski, former national security adviser to President Carter:

Lack of moral and philosophical fibre is fast disqualifying the only available human pilot – still none other than the United States . . . he sees around him a spiritual desolation of unrestrained hedonism . . . have their minds fixated on the instant gratification of their desires and appetites: material, sensual and sexual . . . The lack of binding moral imperatives, he argues, is making the United States unfit to lead the rest of the world. But who else can do so? Nobody is the answer. He looks at Japan and Europe and China and dismisses their challenge, at least for the near future . . . America is peerless, perched on top of the world without true rivals. The challenge comes from within, from American culture . . . it is undermined, he argues, by the empty moral content of its message.[82]

A THIRD GREAT AWAKENING

This suggests a major role for the American religious communities, in effect, a 'Third Great Awakening', to continue their great inheritance of the past of being on the leading edge of the progressive advance of the American nation in all its humanity, compassion and idealism – in short, of helping America to subdue its dark side and move towards its spiritual destiny. For the Bahá'í community there is a particularly important role for at least two major reasons. The first is the clear vision of the coming of the Lesser Peace and the role in that process that is assigned to the United States: a vision that gives the community a unique responsibility for offering the American people sound and realistic advice on public matters. Second, Bahá'ís in America, as elsewhere, should continue to show in their own community an ever-expanding living model of humanity, in all its diversity, living together in harmony and love, as it learns to make the spiritual laws enunciated by Bahá'u'lláh a routine of life.

> Its existence is yet another convincing proof of the practicality of its Founder's vision of a united world, another evidence that humanity can live as one global society, equal to whatever challenges its coming of age may entail. If the Bahá'í experience can contribute in whatever measure to reinforcing hope in the unity of the human race, we are happy to offer it as a model for study. *The Universal House of Justice*[83]

It is surely appropriate to conclude this presentation with the stirring words of Shoghi Effendi in a letter to the American Bahá'í community dated 5 June 1947:

> . . . we cannot fail to perceive the workings of two simultaneous processes . . . each clearly defined, each distinctly separate, yet closely related and destined to culminate, in the fullness of time, in a single glorious consummation.
>
> One of these processes is associated with the mission of the American Bahá'í Community, the other with the destiny of the American nation. The one . . . will be consummated through the emergence of the Bahá'í World Commonwealth in the Golden Age of the Bahá'í Dispensation.
>
> The other . . . received its initial impetus through the formulation of President Wilson's Fourteen Points, closely associating for the first time that republic with the fortunes of the Old World . . . It was further reinforced through the declaration embodied in the Atlantic Charter, as voiced by one of its chief progenitors, Franklin D. Roosevelt. It assumed a definite outline through the birth of the United Nations at the San Francisco Conference . . . It must, however long and tortuous the way, lead, through a series of victories and reverses, to the political unification of the Eastern and Western Hemispheres, to the emergence of a world government and the establishment of the Lesser Peace, as foretold by Bahá'u'lláh and foreshadowed by the Prophet Isaiah. It must, in the end, culminate in the unfurling of the banner of the Most Great Peace, in the Golden Age of the Dispensation of Bahá'u'lláh.[84]

Bibliography

'Abdu'l-Bahá. *Paris Talks*. London: Bahá'í Publishing Trust, 1967.

Bahá'í International Community. *Turning Point for All Nations: A Statement of the Bahá'í International Community on the Occasion of the 50th Anniversary of the United Nations*. New York: Bahá'í International Community United Nations Office, 1995.

The Economist. 31 July 1993.

— 23 November 1996.

Esslemont, J. E. *Bahá'u'lláh and the New Era*. London: Bahá'í Publishing Trust, 1974.

The International Economy. May/June 1991.

Johnston, Douglas. 'Resuscitating Peace: Religious Service to the Political World', Washington, 16 April 1995.

Kidron, Michael and Ronald Segal. *State of the World Atlas*.

Harmondsworth, Middx.: Penguin Books, 5th edn. 1995.

Lee, Kathy. *Prelude to the Lesser Peace.* New Delhi: Bahá'í Publishing Trust, 1989.

New Oxford Review. June 1993.

New York Review of Books. 12 August 1999.

New York Times. 10 April 1991.

Rieff, David. 'The Culture That Conquered the Earth', *Washington Post*, 2 January 1994.

Shoghi Effendi. *The Advent of Divine Justice.* Wilmette, IL: Bahá'í Publishing Trust, 1990.

— *Citadel of Faith: Messages to America 1947–1957.* Wilmette, IL: Bahá'í Publishing Trust, 1965.

— *The World Order of Bahá'u'lláh.* Wilmette, IL: Bahá'í Publishing Trust, 1991.

Tindall, George Brown, and David Shi. *America: A Narrative History.* New York: W.W. Norton & Co., 1996.

The Universal House of Justice. *The Promise of World Peace.* London: Bahá'í Publishing Trust, 1985.

Washington Post. 21 January 1994.

— 31 July 1998.

— 24 October 1998.

— 25 October 1998.

Wills, Garry. *Under God: Religion and American Politics.* New York: Simon and Schuster, 1990.

World Christian Encyclopedia, A Comparative Survey of Churches and Religions in the Modern World, 1900–2000. Oxford: Oxford University Press, 1982.

References

1. America is a continent made up of 35 independent nations. However, it is common practice to use the term America for the United States, perhaps because it is the only nation on the continent to incorporate the word in its national name or because it was the first independent modern State on the continent. In this essay the common practice has been followed as a matter of convenience but no offence is intended to Americans who are citizens of the other 34 American nations.

2. *Washington Post*, 7 February 1999.

3. Tindall and Shi, *America: A Narrative History*, p. 280.

4. Senator William Fulbright, in *New Oxford Review*, June 1993.

5. A reaction in turn to the philosophy of the inherent sinfulness of man which had been propagated by the Christian churches for centuries.

6. The Universal House of Justice, *Promise of World Peace*, para. 26.
7. Shoghi Effendi, *Citadel of Faith*, p. 126.
8. 'Abdu'l-Bahá, quoted in Shoghi Effendi, *Advent of Divine Justice*, pp. 85–6.
9. Universal House of Justice, *Promise of World Peace*, para. 2.
10. See Shoghi Effendi, *World Order*, pp. 203–4 and Lee, *Prelude to the Lesser Peace*.
11. The Bahá'í International Community (BIC) represents the Universal House of Justice at the United Nations with the status of an officially accredited non-government organization (NGO).
12. See Bahá'í International Community, *Turning Point for All Nations*.
13. Thus President Chirac of France told the United States Congress in February 1996, 'Today, as yesterday, the world needs the United States.' *Economist*, 23 November 1996.
14. Tindall and Shi, *America: A Narrative History*, p. 1392.
15. It should be added, however, that the universality of the American melting pot is comparatively recent. Until about 1850 America was still essentially an Anglo-Irish nation. Then for the next hundred years, until the 1960s, the United States was, for all practical purposes, a European nation with suppressed African and indigenous minorities. It is only since then that these minorities have really acquired full citizenship and that Asian and Hispanic Americans have become a significant cultural force in the country.
16. These percentages of population are based on the most recent US Census, that for 1990.
17. The island of Puerto Rico became an American possession after the Spanish–American War of 1898. The main Puerto Rican immigration to the continental United States took place in the immediate post-World War Two period. It might be added that the *mainland* Hispanics were primarily a mix of Spanish and Native American descent, whilst the *island* Hispanics were mostly a mix of Spanish and African. African Americans coming from the Caribbean, with a different experience of slavery which forced on them a culture of self-reliance as a matter of survival, have often progressed further up the economic ladder than mainland African Americans. Well-known Caribbean African Americans have included Marcus Garvey, Malcolm X, Shirley Chisholm, Stokely Carmichael, Harry Belafonte and Colin Powell.
18. *Economist*, 23 November 1996.
19. The crudest examples of discrimination against Asians were 1) the Exclusion Acts which for the period 1882–1943 banned further Chinese immigration and 2) the 1942–4 internment of more than 100,000 Japanese Americans living on the West Coast. Financial

compensation and an apology have recently been offered by the Federal Government for the latter act of injustice.

20. In the first half century of the British North American colonies, until about 1660, the status of the relatively few African involuntary immigrants was ambiguous and was akin to that of the indented servant status of poor English immigrants, i.e. it was a less severely oppressive condition than the slavery of later years.

21. 'Abdu'l-Bahá, *Paris Talks*, p. 178.

22. Most recently, Americans have tried to confront remaining racism in society through public meetings of a presidential commission on race, chaired by the distinguished African American historian John Hope Franklin. It should be acknowledged that two other countries that have had to struggle with a racist past are also showing leadership in this respect. Thus Germany has tried hard in recent years to confront the agony of the Holocaust, while South Africa has set an example of trying to bring reconciliation and closure to the horrors of the apartheid regime through the proceedings of the Truth and Reconciliation Commission, under the chairmanship of Archbishop Tutu, winner of the Nobel Peace prize in 1984.

Racism still soils civil society in many other countries around the world, most evidently in Europe and Australasia, as was once again made evident in the February 1999 Stephen Lawrence Inquiry into the London Metropolitan Police Force.

23. 'Abdu'l-Bahá, quoted in Shoghi Effendi, *Advent of Divine Justice*, p. 37.

24. The vast majority of the indigenous population of America are the American Indians. However, it should not be forgotten that the indigenous population also includes the Polynesians of Hawaii.

25. For example, in both the two earliest colonies: Virginia with the story of Pocahantas, and Massachusetts with help which made possible the first Thanksgiving celebration.

26. Legendary names of the Native American nations include Pocahantas (Powhatans), Tecumseh (Shawnee), Black Hawk (Sauks), Red Cloud (Ogala Sioux), Sitting Bull (Hunkpapa Sioux), Crazy Horse (Ogala Sioux), Geronimo (Apache) and Chief Joseph (Nez Perce).

27. 'Abdu'l-Bahá, quoted in Shoghi Effendi, *Advent of Divine Justice*, p. 55.

28. There was, of course, much intermingling of races on account of sexual exploitation of African American women by European–American men during time of slavery as can clearly be observed in the wide range of colour in the African American community. As in other countries, shades of colour can be a cause of prejudice and tension, even within a family.

29. Often expressed at the personal level by an exceptional interest in genealogy, an interest highlighted by Alex Haley, an African American, in his 1976 book *Roots: The Saga of an American Family*.

30. This connection was recently formalized in the US–South Africa Binational Commission, chaired jointly by the vice presidents of the two countries.

31. An understandable feeling connected with France's supremacy during the two centuries linking Louis XIV, le Roi Soleil, and the Emperor Napoleon, which immediately preceded the two centuries of Anglo-Saxon predominance, *Pax Britannica* in the 19th century and *Pax Americana* in the 20th.

32. It should be added that the connection is reinforced by the existence of French-speaking areas in the United States (Maine and Louisiana) and in addition by colonies of French-speaking Haitian immigrants in New York and elsewhere.

33. 'What is most distinctive about American popular culture is its resolutely popular character . . . its conviction that dreams and realities are, or at least should be, indistinguishable.' David Rieff, 'The Culture That Conquered the Earth', *Washington Post*, 2 January 1994. The point was elaborated in another article: 'The Global Power of US Culture', *Washington Post*, 25 October 1998.

34. Other countries may produce higher quality movies but it is those of America which seem to have most universal appeal.

35. Unitary democracies tend to work best when a nation is ethnically homogeneous and geographically compact. Even such traditional unitary democracies as Great Britain have taken steps recently to decentralize in response to demands for government to be closer to the local community and, therefore, have a more human face.

36. A strong tradition of democracy, equality and freedom was to be reinforced in the 19th century by various new immigrant ethnic groups, e.g. the Scandinavians with experience of relatively free institutions in the home countries, the Irish with their rebellious spirit arising from centuries of resistance to oppression, and the Jews with their strong concern for justice for all minorities arising from their own experience of persecution.

37. Such as Thomas Jefferson, James Madison and George Washington of Virginia, Sam Adams, John Adams and James Otis of Massachusetts, John Dickerson and Benjamin Franklin of Pennsylvania, and Alexander Hamilton of New York.

38. In 1996, the seven smallest states had three representatives each; the three states with the most representatives were California (54), New York (33) and Texas (32).

39. A two-thirds majority is required for impeachment in the House of Representatives and for power to remove the President from office by the Senate.

40. The formal abolition of the international slave trade in cooperation with Great Britain in 1808, restrictions on the extension of slavery into the new territories in the West, etc.

41. More than 600,000 died in the Civil War, about two per cent of the population at that time, or around eight per cent of the adult male population. This may be compared with the loss of some 400,000 lives in the Second World War, representing about 0.3 per cent of the population at that time.

42. Gettysburg Address, 19 November 1863.

43. The 13th Amendment abolished slavery in the United States; the 14th Amendment gave citizenship to all persons born or naturalized in the United States, including former slaves; and the 15th Amendment stated: 'The right of citizens of the United States to vote shall not be denied or abridged by the United States or by any State on account of race, colour, or previous condition of servitude.'

44. European racism reached a peak of intensity and nastiness in the period 1890 to 1945, coinciding with the high tide of the European overseas empires and the fashionable theory of Social Darwinism.

45. The Civil Rights Act of 1964 banned discrimination for voter registration, housing and jobs. That of 1965 specifically forbade use of poll taxes and literacy tests for voter registration and appointed federal examiners to enforce the rules.

46. Native Americans were not given US citizenship until 1924.

47. An early highlight of that movement was the first meeting in the world of women suffragettes at Seneca Falls, New York, in 1848, the same year that the Persian poetess and scholar took off her veil before the nascent Bábí community attending the Badasht Conference, as a symbolic gesture to mark the coming liberation of women.

48. An early precedent in American history of political empowerment of women was the practice of the Iroquois federation of women being responsible for drawing up lists of individuals from which the leaders of the nation would be chosen.

49. Much of the present debate on good governance in the United States focuses on the corrupting role of money in the election of the legislative and executive branches. Nevertheless, the issue that is most frightening for ordinary citizens is the often poor quality of the judicial branch, ranging, on the one hand, from 1) dominance by a self-serving and bloated legal profession, erratic and often

racially biased punishments, unsupervised police forces, prisons run by the most violent inmates, to, on the other hand, 2) an extraordinary amount of physical violence in society, aggravated by a drug and gun culture.

50. America was certainly not the first nation to establish the welfare state, being several decades behind most of Western Europe and Australasia. However, it has pioneered ways to make it more efficient and less burdensome on the economy and it has tried to address the important problem of the debilitating effects of welfare dependency.

51. Wills, *Under God: Religion and American Politics*.

52. Maryland was founded in 1634 initially as a haven for Roman Catholics. The first Jewish congregation in North America was established in New Amsterdam (later New York) in 1656.

53. The Seventh Day Adventist Church is the largest to have its roots in the Adventist movement of the 1830s and 1840s. This was led by William Miller, a Massachusetts Baptist, who initially calculated from biblical prophecy (mostly the Book of Daniel) that the Second Coming of Christ would happen between March 1843 and March 1844. When this did not occur (the First Disappointment) a revised calculation was for 23 October 1844. The apparent lack of fulfilment of the revised prophecy was called the Great Disappointment. The Seventh Day Adventist Church settled for an indeterminate time in the near future.

54. Director of the 1990 survey of religion in America sponsored by the Graduate School and University Center of the City University of New York. *New York Times*, 10 April 1991.

55. *World Christian Encyclopedia*, p. 725.

56. There are quite a few countries where the largest religious community is significantly smaller than 90 per cent, most notably in Africa, the Caribbean and East and South Asia. In India, which is known for its religious diversity and a strong spiritual element in its culture, Hindus make up less than 80 per cent of the population.

57. Tindall and Shi, *America: A Narrative History*, p. 266.

58. 'The men who crafted the First Amendment's clause prohibiting Congress from making "Law respecting an establishment of religion, or prohibiting the free exercise thereof" wanted to be sure that America avoided a government established church . . . there are two orders of magnitude regarding neutrality: neutrality as *among* religions and neutrality as *between* religion and irreligion. The first . . . was what the Framers had in mind and what America practised for most of its constitutional history . . . But then came the doctrine that

holds that government must not merely avoid favouring one religion over another but also avoid favouring religion in general. The inevitable result . . . is outright hostility to religion . . . It's corrosive to our culture . . . now we are being asked in our public life to pretend religion doesn't exist or that it isn't important . . . we've reached the point where everybody's religion is being equally discredited by the state.' William Raspberry, *Washington Post*, 21 January 1994.

59. The Catholic Church is the largest single Christian denomination in the United States (about 30 per cent of all US Christians in 1990, compared with about a quarter of that figure for the next largest denomination, the Southern Baptist Convention), and for more than a century it has been a powerful force in American religious life. Nevertheless, until the 1960s it had something of a siege mentality that came from being a minority in a somewhat unfriendly Protestant environment. The turning point was the election of the first Catholic President (John Kennedy) in 1960 and the reign, 1958–63, of 'the good Pope', John XXIII, who was universally respected and loved.

60. Of 100 Nobel Peace awards made from 1901 to 1998, 18 were given to Americans, the largest contingent of any nation. Though some were awarded to Presidents (Theodore Roosevelt and Woodrow Wilson) and to other government officials, the vast majority (11) were awarded to private citizens.

61. See Johnston, 'Resuscitating Peace: Religious Service to the Political World', *Washington Post*, 16 April 1995.

62. See, for instance, a series of 11 books on religion and ecology produced by the Harvard University Center for Study of World Religions, as reported in *Washington Post*, 24 October 1998.

63. John Louis O'Sullivan, editor of *The United States Magazine and Democratic Review*, quoted in Tindall and Shi, *America: A Narrative History*, p. 563.

64. To put this action in perspective, it might be contrasted with the behaviour of European and Asian imperial powers when they were acquiring new territories.

65. Tindall and Shi, *America: A Narrative History*, p. 595.

66. ibid. p. 563.

67. The American effort may be contrasted with the simultaneous cynical carve-up of the Ottoman Empire by the European imperial powers, France and Great Britain (much to the dismay of Lawrence of Arabia and many others), the consequences of which are still with us today, and with the 45-year long military occupation of Eastern Europe by the Soviet Union after the Second World War.

68. In the crucial vote in the US Senate in November 1919, 49 Senators (51 per cent) voted in favour of the treaty and 35 (36 per cent) voted against, whilst 12 did not vote. To win assent the Constitution required a favourable vote of at least 64 (67 per cent).

69. Critics point out that there is some hypocrisy in present American advocacy of free trade in light of its own long record of protectionism in the 19th and early 20th centuries when it was a developing country. A good debating point, but, nevertheless, the economic case for free trade in the general global interest is overwhelming (*pace* Adam Smith). What is necessary is supervision of the process to ensure a level playing field and to manage fair sharing of transitional costs – functions that almost certainly require a federal world government. As for the connection of free trade and peace, it hardly needs pointing out that disruption by war of a closely integrated global economy will hurt all nations. It might be added that among the strongest supporters of the early peace movement were the Manchester Free Traders, John Bright and Richard Cobden.

70. The US State Department now publishes each year an extremely useful review of human rights conditions around the world, country by country.

71. Former President Carter and others now provide, on an invitation basis, monitoring of election services in countries where credibility in their honesty needs to be established because of past manipulation. This is another example of the American voluntary sector in action.

72. 'Abdu'l-Bahá, quoted in Esslemont, *Bahá'u'lláh and the New Era*, p. 80.

73. President Franklin Roosevelt, First Inaugural Address, 4 March 1933.

74. By 1993, 129 nations, or 68 per cent of the total, representing more than 60 per cent of the world's population, were multi-party democracies. Kidron and Segal, *State of the World Atlas*, pp. 78–9.

75. 'Americans are traditionally uncomfortable with a world role defined solely in terms of "maintaining a global system". That crucial function remains our responsibility; indeed it may be the definition of our responsibility today. But American engagement is given additional energy in this area by the spread of democracy and by basic humanitarian impulses in a world made smaller by global communication.' Peter Rodman, Fellow of the Johns Hopkins Foreign Policy Institute and senior National Security Council, official in the Reagan and Bush Administrations. *The International Economy*, May/June 1991.

76. In 1994, three years after the collapse of the Soviet Union, the United States spent 4.3 per cent of its GNP on defence. This might be compared with the following figures: 3.0 per cent average for all nations; 2.5 per cent average for NATO nations, 3.3 per cent for the UK, 3.4 per cent for France, 1.8 per cent for Germany, 2.0 per cent for Italy, 1.8 per cent for Canada and 1.0 per cent for Japan.

77. 'In an increasingly interdependent world Americans have a growing stake in how other countries govern, or misgovern, themselves. The larger and more close-knit the community of nations that choose democratic forms of government, the safer and more prosperous Americans will be, since democracies are demonstrably more likely to maintain their international commitments, less likely to engage in terrorism or wreak environment damage, and less likely to make war on each other.' Strobe Talbott, US Deputy Secretary of State, quoted in *The Economist*, 23 November 1996.

78. 'There will not be a "single superpower" forever. The global structure of power will inevitably change as other large countries become stronger. The United States would be wise to use its unique current position to help build a strong international order, whose rules of behaviour, decisions, and actions will command universal respect, no matter how global power may be distributed in the future.' Brian Urquhart, former UN Undersecretary-General. *New York Review of Books*, 12 August 1999.

79. Jim Hoagland, *Washington Post*, 10 September 1998.

80. 'It is clear that the US delegation in Rome was not only isolated but profoundly out of touch with the prevailing political climate. Like King Canute commanding the waves to recede, the Americans insisted on special privileges that, however plausible in 1945, were scarcely viable in 1998 . . . US intransigence on positions that struck even staunch US allies as extreme caused American influence in Rome to dissipate as it became clear to other negotiators that the United States was not prepared to sign any treaty that the vast majority of states deemed worth signing.' Diane Orentlicher, Director of the War Crimes Research Office at the American University, *Washington Post*, 31 July 1998.

81. Shoghi Effendi, *Citadel of Faith*, p 127.

82. *Economist*, 31 July 1993.

83. The Universal House of Justice, *The Promise of World Peace*, para. 57.

84. Shoghi Effendi, *Citadel of Faith*, pp. 32–3.

Collective Security as a Means of Ensuring Peace Among the Nations:

The Contribution of the Bahá'í Faith

Danesh Sarooshi[1]

Introduction

The attainment of peace between nations is a long-cherished ideal. The Bahá'í scriptures contain much guidance on the principles that humanity should implement in practice to reach and maintain a lasting peace. Important among these is the concept of collective security. It is this concept that is the focus of this paper. In particular, this paper will examine what the concept means, provide a brief description of how it currently operates under the auspices of the United Nations and, finally, turn to discuss some of the proposals for reform of the concept that may be suggested by Bahá'í scripture.

Our present focus on collective security does not, however, presuppose that its application alone will always be sufficient to achieve an effective long-term peace among States. The study of the conditions necessary to establish and maintain such a peace

162

is a complex enterprise which requires insights and contributions from various fields of study, not just international law: fields such as international relations, history, sociology, social anthropology, social psychology, theories of justice and political theory, to name but a few. However, the contribution that international law has to make is arguably unique since as a subject its focus is on imposing obligations on States. This is of considerable importance in the area of peace and security where, in order to maintain or restore peace, States will in certain cases be required to refrain from, or take, certain action. It is by invoking the binding force of treaties under international law that the concept of collective security makes its contribution to the maintenance of peace. In particular, it was the adoption of the United Nations Charter – the treaty establishing the UN as an international organization – which changed the legal landscape in this area by imposing obligations on UN Member States to have to take collective security measures. As explained below in more detail, this was an important innovation of the UN Charter system as compared to the system contained in the earlier League of Nations Covenant.

The League of Nations and Collective Security

The concept of collective security institutes a system where a collective measure is taken against a member of a community of States that has violated certain community defined values. In the ideal of the system there are three constituent elements. First is the determination by a community of States of the core values which are sought to be maintained as part of the status quo of the community. Second is the determination by an authorized representative of the community that a core value has been violated in a particular case. And third is the determination by the authorized representative of what the response of the community should be to the violation by the recalcitrant State.

These three elements are in existence in the system constituted by the United Nations Charter. However, the earlier, and in fact the first, attempt by States at implementing the concept of collective security when they established the League of Nations

(LON) after the First World War was not so advanced. The aim was nonetheless noble. In the words of its chief advocate, President Woodrow Wilson, the League sought to establish 'not a balance of power, but a community of power; not organized rivalries, but an organized common peace'.[2]

In 1919 the nations of the world established the LON by conclusion of the LON Covenant, an international agreement between States. This Covenant constituted a system of collective security that in the area of taking military action against an aggressor State was decentralized in its application. Thus although the LON Council was given the ability to decide that a certain State had committed, for example, aggression, the decision, however, to take military action against a rogue State was left entirely up to each State. In other words, there was no compulsory requirement to take military action against an aggressor State. This was the major weakness of the LON collective security system. Nonetheless, the LON Council could require States to impose economic sanctions (trading and financial measures) against a recalcitrant State. But even where these economic sanctions were in practice imposed against an aggressor State they were only partial and thus were not effective. For example, the determination by the LON Council that Italy had resorted to an illegal war against Abyssinia (now Ethiopia) within the meaning of Article 16 of the LON Covenant led the Council only to impose temporary, partial and thus ineffective economic sanctions against Italy.[3] The collective security system of the League was not used by States which favoured a policy of appeasement and the world descended into the Second World War.

Despite, however, the failings and ineffectiveness of the LON system of collective security, it did mark a crucial stage in the evolution of the idea that the nations of the world should act collectively in order to deal with a rogue nation. The importance of this has been described by Shoghi Effendi in the following words:

That no less than fifty nations of the world, all members of the League of Nations, should have, after mature deliberation, recognized and been led to pronounce their verdict against an act of aggression which in their judgement has been deliberately committed by one of their fellow-members [Italy], one of the foremost Powers of Europe; that they should have, for the most part, agreed to impose collectively sanctions on the condemned aggressor, and should have succeeded in carrying out, to a very great measure, their decision, is no doubt an event without parallel in human history. For the first time in the history of humanity the system of collective security, fore-shadowed by Bahá'u'lláh and explained by 'Abdu'l-Bahá, has been seriously envisaged, discussed and tested. For the first time in history it has been officially recognized and publicly stated that for this system of collective security to be effectively established strength and elasticity are both essential – strength involving the use of an ade-quate force to ensure the efficacy of the proposed system, and elasticity to enable the machinery that has been devised to meet the legitimate needs and aspirations of its aggrieved upholders. For the first time in human history tentative efforts have been exerted by the nations of the world to assume collective responsibility, and to sup-plement their verbal pledges by actual preparation for collective action.[4]

The international organization which superseded the League of Nations – that is, took over certain of its functions – was the United Nations.[5] The system of collective security was changed for the better with the establishment by States after the Second World War of the UN Charter in 1945. The UN Charter is an international treaty or agreement concluded among the nations of the world that gives life to the UN as an international organi-zation by conferring on it certain objectives to achieve and by giving it certain powers and functions to achieve those objectives. The UN Charter states that the primary object and purpose of the UN Organization is to maintain 'international peace and security, and to that end: to take effective collective measures for the prevention and removal of threats to the peace, and for the suppression of acts of aggression or other breaches of the peace . . .' Our discussion now proceeds by examining briefly how the UN has sought to maintain international peace and security using its collective security system and then by examining what inno-vations the Bahá'í scriptures prescribe for the way in which collective security is currently being used by the UN.

The United Nations and Collective Security

The renewed determination after the Second World War to prevent a recurrence of the scourge of war saw States establish a UN Charter with a relatively advanced collective security system in order to maintain world peace. In particular, Chapter VII of the UN Charter gives the Security Council, an important component organ of the UN, broad powers to take action to deal with threats to world peace.

The Security Council can *require* States as a matter of legal obligation to take certain action against, for example, an aggressor State. We recall from above that this was a failing of the League of Nations system of collective security and as such the UN system represents a significant improvement in this regard. The Security Council has the competence under Article 25 of the Charter to impose a binding obligation on UN Member States to comply with its decisions. This includes, of course, decisions under Chapter VII of the Charter that deal with world peace. In other words, UN Member States are under a legal obligation to carry out against a rogue State what measures the Security Council says should be carried out. The one exception to this position is, as explained below, that States are not obligated to send forces to fight against an aggressor. The reason for this exception is the non-implementation of the Charter provisions dealing with the establishment of a stand-by UN force.

When the Security Council orders the taking of collective security measures to restore peace under Chapter VII, there is a two-stage process that is envisaged. The first is that the Security Council has the power to make a determination under Article 39 of the Charter that specific action by a State constitutes 'a threat to the peace, breach of the peace or act of aggression'. The Council has, in other words, been given by States the power to determine the content of the community values that are to be maintained by the UN collective security system and, moreover, the power to decide when a State is violating these values. This Article 39 determination is a legal prerequisite for the Council to be able to use its other powers under Chapter VII. Once the

Council has made this determination the second stage of the collective security process is its prescription of what measures should be taken by the international community of States to restore the observance by the recalcitrant State of the community value that it is presently violating. The Security Council has the power under Chapter VII to order two main types of measures to be taken against a State to ensure that it respects community values: it can impose economic sanctions and military sanctions.

The Security Council can, under Article 41 of the Charter, impose economic sanctions against a State. The Security Council has imposed economic sanctions against a number of UN Member States in response to their actions that the Council had decided were a threat to international peace. For example, the Security Council imposed economic sanctions against Iraq in resolution 661 in response to that country's invasion of Kuwait.

When imposing economic sanctions the Security Council will, for example, often require that all the world's States must stop trade with, and investment in, the target State's economy. As a result, the population of the country will often suffer owing to shortages of essential food and medical supplies that were being imported into the country before sanctions were imposed. The effect of economic sanctions particularly affects the poorer section of a country's population; while the members of the government whose actions caused the imposition of the economic sanctions are usually not affected. This problem is exacerbated in the case of a dictator of a country whose actions have often led to the imposition of economic sanctions against the country in the first place but who will in no way be affected by the sanctions.

The imposition of economic sanctions is, however, useful since it will often provide diplomatic and other processes of conflict resolution the time they need to try and resolve a situation before the next step of the use of military force is used by the Security Council against the recalcitrant State. However, where economic sanctions are not, or do not look as if they will be, successful then the use of military force is an important, final, collective security measure. This is the two-stage process that the Security Council employed against Iraq. When the economic sanctions imposed against Iraq looked as if they were not going to force Iraq to withdraw from Kuwait, the Security Council as a final measure in resolution 678 authorized UN Member States to use military force against Iraq.

The Security Council is given the power under Article 42 of the Charter to use a military force to fight against an aggressor. This military force was to have been contributed by States to the Security Council under agreements that were to have been concluded between the Security Council and States that wished to contribute to such a UN force. The conclusion of these agreements was provided for by Article 43 of the Charter. However, with the onset of the Cold War soon after the establishment of the UN no State was willing to conclude agreements that would require them to contribute troops to a UN force. The ideological divide during the Cold War between States permeated the UN as an institution and this saw States reluctant to entrust their armed forces to an institution that by definition required cooperation and a unity of purpose. The non-implementation of Article 43 of the Charter has meant that the Security Council cannot require States to contribute troops to a UN force.[6] This does not mean, however, that States cannot contribute troops on a voluntary basis to carry out objectives specified by the Security Council. In fact, it has been the practice of States to contribute troops in many cases to a coalition force to carry out military action when the Security Council has decided that this is needed to restore international peace. For example, in the case of the 1990 Iraqi invasion of Kuwait, the Security Council did not itself form a 'UN force' to fight against Iraqi forces but it did authorize UN Member States to form an *ad hoc* coalition to use force against the invading Iraqi forces.[7] As a result, States contributed troops to a coalition which repulsed Iraqi troops from Kuwait. This combined force was not under UN command and control but under that of the United States. This process of the Security Council delegating its Chapter VII powers to UN Member States to carry out military action on its behalf does not violate the letter[8] or the spirit of the UN collective security system,[9] since the most important feature of a collective security system is that the decision to take action against a State is taken by a central body, in our case the UN Security Council. The means of implementing the decision does not necessarily need to be by all the nations of the world, although this would occur in the ideal of the system.

Bahá'í Innovations to the United Nations Collective Security System

The Bahá'í writings contain a clear statement of its ideal collective security system and it is inextricably linked to the Bahá'í concept of the Lesser Peace. In the *World Order of Bahá'u'lláh*, the former is referred to as 'Bahá'u'lláh's Principle of Collective Security'.[10] Bahá'u'lláh stated in a Tablet to the rulers of nations in His time:

> . . . hold ye fast unto this, the Lesser Peace, that haply ye may in some degree better your own condition and that of your dependents.[11]

Shoghi Effendi has explained that the following passage of Bahá'u'lláh in the same Tablet 'expatiates' on this theme of the Lesser Peace:

> Be reconciled among yourselves, that ye may need no more armaments save in a measure to safeguard your territories and dominions . . . Be united, O kings of the earth, for thereby will the tempest of discord be stilled amongst you, and your peoples find rest, if ye be of them that comprehend. Should any one among you take up arms against another, rise ye all against him, for this is naught but manifest justice.[12]

This is a clear affirmation of the principle that collective action should be taken against an aggressor State. 'Abdu'l-Bahá subsequently went on to elaborate the details of Bahá'u'lláh's principle of collective security, more than 80 years ago, in the following terms:

True civilization will unfurl its banner in the midmost heart of the world whenever a certain number of its distinguished and high-minded sovereigns . . . shall, for the good and happiness of all mankind, arise, with firm resolve and clear vision, to establish the Cause of Universal Peace. They must make the Cause of Peace the object of general consultation, and seek by every means in their power to establish a Union of the nations of the world. They must conclude a binding treaty and establish a covenant, the provisions of which shall be sound, inviolable and definite. They must proclaim it to all the world and obtain for it the sanction of all the human race. This supreme and noble undertaking – the real source of the peace and well-being of all the world – should be regarded as sacred by all that dwell on earth. All the forces of humanity must be mobilized to ensure the stability and permanence of this Most Great Covenant. In this all-embracing Pact the limits and frontiers of each and every nation should be clearly fixed, the principles underlying the relations of governments towards one another definitely laid down . . . the size of the armaments of every government should be strictly limited, for if the preparations for war and the military forces of any nation should be allowed to increase, they will arouse the suspicion of others. The fundamental principle underlying this solemn Pact should be so fixed that if any government later violate any one of its provisions, all the governments on earth should arise to reduce it to utter submission, nay the human race as a whole should resolve, with every power at its disposal, to destroy that government. Should this greatest of all remedies be applied to the sick body of the world, it will assuredly recover from its ills and will remain eternally safe and secure.[13]

It is thus clear that the Bahá'í concept of collective security is only one element, albeit important, of the Bahá'í approach to maintaining peace. The role of collective security is to enforce the provisions of some future type of world constitution adopted by States and their peoples.[14] This is the first important innovation that the Bahá'í principle of collective security requires: that States should conclude a binding treaty (the 'Most Great Covenant') which incorporates the issues that 'Abdu'l-Bahá has expressly mentioned in the quotation above. Reaching agreement on these matters will not be easy in practice and will require a great deal of political will by States. However, it is Bahá'í belief that the peace and security of the world depends on it. Once such an agreement is concluded then collective security can act as the mechanism to ensure enforcement of the agreement's provisions. The body exercising collective security powers may well be a revamped version of the Security Council.

This approach of specifying in express terms the community values that collective security is to maintain is a significant improvement on the current system where the UN Security Council determines on an *ad hoc* basis what constitutes a threat to or breach of the peace or act of aggression and thus what action will trigger a collective security response. The greater certainty provided by the Bahá'í approach can only provide a greater sense of security for States than that which currently exists.

Another innovation that the Bahá'í concept introduces to collective security as it is currently understood is that the government of the rogue State should be removed from power and not just be made to cease its violation of a fundamental community value. Under current international law – in particular the law of the UN – this is clearly not an essential objective of a collective security response by States. This is evidenced by the response of the UN and its Member States to the invasion of Kuwait by Iraq. In responding to the Iraqi invasion, the allied troops only forced Iraqi troops to withdraw from Kuwait. The allies did not go on and remove from power the Iraqi government. This left in power a government that continued to violate international law and the decisions of the Security Council. The subsequent response of the Security Council to this Iraqi government action was to reimpose economic sanctions on Iraq. These sanctions have not to date effected any change in the policy of the government but they have, as noted above, had an adverse effect on the poorer sections of the Iraqi population. Moreover, several UN Member States launched unilateral air strikes against the Iraqi government in an effort to compel compliance.[15] This also met with little or no success. This example does highlight the problem with leaving in power a government that has no respect, or even possibly disdain, for fundamental norms of international law such as, for example, the principle of non-aggression.

However, the measure of removing the government of a State from power would not be appropriate in the context of the present UN collective security system. It would only be appropriate with the broader set of Bahá'í proposals: that the States and peoples of the world conclude and accept the 'Most Great Covenant' and provide therein their consent to such a final measure. It is this consent which would give the collective security system the authority and legitimacy to remove from power the government that violates the terms of the 'Covenant', since this government would no longer have any legal or moral basis to govern its State. It would have shown a flagrant disregard for international law and also the considered view of the majority of its peoples who affirmed the Covenant. The latter would be the case since we recall that, according to 'Abdu'l-Bahá, the Covenant should be ratified by all the peoples of the world: it must obtain the 'sanction of all the human race'. Accordingly, an international force would be acting with international and local legitimacy were it to remove from power a government that had transgressed any of the fundamental provisions of the Covenant, since the force would have received a mandate to act in such a manner from all the peoples of the world as well as, importantly, the peoples of the particular nation.

The removal of a government from power as a collective security response has in any case already arguably occurred in the case of the Security Council's response to the overthrow within Haiti of the democratically elected President Aristide in September 1991. After the failure of protracted negotiations between the coup leaders and President Aristide, who was living in exile in the US, to restore democratic rule within Haiti, the Security Council decided finally to impose economic sanctions (an oil and arms embargo) against Haiti in resolution 873. The Security Council went even further in its subsequent resolution 940 when it decided that economic sanctions were not sufficient to dislodge the coup leaders from Haiti and it authorized military forces of UN Member States to enter Haiti to implement the Governors Island Agreement.[16] In response to an imminent invasion by these forces, the coup leaders agreed to the immediate restoration of the government of President Aristide. After this agreement by the coup leaders to step down, a multinational force spearheaded by the US entered Haiti in an action known as 'Operation Uphold Democracy' in order to provide a secure environment and ensure the smooth transition of power within the State.[17] The importance of this case is that the Security Council decided for the first time that the continuation of a democratic government within a UN Member State is a community value that it wished to protect and maintain using its collective security powers under the Charter and, more importantly for present purposes, that it was willing to remove a non-democratic government from power and restore the democratic government. Despite the positive result in the case of Haiti, there were serious concerns expressed over the operation's international legitimacy.

What we mean by international legitimacy in this context is that the UN when it takes action to deal with threats to world peace can be said to be acting on behalf, and with the support, of the majority of the world's nations and peoples. It is clear that not every action by the Council under Chapter VII would thus be seen as being legitimate,[18] even where, strictly speaking, that action may be lawful. A lawful position is not always a legitimate one.[19] The main issue concerning legitimacy that arose in the case of Haiti was whether the removal of a government from power is a legitimate objective of a collective security response. This is where the Bahá'í approach of expressly providing in a treaty the principles and values that collective security is to maintain together with the agreement of the nations and peoples of the world that a collective security response can involve the removal of the government is of importance, since it provides a degree of legitimacy for such action that does not currently exist. Moreover, the incorporation into the 'Most Great Covenant' of the community values that collective security is to maintain has the further advantage in terms of legitimacy that these will have been agreed to by all States that have ratified the agreement; while under the current UN system it is only the members of the Security Council who decide what are the community values.

There is also a more general issue of legitimacy concerning

the present use of collective security that a Bahá'í approach would assist in resolving. This issue relates to the legitimacy of the decision-making processes of the Security Council when exercising its collective security powers. The main point that arises here concerns the veto power that the five Permanent Members of the Security Council possess over, among others, decisions relating to collective security made by the Council. The five Great Powers that emerged from the Second World War – the United States, the United Kingdom, the former Soviet Union (now replaced on the Council by Russia), China and France – have been designated by Article 23(1) of the UN Charter as 'Permanent Members of the Security Council'. In addition to having the right to permanent representation on the Security Council – the other ten members of the Security Council being elected on a two-yearly basis – Article 27(3) of the Charter gives the Permanent Members the power to veto decisions of the Security Council. This power of veto of the five Permanent Members means that they exercise greater weight than the ten Non-Permanent Members in the decision-making processes of the Council. This does not sit easily with the Bahá'í administrative principle of consultation which suggests that persons who are part of a decision-making organ should have an equal right to participate and vote when making a decision. Application of this principle to our case may suggest that every State in the Security Council should have an equal right to participate in the decisions of the Council. That is, the process of decision-making would have to be changed to ensure that no State possesses the power to veto decisions that were acceptable to a majority of the Council. The Bahá'í International Community has itself made such a proposal, first in 1955 and more recently in 1995 when it stated concerning UN reform that there should be gradual elimination of the concepts of 'permanent membership' and 'veto power'.[20] Such innovations are also important for the long-term legitimacy of action by the Security Council, since the Security Council must be perceived by States to be acting to ensure international peace and not just the achievement of its members' own individual interests. The abolition of the veto power – if it were to take place – would assist greatly in reassuring States who are not members of the Security Council that the Council was genuinely acting 'on their behalf', in the words of Article 24 of the Charter, and not just in those cases where the Permanent Members agreed.

Concluding Remarks

The operation of an effective collective security system is one of the most urgent needs facing international society. We have seen in the last few years what happens when the system does not operate: for example, the genocide of an estimated 800,000 people in Rwanda in the space of less than four months in 1994. The establishment of an effective collective security system – or for that matter peace – does not, however, depend on political agreements alone.[21] It depends on the political will of nations, and this in turn depends, largely, on the peoples of the world wanting such a system to work. Put differently, a genuine acceptance of the organic unity of the world is the essential precondition for lasting peace. In the illuminating words of Bahá'u'lláh: 'The well-being of mankind, its peace and security, are unattainable unless and until its unity is firmly established'.[22] An essential part of this unity, Bahá'u'lláh explains, is the following: 'It is not for him to pride himself who loveth his own country, but rather for him who loveth the whole world. The earth is but one country, and mankind its citizens'.[23] It is this more inclusive loyalty of persons as citizens of the world that will ensure the effective operation of a future collective security system and is the surest guarantor of peace among the nations. The Bahá'í approach of concluding a 'Most Great Covenant' will allow full expression to be given to the considered view of the peoples and governments of the world and it also gives a future international executive the authority and legitimacy to take effective collective security measures. This system, Bahá'í scripture predicts, will preside over what Bahá'ís term 'the Lesser Peace'.

Bibliography

'Abdu'l-Bahá. *The Secret of Divine Civilization*. Wilmette, IL: Bahá'í Publishing Trust, 1990.

Alvarez, J. 'Judging the Security Council', *American Journal of International Law*, no. 90, 1996.

Arangio-Ruiz, G. '"The Federal Analogy" and UN Charter Interpretation: A Crucial Issue', *European Journal of International Law*, vol. 8, 1997.

Bahá'í International Community. *Proposal for Charter Revision Submitted to the United Nations by the Bahá'í International Community*. Wilmette, IL: National Spiritual Assembly of the Bahá'ís of the United States, 1955.

— *Turning Point for All Nations: A Statement of the Bahá'í International Community on the Occasion of the 50th Anniversary of the United Nations*. New York: Bahá'í International Community United Nations Office, 1995.

Bahá'u'lláh, *Gleanings from the Writings of Bahá'u'lláh*. Wilmette, IL: Bahá'í Publishing Trust, 1983.

Brownlie, I. 'The Decisions of Political Organs of the UN and the Rule of Law', in MacDonald, *Essays in Honour of Wang Tieya*. The Hague: Kluwer, 1993.

Caron, D. 'The Legitimacy of the Collective Authority of the Security Council', *American Journal of International Law*, no. 87, 1993.

Cassese, A. (ed.). *UN Peace-Keeping: Legal Essays*. Alphen aan den Rijn: Martinus Nijhoff, 1978.

Claude, I. 'Collective Legitimization as a Political Function of the UN', *International Organization*, no. 20, Summer 1966.

Crawford, J. 'The Charter of the United Nations as a Constitution', in Fox, *The Changing Constitution of the United Nations*. London: British Institute of International and Comparative Law, 1997.

Dinstein, Y. *War, Aggression and Self-Defence*. Cambridge: Cambridge University Press, 1994.

Expenses case, International Court of Justice Reports: *Pleadings, Oral Arguments, Documents*, 1962.

Fassbender, B. *UN Security Council Reform and the Right of Veto: A Constitutional Perspective*. The Hague: Kluwer Law, 1998.

Fox, H. (ed.). *The Changing Constitution of the United Nations*. London: British Institute of International and Comparative Law, 1997.

Franck, T. 'Legitimacy in the International System', *American Journal of International Law*, no. 82, 1988.

— 'The "Powers of Appreciation": Who is the Ultimate Guardian of

UN Legality', Editorial Comment, *American Journal of International Law*, no. 86, 1992.

Herdegen, M. 'The 'Constitutionalization' of the UN Security System', *Vanderbilt Journal of Transnational Law*, no. 27, 1994.

Higgins, R. 'A General Assessment of UN Peace-Keeping', in Cassese (ed.). *UN Peace-Keeping: Legal Essays*. Alphen aan den Rijn: Martinus Nijhoff, 1978.

International Status of South West Africa case, *International Court of Justice Reports*, 1950.

Kritsiotis, D. 'Legality of the 1993 US Missile Strike on Iraq', *International & Comparative Law Quarterly*, no. 45, 1996.

Link, A. (ed.). *The Papers of Woodrow Wilson*. Princeton: Princeton University Press, 1982.

MacDonald, R. St. J. (ed.). *Essays in Honour of Wang Tieya*. The Hague: Kluwer, 1993.

Malone, D. *Decision-Making in the UN Security Council*. Oxford: Oxford University Press, 1999.

Miller, A. 'Universal Soldiers: UN Standing Armies and the Legal Alternatives', *Georgetown Law Journal*, no. 81, 1993.

Murphy, S. 'The Security Council, Legitimacy, and the Concept of Collective Security After the Cold War', *Columbia Journal of Transnational Law*, no. 32, 1994.

Reisman, W.M. 'The Constitutional Crisis in the United Nations', *American Journal of International Law*, no. 87, 1993.

Repertory of Practice of UN Organs, Supplement no. 3, vol. 2.

Sarooshi, D. *The United Nations and the Development of Collective Security*. Oxford: Oxford University Press, 1995.

Security Council Summit Meeting, 1992. Statement by the Federal Chancellor of Austria, Mr Vranitzky. S/PV.2981.

Shoghi Effendi. *The World Order of Bahá'u'lláh*. Wilmette, IL: Bahá'í Publishing Trust, 1991.

Simma, B. 'From Bilateralism to Community Interest in International Law', *Recueil des cours*, no. 250, The Hague, 1994.

Weiss, T. 'Overcoming the Somalia Syndrome – Operation Rekindle Hope?' *Global Governance*, vol. 1, no. 2, 1995.

Weston, B. 'Security Council Resolution 678 and Persian Gulf Decision Making: Precarious Legitimacy', *American Journal of International Law*, no. 85, 1991.

Wilson, Woodrow, 'Address to the US Senate', 22 January 1917, in Link, *The Papers of Woodrow Wilson*, vol. 40. Princeton: Princeton University Press, 1982.

References

1. Danesh Sarooshi: Senior Lecturer in Public International Law, University College London, University of London.
2. Woodrow Wilson, 'Address to the US Senate', 22 January 1917, in Link, *The Papers of Woodrow Wilson*, vol. 40, p. 536.
3. See Dinstein *War, Aggression and Self-Defence*, p. 278.
4. Shoghi Effendi, *World Order*, pp. 191–2.
5. For a description by the International Court of Justice of how the UN took over certain of the functions of the League of Nations, see *International Status of South West Africa* case, *International Court of Justice Reports (1950)*, p. 128.
6. See also *Repertory of Practice of UN Organs, Supplement no.3*, vol. 2, p. 244; and Higgins, 'A General Assessment of UN Peace-Keeping', Cassese, *UN Peace-Keeping*, p. 4.
7. For further examples, see Sarooshi, *The United Nations and the Development of Collective Security*, chapter 5.
8. There are, however, important limitations which the Security Council must observe when delegating its Chapter VII powers for these delegations to be lawful. See ibid.
9. In fact, some States see such delegations of power – or authorizations – as a novel way to ensure that the Charter system of maintaining or restoring international peace and security remains effective. See, for example, the statement by the Federal Chancellor of Austria, Mr Vranitzky, in the Security Council Summit Meeting in 1992. See also Miller, 'Universal Soldiers: UN Standing Armies and the Legal Alternatives', *Georgetown Law Journal*, no. 81, 1993, p. 776; and Weiss, 'Overcoming the Somalia Syndrome – Oper-ation Rekindle Hope?' *Global Governance*, vol. 1, no. 2, 1995, p. 177.
10. Shoghi Effendi, *World Order*, p. 191.
11. Bahá'u'lláh, *Gleanings*, p. 254.
12. ibid.
13. 'Abdu'l-Bahá, *Secret of Divine Civilization*, pp. 64–5.
14. Interestingly, the view has already been expressed that the present UN Charter can be characterized in many ways as a 'constitution', see, for example, the statement by the representative of the US Government in the oral proceedings in the *Expenses* case, International Court of Justice Reports: *Pleadings, Oral Arguments, Documents 1962*, p. 427; Crawford, 'The Charter of the United Nations as a Constitution', in *The Changing Constitution of the United Nations*, p. 3; Simma, 'From Bilateralism to Community Interest in International Law', *Recueil des cours*, no. 250, pp. 258–62; Franck, 'The "Powers of Appreciation": Who is the Ultimate Guardian of

UN Legality' (Editorial Comment), *American Journal of International Law*, no. 86, 1992, p. 521; Reisman, 'The Constitutional Crisis in the United Nations', *American Journal of International Law*, no. 87, 1993, p. 83; Fassbender *UN Security Council Reform and the Right of Veto*, pp. 89–115; and Herdegen, 'The "Constitutionalization" of the UN Security System', *Vanderbilt Journal of Transnational Law*, no. 27, 1994, p. 150. But cf. Arangio-Ruiz, '"The Federal Analogy" and UN Charter Interpretation: A Crucial Issue', *EJIL*, no. 8, 1997, p. 1.

15. For the legal considerations relating to this action, see e.g. Kritsiotis 'Legality of the 1993 US Missile Strike on Iraq', *International & Comparative Law Quarterly*, no. 45, 1996, p. 162.

16. The relevant section of resolution 940 provides: '[The Security Council] . . . 4. *Acting* under Chapter VII of the Charter of the United Nations, [the Security Council] authorizes Member States to form a multinational force under unified command and control and, in this framework, to use all necessary means to facilitate the departure from Haiti of the military leadership . . . the prompt return of the legitimately elected President and the restoration of the legitimate authorities of the Government of Haiti, and to establish and maintain a secure and stable environment . . . on the understanding that the cost of implementing this temporary operation will be borne by the participating Member States . . .'

17. For a detailed exposition of this operation, see Malone, *Decision-Making in the UN Security Council*.

18. cf. the view that because the UN is not responsible to individuals but only States, that it has no legitimacy at all to use force. In other words, there is no constituency from which the UN could draw such a mandate or authority. For a Bahá'í response to this problem, see text that follows below.

19. See also Claude, 'Collective Legitimization as a Political Function of the UN', *International Organization*, no. 20, Summer 1966, p. 367.

A collective security system maintains the status quo of a particular community. It is thus of considerable importance that the values which the system maintains are those which the majority of States in the world are dedicated to upholding. In other words, the system must be 'legitimate'.

The legitimacy of action by the Security Council under Chapter VII of the UN Charter has been the source of considerable academic discussion. On the issue of the legitimacy of collective enforcement measures by the Security Council, see Alvarez, 'Judging the Security Council', *American Journal of International Law*, no. 90, 1996, p. 1; Brownlie, 'The Decisions of Political Organs of the UN and the Rule of Law', in *Essays in Honour of Wang Tieya*, p. 91; Caron, 'The Legitimacy of the Collective Authority of the Security Council', *American Journal of International Law*, no. 87, 1993, pp. 556–88; Claude, 'Collective Legitimization as a Political Function of the UN', *International Organization*, no. 20, Summer 1966, p. 367; Franck, 'Legitimacy in the International System', *American Journal of International Law*, no. 82, 1988, p. 705; Murphy, 'The Security Council, Legitimacy, and the Concept of Collective Security After the Cold War', *Columbia Journal of Transnational Law*, no. 32, 1994, p. 201; and Weston, 'Security Council Resolution 678 and Persian Gulf Decision Making: Precarious Legitimacy', *American Journal of International Law*, no. 85, 1991, p. 516.

20. See *Proposal for Charter Revision Submitted to the United Nations by the Bahá'í International Community*, p. 6; and *Turning Point for All Nations*, p. 11.

21. See *The Promise of World Peace*, p. 12.

22. Bahá'u'lláh, *Gleanings*, p. 286.

23. ibid. p. 250.

An International Legal Order

Rod Rastan

Introduction: The Bahá'í Model of World Order

Bahá'í discussion of world order is principally formulated along a two-stage approach. The first stage, referred to as the Lesser Peace, is described as essentially a minimalist first step towards world order, espoused by States through force of functional necessity. The second stage, the Most Great Peace, the spiritual unity of the human race, is envisaged as the eventual goal: described as a fully-fledged federal world governance system that is built upon and sustained by a universal spiritual foundation.[1] In terms of the current state of world affairs, the Universal House of Justice, the international governing body of the Bahá'í Faith, has in recent years noted 'signs of the emergence of the Lesser Peace'.[2]

Bahá'í literature on the subject by the Central Figures of the Faith, Shoghi Effendi and the Universal House of Justice, describes a process of gradual maturation towards world order. As part of this process the emergence of a number of key international institutions and mechanisms are referred to. These are outlined in Shoghi Effendi's[3] discussion of the model of world order foreseen as including, *inter alia*, the establishment of an international executive with supreme, unchallengeable and enforceable authority; a world parliament with legislative powers; a supreme tribunal 'whose judgement will have a binding effect even in such cases where the parties concerned did not voluntarily agree to submit their case to its consideration',[4] which 'will adjudicate and deliver its compulsory and final verdict in all and any disputes that may arise between the various elements constituting this universal system';[5] and 'a single code of international law – the product of the considered judgement of the world's federated representatives – [which] shall have at its sanction the instant and coercive intervention of the combined forces of its federated units'.[6] At the same time, the principle that guides this process is one described as being based upon decentralization and diffusion of governance to the lowest appropriate level.[7]

These key features form what Shoghi Effendi terms 'in its broadest outlines, the Order anticipated by Bahá'u'lláh, an Order that shall come to be regarded as the fairest fruit of a slowly maturing age'.[8] This model forms the vision of world order associated with Bahá'u'lláh's name and is one that will evolve gradually, through 'a slowly maturing age', towards the Most Great Peace. In contrast, the early stages of the emergence of the Lesser Peace are of an infinitely more limited scope. As Shoghi Effendi distinguishes:

> No machinery falling short of the standard inculcated by the Bahá'í Revelation, and at variance with the sublime pattern ordained in His teachings, which the collective efforts of mankind may yet devise can ever hope to achieve anything above or beyond that 'Lesser Peace' to which the Author of our Faith Himself alluded in His writings . . .
>
> The Most Great Peace, on the other hand, as conceived by Bahá'u'lláh – a peace that must inevitably follow as the practical consequence of the spiritualization of the world and the fusion of all its races, creeds, classes and nations – can rest on no other basis, and can be preserved through no other agency, except the divinely appointed ordinances that are implicit in the World Order that stands associated with His Holy Name.[9]

What then is the Lesser Peace? As indicated in this passage, its emergence will not signal the establishment of the institutions and mechanisms outlined above but will rather signal certain first stages in a long process which may suffer gains and losses. As the Universal House of Justice states, peace 'must mature through a long period of evolution, *with its attendant tests, setbacks and conflicts*, towards the moment when it will have emerged, under the direct influences of God's Faith, as the Most Great Peace'.[10] Similarly, the Bahá'í International Community, the NGO representation of the Faith at the United Nations, writes, 'The central spiritual issue facing all people . . . whatever their nation, religion, or ethnic origin, is that of laying the *foundations* of a global society that can reflect the oneness of human nature'.[11] What we may therefore anticipate is not for current international institutions and actors, be they States or regional and international groupings such as the EU, NATO or the UN, or international courts, arbitration and monitoring bodies, to take on the permanent shape or form anticipated by Bahá'u'lláh – it may be far too early to expect such developments. Neither should we expect only positive trends with the emergence of the Lesser Peace, for the Universal House of Justice writes of an evolution with attendant 'tests, setbacks' and even 'conflicts', meaning such a process will be challenged, will suffer reverses and even encounter conflicts, armed or otherwise. Instead, we should look for seeds and processes: namely, whether the world is responding to the crises in international affairs and whether it is awakening to the need for experimentation and flexibility, to the need and possibility for movement towards the kind of federated system outlined by Bahá'u'lláh.[12]

In a sense, this has been a process at play during the course of the whole century. In *Peace Among the Nations*, the Bahá'í International Community Office of Public Information explains: 'The attainment of peace in the political realm is discernible through the working of a process that can be seen as having been definitely established in the twentieth century . . .'[13] It again notes, however, that 'before the peace of nations matures into a comprehensive reality, it must pass through difficult stages, not unlike those experienced by individual nations until their internal consolidation was achieved'.[14] The Lesser Peace, referred to as 'the political unity of nations', is then defined:

> The political unity of nations implies the achievement of a relationship among them that will enable them to resolve questions of international import through consultation rather than war and that will lead to the establishment of a world government.[15]

The definition is broad and non-exhaustive. No reference is made here to binding pacts or treaties or to specific institutions as necessary bases for the Lesser Peace, although such modalities may to a certain extent be implied in the phrase 'achievement of a relationship among them'. The appropriate mechanisms for world order, nonetheless, are anticipated as *evolving* along a gradual path with attendant 'tests, setbacks and conflicts'. As such, the Lesser Peace should not be seen as a *fin de siècle* signifying the immediate cessation of all wars and conflicts but rather as the beginning of a new *increasingly* unified, integrated and coherent, but by no means perfect, approach in international affairs to the ordering of collective life on the planet. Indeed, the very notion of collective security adumbrated by Bahá'u'lláh envisages the occurrence of future wars and conflicts to which an international community will be called upon to respond by military and other means. These initial efforts, which in their early stages will perforce be experimental, selective, inconsistent in application and at times possibly defective in developing best practices from painful lessons learned, will, critically, progress in *a gradual process* until peace 'matures into a comprehensive reality'.[16] In the light of the perspective on the implications of the concept elaborated by Shoghi Effendi and the Universal House of Justice, *Peace Among the Nations* suggests that the Lesser Peace 'can already be detected on the political horizon'.[17]

The purpose of the present paper is to analyse the topic of international judicial bodies and the emergence of a system of international rules and regulations governing accountability, as correlated to a vision of world order based on the Bahá'í writings. As a preliminary basis, the first part provides a broad review of current judicial and quasi-judicial structures that exist. It discusses the level to which States are bound and, alternatively, the rights and responsibilities incumbent on individuals under international norms. (Space does not permit discussion of the responsibility of corporations and other international organizations or associations). These norms and institutions are then assessed in practice and a concluding section examines their compatibility with Bahá'í concepts of international peace and security.

The World's Judiciaries

State Responsibility under International Law

A hundred years ago, a few short years following the ascension of Bahá'u'lláh, the major powers of the 19th century convened a conference of 26 States for the purpose of discussing international peace and disarmament. Confronted with the increasingly unbearable burdens of an arms race in Europe and the heightened threats of instability, the Hague International Peace Conference of 1899 was described as 'the first truly international assembly meeting in time of peace for the purpose of preserving peace'.[18] The Peace Conference set itself the three highly ambitious and ultimately unattained goals of world disarmament, the resolution of international disputes through peaceful mechanisms that would avert resorting to war and the articulation of a set of regulations to minimize unnecessary suffering in wartime. Ultimately the stronghold of state sovereignty proved unwilling to cede to the demands of international regulation and adjudication by a superior authority. Nonetheless, a number of tentative steps were taken. Notable among these was the formulation of two Conventions for the laws of war on land and on sea, known today as the Hague laws of war.[19] At the same time, a third Convention on the Pacific Settlement of Disputes provided for the establishment of a Permanent Court of Arbitration, through which States could refer any disputes to peaceful settlement as an alternative to war.[20] The Permanent Court of

Arbitration, although permanently seated in the Hague, was neither permanent with respect to its activity, nor a court given the non-professional character of its arbitrators, who were in fact appointed by the parties to the dispute themselves. Most crippling of all, the mechanism allowed the exclusion of any matters affecting the 'vital interests' of the parties concerned, thereby undermining one of the principal purposes of the institution, namely averting resort to the use of force by downsizing its purview to matters of essentially minor concern. A second Hague Peace Conference in 1907, which attempted to readdress the three themes of the original Peace Conference, fared little better. Among its outcomes, it managed to revise the Convention regarding the Court of Arbitration with improved rules of procedure but the fundamental weakness of the fora remained such that in 80 years little over 20 cases have been referred to the body.

The work of these conferences had some impact on the establishment in 1907 of a Central American Court of Justice, which operated from 1908. The Court, however, rendered only two insignificant cases in its first decade and was formally dissolved in 1918.[21] Following the First World War, the newly created League of Nations returned to the issue of international adjudication raised at the Hague Peace Conferences. The Permanent Court of International Justice (PCIJ) was established in 1922, composed of a bench of professional judges competent to hear and determine any dispute of an international character submitted to it by the parties to the dispute. At the same time, the Court could give an Advisory Opinion upon any dispute or question referred to it by the Council or by the Assembly. At the time of its establishment, there was an ancillary proposal to establish a 'High Court of International Justice' as a special chamber of the PCIJ to deal with the international criminal conduct of individuals. The proposal was defeated but periodically reared its head in different guises during the course of the century. The PCIJ was a significant advance in international legal proceedings and passed down its basic structure almost unchanged to its heir, the International Court of Justice, established under the Charter of the United Nations in 1945.

As was the case for its predecessor, litigation before the International Court of Justice (ICJ) is strictly confined to inter-State disputes and subject to voluntary adjudication. Pursuant to Article 36 of the Statute of the ICJ, however, State Parties to a particular international agreement may provide a jurisdiction clause granting recourse to the Court in the event of a dispute between the parties over the interpretation or application of a treaty. There are several hundred treaties containing such a clause, although they are typically in the form of annexed proto-cols requiring separate and often unforthcoming consent. Alternatively, a State may accept the compulsory jurisdiction of the Court in the event of any legal dispute in reciprocal effect to a similar declaration made by another State. Acceptance of the so-called 'optional clause' is typically riddled with wide-ranging reservations on conditionality, providing for exclusion of matters that affect, in the familiar refrain, the 'vital interests' of a State. While 60 such declarations of States are at present in force, the value of the optional clause remains doubtful. Additionally, although the findings of the Court are binding on the parties to a particular case, the ICJ remains essentially a forum for voluntary adjudication operating with a highly exceptional caseload. Its caseload is typically concerned with relatively minor disputes such as frontier disputes or maritime delimitation and it is ulti-mately dependant on the goodwill of the parties to the dispute themselves to guarantee enforcement.[22] Where the Court has been seized of a politically sensitive issue, acceptance of its rulings has proved controversial and remained contested.[23] Despite the Court being the principal judicial organ of the United Nations, the Charter does not expressly empower it to apply, and the Court has on a number of occasions refused to exercise, the power of constitutional review over the legality of the actions of organs of the United Nations such as the Security Council. Recent pronouncements in the *Lockerbie* and *Bosnia* cases, however, have shown that the Court is at least willing to deliberate in concrete contexts on the consistency of the Council's actions with the Charter.[24]

One may contrast the International Court of Justice with

another forum dealing with inter-State disputes: the Court of Justice of the European Communities, in Luxembourg. Whereas like the International Court of Justice the decisions of the European Court of Justice are binding, the latter's jurisdiction is both compulsory and enforceable, making it a far more powerful institution than the International Court of Justice. The European Court of Justice acts in many ways not wholly dissimilar to a federal constitutional court for parties to the EC treaty. The normative authority of EC law supersedes that of national law and is self-executing in national legal systems. Certain rules of EC law are directly enforceable in national courts and take precedence over contradictory national rules; while a number of areas, notably the sphere of external trade policy, operate under the exclusive competence of the Court of Justice. At the same time, the competence of the Court extends to judicial review of Community decisions. This reflects far more the supranational framework that the Bahá'í writings espouse. It is worth noting, however, that the 1992 Treaty of European Union (Maastricht), while consolidating the powers of the Courts of Justice in the traditional areas of the EC treaty, does not extend any superior authority for the Court into the two important new pillars of Common Foreign and Security Policy and Cooperation in Justice and Home Affairs, which essentially remain at the level of intergovernmental, as opposed to supranational, cooperation.[25]

In a broad sweep of other international fora, all in all, there are currently more than 25 permanent standing international courts or quasi-courts, inspection panels and monitoring bodies to which States, international organizations, corporations, individuals and associations may bring international claims.[26] Binding specialized procedures exist under other international conventions such as the Hamburg Court governing the application of the 1982 Law of the Sea Convention, dispute resolution mechanisms established under the World Trade Organization, as well as the more limited judicial functions carried out by the United Nations Compensation Commission dealing with Iraq's liability for its invasion and occupation of Kuwait.[27] International arbitration between States and private actors such as foreign corporations has for years given access for non-State entities to direct litigation under international law[28] and has developed, as in the Iran–US Claims Tribunal, into attributing substantive international legal rights to private individuals bringing an action against a foreign State.[29] States may also be brought to account through both inter-State and individual petitions under the plethora of international and regional human rights mechanisms established in the last 50 years that incur State liability for violations against individuals. Notable among these are the quasi-legal, supervisory functions exercised by bodies such as the UN Human Rights Committee established under the International Covenant on Civil and Political Rights and the UN Committee for the 1984 Torture Convention.[30] There are also a number of regional judicial bodies such as the European Court of Human Rights under the Council of Europe, with its seat in Strasbourg, the Inter-American Court of Human Rights under the Organization of American States, and the anticipated African Court on Human and Peoples' Rights under the Organization of African Unity.[31] Whereas the crucial question of the enforcement in national courts of decisions and judgements passed down from such bodies remains a highly contentious issue, the European Court of Human Rights, together with the European Court of Justice noted above, stand apart in being empowered by State Parties with the capacity to review a judgement of a national court and to give a binding pronouncement which is directly enforceable in domestic law. Such findings may, in addition, implicate the State in changing its laws and paying compensation to the aggrieved party.

The provision of this kind of direct enforcement in national courts for the rulings of international courts and tribunals is presently absent beyond the confines of Europe but would be a crucial aspect for the emergence of a system with 'unchallengeable authority' as envisaged in Bahá'í literature. Such authority would be unchallengeable both in terms of its legitimacy and in its backing by remedial enforcement measures. Where national bodies are able to exercise effective discretion over the implementation or even recognition of international rulings, or are able to channel such rulings through domestic modalities that mute their impact, the whole notion of an international legal order can be considerably diminished. The capacity for judicial review and accountability for actions and decisions taken by the highest international executive body, currently the Security Council, would appear a further necessary aspect of the Bahá'í model. Shoghi Effendi refers to the system as one in which 'Force is made the servant of Justice',[32] implying accountability and scrutiny of the use of force, and perhaps in its broadest sense, 'power' at any level. At the same time, implicit in calls for a 'world tribunal' which 'will adjudicate and deliver its compulsory and final verdict in all and any disputes that may arise between the various elements constituting this universal system',[33] is the need for the judgements, decisions, advisory opinions and preliminary rulings on interim measures[34] of bodies such as the World Court to be given both mandatory and enforceable form. While further international standards are being developed, perennial debates in the International Law Commission attest to the difficulties faced in the definition and enforcement of notions of State responsibility in a system founded on sovereign discretion.[35] As Gilbert puts it, 'The concept of punishment for criminal behaviour manifestly cannot be applied in a straightforward manner to the treatment of offending States, for, in part, it implies a vertical society. Yet it is an essential element of crime.'[36]

The Individual under International Law

As the post-World War II proceedings in the *Flick* case affirmed,

> It can no longer be successfully maintained that international law is concerned only with the actions of sovereign states and provides no punishment for individuals . . . International law, as such, binds every citizen just as does ordinary municipal law . . . The offender in either case is charged with personal wrong and punishment falls on the offender in *propre persona*. The application of international law to individuals is no novelty.[37]

Two questions are relevant here: what acts are considered international crimes attracting individual criminal responsibility and who has jurisdiction to try the offender? This latter aspect falls into two parts. The first is the grounds by which a State may seize jurisdiction. Jurisdictional grounds can range from situations where a State or its national is directly involved in the incident (as victim, offender or by the offence occurring on the territory of the State), to where a State has no link whatsoever with the crime but has taken the alleged offender into custody under the principle of universality. Under universal jurisdiction, the crime may have been committed by a foreign national against another foreign national on foreign soil, as in the *Pinochet* case, but a third State on whose territory the accused is found may take him or her into custody. Jurisdiction is ceded as a matter of international public policy[38] because the offender 'is treated as an outlaw, as the enemy of all mankind – *hostie humanise generis* – whom any nation may in the interests of all capture and punish'.[39] Only a limited number of crimes attract universal jurisdiction. The crime of piracy is the classical instance of the application of universal jurisdiction over individuals under customary law[40] but the modern-day customary law classification may be said to include slavery,[41] genocide,[42] apartheid[43] and certain categories of war crimes, particularly with respect to violations of the 1907 Hague Convention IV and grave breaches of the 1949 Geneva Conventions.[44]

The second issue deals with the obligation incumbent on States to give effect to their jurisdiction; that is, whether there is mere authorization under international law for a State to assert jurisdiction over a particular crime or if it is under a mandatory duty to do so. Treaty obligations with respect to international crimes typically carry an *aut dedere aut judicare* (try or extradite) formulation whereby the State concerned must either prosecute the individual or extradite him or her to a State that will. International crimes under various multilateral treaties envisaging this form of jurisdiction include slavery,[45] piracy,[46] genocide,[47] apartheid,[48] counterfeiting of currency,[49] war crimes,[50] drug trafficking,[51] hijacking[52] and sabotage of aircraft,[53] sabotage on the high seas,[54] attacks on diplomats,[55] the taking of hostages[56] and torture.[57] It may be correct to say, however, that these Conventions do not impose a mandatory obligation on States but merely *permit* or, more correctly, grant *international grounds* for a State to prosecute and punish those it deems offenders.[58] The absence of a mandatory nature can be said to occur because no supervisory body exists to enforce these international rules against a State that fails to exercise its duty to try or extradite. The system operates outside of an institutional context that would convert a general legal duty into a mandatory responsibility incurring State sanction. Additionally, where domestic prosecutions do occur, the absence of the precedent setting value of decisions and judgements produced by alternative national fora, together with disparities and inconsistencies in the application of the same laws, may, as one commentator has noted, serve 'to break down the aggregate international rule of law rather than solidify it'.[59] International criminal jurisdiction, thus, displays little semblance to a universal system.

The alternative to national prosecutions is trial by international tribunals. The International Military Tribunals at Nuremberg and Tokyo were perhaps less than international and more examples of the exceptional exercise of territorial jurisdiction of the Allied Powers over occupied territory. They were also less than consistent in their application of the law, by dint of trying Axis war criminals while ignoring offences committed by Allied personnel. The establishment of the International Criminal Tribunals for the former Yugoslavia[60] and Rwanda[61] are clearer examples of international prosecution and enforcement of the norms governing the conduct of individuals. In these instances, each Tribunal has primary jurisdiction over national courts for crimes within its jurisdiction. Having been established by the Security Council acting under Chapter VII of the UN Charter, they theoretically enjoy the backing of the Council in the enforcement of their rulings and in the mandatory weight of their pronouncements. In practice, however, the Tribunals have not been able to enforce compliance from States, and the Security Council, being an internally divided political body, has not intervened in the way that domestic mechanisms may be expected to in order to enforce judgements on the national level. At the same time, without specific policing capacities, the Tribunals have not been able to independently effect the apprehension of indictees and have had to rely on often unforthcoming cooperation from States or, in the case of Bosnia, the delegated security arm of SFOR in order to bring suspects to trial.[62]

Shoghi Effendi discusses 'a single code of international law' which would 'have at its sanction the instant and coercive intervention of the combined forces of the federated units [of the world community]'.[63] This is typically applied to considerations of a collective security framework for inter-State disputes but arguably an aspect of that collective security regime would demand the 'instant and coercive intervention of the combined forces of the federated units' in the apprehension and investigation of individuals suspected of serious offences against international norms. It would appear untenable in such a system for an alleged international criminal to be able to roam the world freely or to take shelter behind the sovereignty of a shielding State. Without a consistently applied international criminal law regime, that 'single code of international law' would mean little. To enforce such a regime, however, some kind of independent supervisory body would be needed to ensure the compliance of States with their legal obligations. This topic is returned to below in analysis of the International Criminal Court.

Habitual Lawfulness?

It should be acknowledged that on a day-to-day level, the vast body of international treaties and practices are generally upheld and operate effectively. From the Universal Postal Union to aviation law and law of the sea, international sale of goods to the law of treaties, conflict of jurisdictions to diplomatic immunity, as well as international law that has been incorporated into national law, there is much of a legal system that covers most, if not all, aspects of international life. As one scholar notes, 'the vast majority of such engagements are continuously, honestly, and regularly observed even under adverse conditions and at considerable inconvenience to the parties . . . The record proves that there is a "law habit" in international relations."[64] This is the functional core of international life. As Brierly notes:

> The volume of this work is considerable, but most of it is not sensational . . . That does not mean that the matters to which it does relate are unimportant in themselves; often they are very important to particular interests or individuals. But it means that international law is performing a useful and indeed a necessary function in enabling states to carry on their day-to-day intercourse along orderly and predictable lines.[65]

This elaborate flow and interchange of international rights and duties are voluntarily observed by States and individuals because it is in their general interest to do so. Beyond this functional core, however, lie a minority of difficult but high-profile cases in which the participants view their interests best served by non-compliance with the law. These situations demand the exercise of scrutiny by a legitimate international authority and a capacity for binding enforcement powers. Yet it is precisely this supranational authority and power that most troubles States. An international legal order, however, cannot rest on voluntary compliance alone.

Summary

There exists, in piecemeal fashion and subject, except in the case of Europe, to a State-centric principle of strict consensualism, the early glimpses of a system of international liability and adjudication under a system of rules and regulations as envisaged by Bahá'u'lláh. On a general level, the system bears up well under routine disputes settlement or when dealing with issues of minimal political volatility. Its fragility is exposed, however, when confronted with a crisis situation such as Bosnia or Rwanda, with terrorist incidents such as Lockerbie or Nairobi or in dealing with international pariahs such as Saddam Hussain, Slobodan Milosevic, or retired dictators such as Augusto Pinochet or Idi Amin. At such times, efforts to implement those same international norms and standards can threaten to throw the delicate balance of diplomacy and law into chaos. The current situation is clearly not a stable basis for world order.

The deficiencies of the international system to deal with the major issues of international concern was one of the principal motives behind initiatives undertaken by the Russian and Dutch governments, on the occasion of the centenary of the Hague International Peace Conference, to convene a peace conference in 1999 to return the international community to the original three agenda goals of disarmament, the laws of war and the peaceful settlement of disputes. Three reports were commissioned from international experts in each field, providing critical analysis of developments over the course of the century and offering recommendations for viable enhancement and reform.[66] These formed the basis of intergovernmental discussions, as well as those of a parallel international civil society campaign and conference, the Hague Appeal for Peace.[67] Their outcomes in turn were fed into the much heralded Millennium session of the General Assembly (September 2000) and the related civil society Millennium Forum (May 2000). At the same time, a Millennium Summit of world leaders was held, described by the UN as 'most likely to become the largest-ever gathering of Heads of State and Heads of Government',[68] and of all international conferences and gatherings over the course of the last century perhaps the one that most closely resembled Bahá'u'lláh's call for a convocation of world leaders to elaborate an enduring framework for international peace and security.[69] These events were noted by the Universal House of Justice in its annual Ri ḍván Message 2000. There is thus a measure of activity on all fronts by both governments and civil society. The backdrop of the Kosovo bombings at the Hague Conference in May 1999 and the more recent tragedy in East Timor, however, have served to heighten the focus of the public at large to the ongoing series of crises that seem to grip the world's affairs on a daily basis. Thus, as a preliminary assessment, the international community may be said to be at least notionally 'awake' and to be taking a number of active steps forward. Below, analysis is offered on the quality of proposals tabled and the effectiveness of efforts undertaken, in the context of the application of international laws and standards in practice.

International Law in Practice

State Responsibility: The Decentralization of International Dispute Settlement

The European Court of Justice, which like many features of European integration may prove to be a precursor of later development in the international sphere, has formulated a constitutional framework to its jurisprudence and may, indeed, be drawing us nearer to the goal of a federated Europe. Here, the common stated goal of 'ever closer union' is made possible through an infrastructure of basic political institutions – an Assembly, a Council, a Commission and a Court of Justice – which share legislative, executive and judicial powers. In contrast, on the current international scene, the role and context given the principal organs of the United Nations is quite different. The General Assembly is not a legislative body, nor the Security Council truly an executive, nor the International Court of Justice a judiciary in the domestic sense, lacking as they do the necessary powers to perform these functions. At the same time, the UN Charter fails to possess the comprehensive, definitive and peremptory nature of a 'constitution' or even of the 'foundation' and supplemental treaties of the European Union, nor can the Member States of the United Nations themselves be said to constitute a 'community' in any strict sense of the basic political, economic, legal or cultural affinities that would provide a clearly delineated context to these organs.[70] For the immediate future into which the Lesser Peace is unfolding, it may indeed be premature to expect the International Court of Justice to emerge as a centralized 'principal judicial organ' of the international community along 'federal' European lines.

Indeed, one of the features of the gradual emergence and increasing reference to international law and to mechanisms for the peaceful settlement of disputes, has meant that international dispute settlement, rather than consolidating under the authority of the International Court of Justice, has diversified into the range of specialized and decentralized courts and proceedings noted above. This proliferation of law-making and adjudicating bodies in often overlapping areas of competence may give rise to concerns regarding the long-term ability of the emerging system to retain its consistency, integrity and coherence. Diversification is to be expected, as States look away from the cumbersome procedures of the World Court to more specialized settlement mechanisms. It is part of the drive to sharpen the efficiency of international law as it progresses into ever-wider fields of competence. What is important as far as an emerging international system is concerned, however, is that the norms and principles underlying the rules being applied by these multiple judiciaries or dispute settlement panels do not, through diversification, lead to fragmentation[71] but rather somehow retain their cogency and authority.

In the Hague Centennial Report on the Peaceful Settlement of Disputes,[72] the authors offer a number of responses that envisage a new role for the International Court of Justice. The potential of the ICJ is viewed less as a centralized court of appeal for routine dispute settlement between States – unlikely given the above-mentioned decentralized trend of dispute settlement – but rather as serving a constitutional function in identifying and perfecting the basic norms and principles of international law.[73] Such a guiding role is suggested in order to establish a structured legal order for international society to which other specialized courts, intergovernmental organizations and domestic judiciaries could refer:

> Because international society is becoming more decentralized, the need to identify the basic governing principles of international law becomes more evident since it is this element that ensures its integration and coherence. It is not perhaps a question of adopting a Constitution for the world community, although the time will come for this specific step, but certainly it is a question of developing such principles . . . as are essential for the integration of the law,

transformation, delegation of power, intrinsic limitation of power, the supremacy of the law, the supremacy of social interest and social responsibility.[74]

National courts are also recommended being given access to the Court with respect to the interpretation of principles of international law in domestic cases, leaving aside consideration of the merits in a particular case. This would make the ICJ a court of reference for international law, much in the same way that the European Court of Justice functions with respect to Community law under Article 234 (formerly Article 177 of the Treaty of Rome).[75] At the same time, responding to the increased variety of participants in the international arena, an expanded use of the advisory functions of the ICJ in dealing with questions involving basic principles of international law is proposed on general licence to intergovernmental organizations, their organs, the UN Secretary-General and eventually to non-governmental organizations, corporations and even individuals (subject to clearance by some form of specialized committee or pre-trial chamber).[76] Such an increased emphasis on the principles of international law would aim at keeping the foundation of the international legal community intact through countering the feared explosion of contradictory international jurisprudence. The feasibility of such a proposal is highlighted by the precedent of a number of important judgements noted above where the Court has already exercised such a review role, albeit in a limited capacity.[77] The structure of the emerging legal order would thereby be held together through a relatively uniform interpretation of its basic underlying principles, which would in turn help to ensure the universality of the system.[78]

The proposal is echoed in a 1995 submission by the Bahá'í International Community to the United Nations on the occasion of its 50th anniversary. In *Turning Point for All Nations*, amongst a wide range of proposals aimed at reforming and reinvigorating the UN system and its principal organs, the BIC calls for the coordination of the numerous thematic courts and tribunals:

The World Court [ICJ] should act as an umbrella for existing and new thematic courts, that arbitrate and adjudicate international cases within specific thematic domains.

Early components of a unified system can already be found in the specialized courts for arbitration of such matters as commerce and transportation, and in the proposals for such bodies as an International Criminal Court and a Chamber for Environmental Matters. Other issue areas that might need to be addressed under such a system would include courts for international terrorism and drug trafficking.[79]

The newly negotiated International Criminal Court (see below) indeed highlights the need for greater coordination among the various international fora. The ICC will operate independently from other international courts and tribunals, both in terms of jurisdiction and in its interpretation and application of substantive crimes. However, it is possible for the Court, as with the current *ad hoc* tribunals, to come into conflict with other international bodies where a matter overlaps on competence. The subject matter of an ICC prosecution against an individual, for example, may at the same time touch on parallel proceedings brought by an interested State before the ICJ. At the same time the European Court of Human Rights, or some other regional body, may theoretically be petitioned by the accused, alleging a violation of his or her rights under that instrument by the apprehending State (if a State Party) in its transfer proceedings to the ICC.[80] Meanwhile, the subject matter from which the situation arose may be under concurrent consideration by the Security Council, which may itself decide temporarily to stay the excercise of jurisdiction by the ICC (under article 16 of the ICC Statute). It is hoped that if such a hypothetical situation arose, in practice it would be resolved through informal, possibly diplomatic, channels. But this is obviously far from satisfactory as far as a *system* is concerned and only serves to highlight the need for greater coherence in the face of an increasingly diversifying legal order.

The Hague Report also suggests greater reference be made to the Court in institutional dispute settlement, particularly in the context of the UN Charter. This would envisage greater linkages between the responsibilities exercised by the Security Council, the General Assembly, the Secretary-General and the International Court of Justice, in order for them to operate as an integrated, rather than a fragmentary and often internally competing, system. This would be particularly appropriate in the field of the maintenance of international peace and security.

> Inevitably [*sic*] there is scope for a certain tension to develop between a political organ [e.g. the Security Council] in the exercise of its functions and the 'principal judicial organ of the United Nations' . . . Although it is highly unlikely that any court would find it appropriate to substitute its own discretionary decision for a decision taken by an organ given the authority to exercise that discretion and engaged in doing so while dealing directly under pressure of time with the facts as they unfold, there seems no reason why a court may not evaluate the exercise of a discretion, and decide whether or not the constitutional limits placed on that discretion were observed.[81]

On the general level, the idea finds resonance in the broad BIC statement that 'In any system of governance, a strong judicial function is necessary to moderate the powers of the other branches and to enunciate, promulgate, protect and deliver justice', and that 'justice is a thread that must be woven into the consideration of every interaction, whether in the family, the neighbourhood, or at the global level'.[82] The above proposals may go some way towards evolving an integrated systematic approach such as that outlined by Shoghi Effendi, in which the as yet diversified law-making bodies would defer to the guiding role of a central judicial authority, acting in the pseudo-constitutional capacity of safeguarding the coherence and integrity of the law. Proposals for a possible power of judicial review over the actions of organs of the United Nations, and specifically the Security Council, would work further towards the model of a supreme tribunal that 'will adjudicate and deliver its compulsory and final verdict in all and any disputes that may arise between the various elements constituting this universal system'.[83] While the longer term Bahá'í model for world order would be one founded on a world constitution, with corollary executive, legislative and judicial organs, such a framework, in the more immediate term, would enable the principal organs of the United Nations system, if not other institutional systems, to become closely integrated such that law had the backing of executive force and that force itself had the legitimacy of judicial scrutiny and accountability.

Individual Liability – An Emerging International System

As noted above, the sphere of international practice in the enforcement of individual criminal liability has traditionally been regulated via the national level. The regime of relying principally on the domestic prosecution of internationally criminalized conduct, however, has proved both ineffective and unsatisfactory. The fact that even the developed democracies of Western Europe, in their prosecution of Nazi war criminals and in the enactment of legislation to give domestic effect to their obligations to cooperate with the Yugoslav and Rwandan Tribunals, have had difficulty in fulfilling their humanitarian law obligations, demonstrates clearly the inefficiency of relying solely on national courts to repress the commission of international crimes and the need for a permanent International Criminal Court to ensure the homogenous application of international criminal law.[84]

The Rome Statute establishing a permanent International Criminal Court (July 1998)[85] consolidates a number of the most fundamental international norms related to crimes of mass violence, as well as rectifying the absence of a permanent corollary to the two *ad hoc* International Criminal Tribunals for Rwanda and the former Yugoslavia. The ICC, which will come into effect once 60 States have ratified its Statute,[86] will exercise jurisdiction over the war crimes, genocide, crimes against humanity and aggression within the jurisdictional delimitation of its State Parties.[87] In contrast to the two ad hoc tribunals, however, and in line with the established legal principle of the exhaustion of local remedies rule, the jurisdiction of the ICC will be *complementary* to national courts. This means that the Court will not be in a strictly hierarchical relation with national bodies but will act as a safety net where a State Party is genuinely unable or unwilling to prosecute offenders itself. Given this complementarity aspect granting primacy to State Parties, and owing to the anticipated notoriety of a case being launched against a State's nationals at the international level, the ICC should, nonetheless, by its very existence, serve as a catalyst for the domestic prosecutions of internationally criminal conduct. One of the biggest contributions the establishment of the ICC might make could well be its contribution to the emergence of a baseline standard for the prosecution of crimes of mass violence by domestic courts. Its establishment by treaty, however, means that unless the Security Council invokes its Chapter VII mandatory powers, the Court will be limited in its ability to extend its reach to nationals of non-State Parties.[88] Until the ICC becomes truly universal through widespread ratification, large gaps in the shaping of an international system will remain, for it is precisely those States with pariah tendencies, or those in delicate transitions to democracies, which are most unlikely to want to join the new Court. There will, therefore, still be much for 'like-minded' governments to legislate upon in order to fill in these gaps. This would mean ensuring that their domestic courts have statutory authority to try serious offenders that fall within their jurisdiction under national laws based on universal jurisdiction, passive personality doctrine[89] or domestically executable international treaty obligations; as well as extending the number and range of their treaties for extradition and mutual cooperation in criminal matters.

As to possible future directions, while the ICC is not in any sense an international human rights court, dealing as it does with individual liability for serious crimes of mass violence, it may be possible for the Court to presage future engagement in such areas. Since much of its work will revolve around human rights related norms as they impinge on international humanitarian law, the ICC will show, at the very least, the viability of international adjudication in examining the application of these norms. Additionally, should the ICC garner a measure of international credibility for its judgements and for its working relationship with States, it may be conceivable for the Assembly of State Parties to consider empowering the ICC to exercise jurisdiction over any treaty dealing with international crimes of individual liability, where parties voluntarily request adjudication by the Court.[90] This would not require the articulation of specific treaty crimes in the Statute but could be a general opt-in provision signalling the availability of the Court to act as a neutral forum for the settlement of disputes under the *aut dedere aut judicare* regime of numerous bilateral and multilateral Conventions. The curious *ad hoc* measures arrived at in the *Lockerbie* case of conducting trial proceedings under Scottish law in the Netherlands on a former US military base highlight the possible benefits deriving from such a proposal: for whereas the pertinent 1971 Montreal Convention includes a standard clause referring issues of treaty interpretation to the International Court of Justice, no permanent neutral international forum exists in which the alleged offenders may be tried.

The ICC could at the same time exercise a capacity for supervision and technical assistance in the restructuring or reconstruction of national penal systems with a view to generating greater coherence in the prosecution of international crimes. This is envisaged in the Statute itself. Operating under principles of complementarity that give primacy to national fora and set high admissibility criteria to the initiation of trials, it is quite possible that the ICC will have a highly exceptional caseload, functioning as a part-time institution only brought off the shelf via Security Council referrals. The Prosecutor is, however, empowered to request a chamber of the Court to review criminal proceedings that have been deferred to national authorities (Article 18). Thus, beyond assessing the admissibility criteria for the submission of cases that have been referred to it, the Court can review the *bona fides* of trial proceedings undertaken by any State Party in respect of the crimes within its jurisdiction. It may thereby be conceived that one of the early, if not main functions of the ICC would be to operate in this alternative supervisory capacity, as an international guardian over the application of the law by domestic courts. Such a role would ensure that even in the absence of referrals to international adjudication, the ICC will, nonetheless, play an important role in supervising the uniform application of jurisdiction over humanitarian norms by proxy.

Political Will: International Cooperation and Enforcement

A final note touches on the legal framework governing obligations incumbent on States towards international bodies. National law, of course, has a procedural role in implementing cooperation required under treaty obligations but to extend a discretion over substantive interpretative powers for States to determine the extent of their obligations would grant an effective *carte blanche* on any issue. As the Trial Chamber of the ICTY has held in the *Blaskic* case:

> Although it is a general principle of international law that it is for the State to determine how it will fulfil its international obligations, a State cannot impose conditions of form on the fulfilment of these obligations by enacting national legislation which results in the derogation thereof.[91]

Similarly, rulings and judgements from international judicial bodies must needs be automatically recognized and not become subject to the scrutiny of the national courts concerned. Judgements, however, may still prove ineffective without the ability of an international court to enforce its will against a recalcitrant State. In such a situation, an international court would have to rely on the enforcement arm of the Security Council or that of a delegated enforcement agency, much in the same way the ICTY has relied upon SFOR and cooperating States to give effect to an enforcement jurisdiction. If international judicial rulings cannot become effective against non-compliant States without the intervention of a distinct political body like the Security Council, operating under unrepresentative and undemocratic voting procedures, one may question how effective such rulings can be. While there may be a distinction between judicial and enforcement jurisdiction, the practical effect in administering justice may remain much the same by leaving international judicial bodies dependent upon the discretion of political executives to give effect to their decisions. In the case of the former Yugoslavia, in spite of the mandatory nature of ICTY's orders, the Tribunal has not been able to rely on the Security Council to take any decisive action to enforce its rulings despite notifying its parent body on a number of occasions of the failure of certain States to cooperate and comply with their obligations.

In the current polycentric international order lacking a coordinated policing capacity to enforce the rulings of its multiple judiciaries, international law will typically not be able to function effectively without either the voluntary consent of States or the backing of an executive authority, such as the Security Council. Discussion of enhancement and reform of international bodies must therefore be balanced by the *realpolitik* that guides the whole framework. In a system lacking real political will, institutional mechanisms for world order will always remain half-baked and inadequate. As 'Abdu'l-Bahá notes, 'any agency whatever, though it be the instrument of mankind's greatest good, is capable of misuse. Its proper use or abuse depends on the varying degrees of enlightenment, capacity, faith, honesty, devotion and highmindedness of the leaders of public opinion.'[92] The key issue thus is more one of political will and enlightened leadership than law.

Such leadership is contrasted with a school of 'neutrality' that continues to exercise most influence in diplomatic circles and is reflective of an amoral postmodernist view of the world. It is a position of non-engagement and non-confrontation, of balancing off perceived evils against one another, and by thus negating the possibility for value judgements, removing the moral imperative to act or intervene. Veteran Bosnian war journalist Ed Vulliamy describes this neutrality as a form of diplomatic appeasement:

> 'Appeasement' is a pejorative and historically tendentious term but it seems a good enough word to describe three years of diplomat-to-diplomat barter between the leaders of the democratic West and Radovan Karadzic – now a fugitive wanted for war crimes – beneath the chandeliers of London, Geneva and New York; or the matey soldier-to-soldier dinners of lamb and suckling pig shared by successive United Nations generals with their opposite number, General

Mladic – likewise fugitive and wanted – whose death squads perpe-
trated the Srebrenica massacre, on his personal orders and in his
presence. After so much handshaking and negotiation while these
two men were very publicly engaged in their foul pogrom, it is
curious to see the international establishment baying for their
capture, now that it is too late and their work is done.[93]

Hesitancy to commit, or interest to uphold, international order
with force, despite resultant costs, finds echo in hundreds of
conflicts and structural ills around the world. It is demonstrative
of the perennial tug-of-war between a statically conceived international order and the demands of international justice. The
Universal House of Justice calls it 'a paralysis of will'.[94] It may
not therefore be surprising that an appeal for values-driven
policy-making and visionary leadership forms the concluding 'A
Call to World Leaders' in the BIC's *Turning Point for All Nations*:

> Above all else, leaders for the next generation must be motivated by
> a sincere desire to serve the entire community and must understand
> that leadership is a responsibility; not a path to privilege. For too
> long, leadership has been understood, by both leaders and followers,
> as the assertion of control over others. Indeed, this age demands a
> new definition of leadership and a new type of leader.
> . . . They must be committed to and guided by principles,
> thereby acting in the best long-term interests of humanity as a
> whole.[95]

It is, therefore, not better laws and institutions that we need but
better enforcement of those laws and the better use of those
structures.[96] And that can only come about through a fundamental change of political will and re-analysis of what State
interest is. As the UN Secretary-General noted recently,

> The world has changed in profound ways since the end of the cold
> war, but I fear our conceptions of national interest have failed to
> follow suit. A new, broader definition of national interest is needed
> in the new century, which would induce states to find greater unity
> in the pursuit of common goals and values. In the context of many
> of the challenges facing humanity today, the collective interest *is* the
> national interest.[97]

Conclusion: Asking the Impossible?

State Sovereignty

It is difficult to trace the development of any kind of 'international rule of law' where States retain a primary and often unquestionable sovereignty, unwilling to cede to the compulsory examination of their interpretation and application of international law by a higher authority. We still clearly have a long way to go before we realize the Bahá'í vision of a supreme tribunal to which all disputes and differences will be referred and whose judgements 'will have a binding effect even in such cases where the parties concerned did not voluntarily agree to submit their case to its consideration'.[98] A positive direction can nonetheless be traced. In the words of the Trial Chamber of the ICTY:

> . . . the impetuous development and propagation in the international community of human rights doctrines, particularly after the adoption of the Universal Declaration of Human Rights in 1948, has brought about significant changes in international law, notably in the approach to problems besetting the world community. A state-sovereignty-orientated approach has been gradually supplanted by a human-being-orientated approach. Gradually the maxim of Roman law *hominum causa omne jus constitutum est* (all law is created for the benefit of the human being) has gained a firm foothold in the international community as well.[99]

Similarly, Kofi Annan, seizing on the historic moment for reflection and reorientation afforded by the Millennium in the Western calendar, has affirmed,

> State sovereignty, in its most basic sense, is being redefined – not least by the forces of globalization and international cooperation. States are now widely understood to be instruments at the service of their peoples, and not vice versa. At the same time individual sovereignty – by which I mean the fundamental freedom of each individual, enshrined in the charter of the UN and subsequent international treaties – has been enhanced by a renewed and spreading consciousness of individual rights. When we read the charter today, we are

more than ever conscious that its aim is to protect individual human beings, not to protect those who abuse them.[100]

The exercise of jurisdiction over international crimes is arguably no longer one that can be left to the dialect of legislative relativism. For a credible rule of law regime to emerge, obsolete notions of sovereignty must cede this obstinacy, if only through force of international crises, to the incessant needs of a world of both integrated problems and integrated solutions.[101] Though States continue to invest high regard in the notion of voluntary cooperation by enlightened parties, the experience of the Yugoslav Tribunal, to the contrary, has been that States, including third party States, even under Chapter VII mandatory compulsion, may actively block judicial processes. Current notions of state sovereignty will thus battle hard against the emergence of a 'supreme tribunal' regulated with the coercive powers of an international legal order.

Shoghi Effendi writes,

> . . . for this system of collective security to be effectively established strength and elasticity are both essential – strength involving the use of an adequate force to ensure the efficacy of the proposed system, and elasticity to enable the machinery that has been devised to meet the legitimate needs and aspirations of its aggrieved upholders.[102]

We may speculate what is meant by 'elasticity' here but presumably it may refer to the hardened and sacrosanct notion of state sovereignty: suggesting an elasticity that would allow for the exercise of power in an international system at the most appropriate level. To our present concern of international law, both strength and elasticity are required of national jurisdictions and penal systems to allow for the gradual development of an international system through the consistent and homogenous application of law that is within the purview of a credible international authority. The overriding concern must thus squarely rest with the positive imperatives of international peace and security and not with the unwarranted fear of overreaching and politicized interventionism into state jurisdictions.

It is a question of redefining sovereignty. As one leading legal scholar, Thomas Franck, puts it:

> As we enter the third millennium, there is much evidence of a global community, emerging out of a growing awareness of irrefutable interdependence, its imperatives and exigencies . . . This emergent sense of global community is often, but should not be, seen as alternative to, or competing with, the basic community of the State. *Communitas* can be concentric and overlapping. Society is starting to perceive of itself as a community of States and, simultaneously, as a community of persons. It is not a matter of abandoning concepts of state sovereignty but of recognizing in law what is increasingly evident in social and cultural practice: the striation of identity to accommodate multiple identifications.[103]

At the same time, it must be acknowledged that human security, as with peace, encompasses more than the mere absence of conflict. As Kofi Annan has noted,

> . . . Today, security is increasingly understood not just in military terms, and as far more than the absence of conflict. It is in fact a phenomenon that encompasses economic development, social justice, environmental protection, democratization, disarmament and respect for human rights. These goals – these pillars of peace – are interrelated. Progress in one area begets progress in another. But no country can get there on its own. And none is exempt from the risks and costs of doing without.[104]

Finally, within the broader construct of international public policy of which *ex post facto* accountability must form one part, a vision must guide the analysis of statesmen that puts priority on preventative diplomacy and on enabling rapid and consistent institutional response to global crises. John Huddleston remarks,

> It is surely clear that present reactive and ad hoc approaches to maintenance of peace are grossly inadequate even to handle relatively minor outbreaks of violence and would certainly be utterly powerless to contain and stop any major conflict. It is only rational to ask that a start be made in thinking seriously about a systematic

approach, which inevitably involves moving from world confederation to world federation.[105]

Pinochet's Point

The battle between international law and domestic sovereignty
crystallized in the public eye best perhaps in the *Pinochet* case.
One argument raised by Chilean lawyers was that to disregard
state sovereignty, in the instance with respect to former head of
state immunity, would throw the delicate balance of the international system into chaos. International law, it was argued, is
premised on a set of assumptions about the rules of the game,
about very clear demarcations where international law stops and
where national discretion takes over. As such, while the efforts of
Spanish judge Garzon to persuade Britain to extradite Pinochet
may have been an excercise in 'justice without borders', as one
commentator has noted, 'borders are akin to fences, and good
fences make good neighbours'.[106] Senator Jesse Helms of the US
Foreign Relations Committee has similarly asked: 'The point is
this: Who decides who stands trial and who goes free in this brave
new world of "global justice"? Some self-appointed Spanish
judge? Some foreign prosecutor in an International Criminal
Court? Or the free peoples of sovereign democratic nations?'[107]
What about other leaders, it is asked. Will they too be arrested as
soon as they step abroad?

The answer to all of the above should surely be a resounding
'yes'. If a nexus of policy intent (as opposed to incidental causal-
ity) and of clear command and control can be established linking
an official to an international crime, then surely he or she must
be held accountable. That is precisely the duty of States under
international law, albeit a duty that has seldom been put into
effect.[108] As the House of Lords held in the *Pinochet* case, diplomatic immunity cannot be used as a shield against the
commission of international crimes by State officials. Similarly,
the Appeals Chamber of the Yugoslav Tribunal has emphasized,

. . . It would be a travesty of law and a betrayal of the universal need for justice, should the concept of state sovereignty be allowed to be raised successfully against human rights. Borders should not be considered as a shield against the reach of the law and as a protection for those who trample underfoot the most elementary rights of humanity.[109]

Until such a principle is universally and consistently upheld, States will continue to be faced with the intractable deficiencies of the international dilemma: where, just as in the domestic domain, only the guarantee of order and the rule of law can ultimately safeguard the freedoms and legitimate interests of its participants.

Where There's a Will?

In one celebrated analogy, the political unification of the world during the Lesser Peace is expressed as the forging of the disjointed limbs of humanity into a single unified body; but one that is paralysed, unable to act, indeed lifeless. The next stage is for life to be breathed into it.[110] As applied to the body of the current international community, all the essential components are in many ways there, if only in prototype and underdeveloped form and operating with nominal coordination. What is missing is the international will to give the system life and purpose. Absent is the vision that recognizes the need and interest to genuinely address and resolve global issues. For the noted legal scholar Philip Allott, it is fundamentally a question of envisaging a world revolution 'not on the streets but in our minds':

> . . . there is a direct connection between things which we find intolerable in the world situation and these [*sic*] structural faults in the world system.
>
> And that direct connection is located nowhere else than in our own minds.[111]

> If the role of philosophy in human self-surpassing and self-perfecting is not restored . . . then the development of the international legal system is condemned to be an impoverished product of an impoverished human consciousness.[112]

And yet, such a universal reorientation can only come about in the final analysis from widespread adherence to a set of deeply shared and profoundly felt values and norms. In many ways the story of the 20th century has been a search for such an ethos for mass mobilization. From appeals to nationalism, to fascism, Communist ideals and religious fanaticism, to the capitalist consumer culture – all have signally failed to nourish and sustain a sense of purpose and direction for the course of national life, let alone act as a wellspring for international prosperity. In the face of widespread apathy towards institutions and the poverty of modern-day politics and philosophy, the conviction that some benevolent source of motivation is needed cannot surely be doubted. That the Bahá'í Faith distinguishes itself precisely in its claim to being uniquely able, at this stage in history, to fulfil that role, is one that warrants careful and impartial investigation. It is only through the channelling of such a motivational consciousness, however, that long-guarded national self-interest can be replaced by genuine concern for the common interest.[113]

Commenting on the technological progress of Western nations in developing weapons of mass destruction, Bahá'u'lláh writes: 'The purging of such deeply-rooted and overwhelming corruptions cannot be effected unless the peoples of the world unite in pursuit of one common aim and embrace one universal faith. Incline your ears', He urges world leaders and the peoples of the earth, 'unto the Call of this Wronged One and adhere firmly to the Lesser Peace.'[114] 'Abdu'l-Bahá similarly states,

Today the world of humanity is in need of international unity and conciliation. To establish these great fundamental principles a propelling power is needed. It is self-evident that the unity of the human world and the Most Great Peace cannot be accomplished through material means. They cannot be established through political power, for the political interests of nations are various and the policies of peoples are divergent and conflicting. They cannot be founded through racial or patriotic power, for these are human powers, selfish and weak. The very nature of racial differences and patriotic prejudices prevents the realization of this unity and agreement. Therefore, it is evidenced that the promotion of the oneness of the kingdom of humanity, which is the essence of the teachings of all the Manifestations [Prophets] of God, is impossible except through the divine power and breaths of the Holy Spirit. Other powers are too weak and are incapable of accomplishing this.[115]

The Bahá'í writings assert that the 'propelling power' to bind nations and people in common interests derives from the ancient and terrific potency of religion, as expressed in a universal faith whose central mission is to 'unify the contending peoples and kindreds of the earth'.[116] Mindful of the expansionist excesses committed in the name of religion throughout history, its guiding values and its experience in building a model of world community from the variegated backgrounds, creeds and races of its adherents, offers compelling relief and invites analysis. At the heart of its appeal is the challenge to move beyond mere interdependence and damage limitation to laying the groundwork for a fundamental reorientation of political and collective will.

Conclusion

The meaning and measure of human progress are difficult to establish. A fair general judgement might be that material progress has not been matched by spiritual progress . . . [we must find] within ourselves another capacity, the capacity to form the idea of the ideal – the ideal of a better human future which we can choose to make the actual . . . To overcome the tyranny of the actual, to overcome the ignorant and infantile belief that the actual self-organizing of humanity is necessary and inevitable, we need only recall and recover our extraordinary power constantly to re-conceive the ideal, in order yet again to choose to make it actual.[117]

While we yet await the maturation of international will, the birth of international judiciaries will stand as one of the 20th century's most enduring legacies to the future. Their emergence to supranational autonomy from a world threatening to be consumed by its own rapacious anarchy is a stage that must needs inevitably be reached. Although norms and standards, even a number of institutions with binding powers, have emerged, their effectiveness and ability to coordinate national bodies remain largely in the shackles of moribund debates over sovereignty, national interest and political will. This may rightly be the shape and form of the first stirrings of the Lesser Peace. As such, the emergence of an international legal order is only half complete, or in another analysis, but barely begun. Accordingly, just as in the domestic domain, where justice and the rule of law form the cornerstone of every durable system for peace and security, so the application and enforcement of a system of international liability will form one of the key challenges to a 21st century grappling with the unfoldment and maturation of the Lesser Peace.

Bibliography

'Abdu'l-Bahá. *The Promulgation of Universal Peace*. Wilmette, IL: Bahá'í Publishing Trust, 1982.
— *The Secret of Divine Civilization*. Wilmette, IL: Bahá'í Publishing Trust, 1990.
'Advisory Opinion on the Legality of the Threat or Use of Nuclear Weapons', *ILM*, vol. 35, 1996.
Allott, Philip. 'The Concept of International Law', *European Journal of International Law*, vol. 10, no. 1, 1999.
— *Eunomia. New Order for a New World*. Oxford: Oxford University Press, 1990.
— 'International Law and International Revolution: Reconceiving the World'. Josephine Onoh Memorial Lecture 1989. Hull: Hull University Press, 1989.
Annan, Kofi A. Address at Cedar Crest College, Allentown, Pennsylvania, 13 September 1997. SG/SM/6325.
— 'Two concepts of sovereignty', in *The Economist*, 18 September 1999.
Bahá'í International Community Office of Public Information. *Peace Among the Nations*. Statement in response to a question about the Lesser Peace and the catastrophic events of the end of the Twentieth Century, 20 March 1999. Haifa: Bahá'í International Community Office of Public Information, 1999.
— *Turning Point for All Nations: A Statement of the Bahá'í International Community on the Occasion of the 50th Anniversary of the United Nations*. New York: Bahá'í International Community United Nations Office, 1995.
— *Who is Writing the Future? Reflections on the Twentieth Century*. New York: Office of Public Information, February 1999.
Bahá'u'lláh. *Gleanings from the Writings of Bahá'u'lláh*. Wilmette, IL: Bahá'í Publishing Trust, 1983.

— *Tablets of Bahá'u'lláh revealed after the Kitáb-i-Aqdas*. Haifa: Bahá'í World Centre, 1978.

Bergsmo, Morten. 'The Jurisdictional Regime of the International Criminal Court (part II Articles 11–19)'. *European Journal of Crime, Criminal Law and Criminal Justice*, vol. 6, no. 4, 1998.

Bhattacharyya, Rupa. 'Establishing a Rule-of-Law International Criminal Justice System'. *Texas International Law Journal*, vol. 31, no. 96.

Brierly, James L. *The Law of Nations*. New York: Oxford University Press, 6th edn., 1963.

Brownlie, Ian. *Principles of Public International Law*. Oxford: Clarendon Press, 1990.

'Europe Survey', in *The Economist*, 23 October 1999.

Ferencz, B. *An International Criminal Court; A Step Toward World Peace: A Documentary History and Analysis*, vol. 2. New York: Oceana Publications, 1980.

Fox, Hazel and A. Meyer (eds.). *Effecting Compliance*. London: British Institute of International and Comparative Law, 1993.

Franck, Thomas. *Fairness in International Law and Institutions*. Oxford: Clarendon Press, 1997.

Gilbert, G. 'The Criminal Responsibility of States'. *ICLQ*, vol. 39, no. 345, 1990.

Helms, Jesse. 'And After Pinochet?' *Washington Post*, 10 December 1998.

Huddleston, John. 'Another Look at Achieving Peace by the Year 2000', *Journal of Bahá'í Studies*, vol. 2, no. 51, June 1999.

Hudson, Marley A. *The Central American Court of Justice*. *American Journal of International Law*, vol. 20 (1926) Special Supplement; ibid. vol. 26 (1932), ibid. vol. 29 (1935) Special Supplement.

Jennings R. and A. Watts. *Oppenheim's International Law*.

Jessup P.C. *A Modern Law of Nations*: An Introduction, 1948.

Lauterpacht, E. *Aspects of the Administration of International Justice*. Cambridge: Grotius, 1991.

Lauterpacht, H. *International Law: Being the Collected Papers of Hersch Lauterpacht, vol. 1, The General Works (Collected Paper)*. Cambridge: Cambridge University Press, 1970.

'Libya v. US; Libya v. UK'. *International Court of Justice Report*, 1992.

Marschik, Axel. 'European Approaches to War Crimes', in McCormick and Simpson, *The Laws of War Crimes: National and International Approaches*. The Hague: Kluwer, 1997.

McCormick, Timothy L.H. and Gerry J. Simpson (eds.), *The Laws of War Crimes: National and International Approaches*. The Hague: Kluwer, 1997.

The Millennium Assembly of the United Nations: Thematic framework for the Millennium Summit. Report of the Secretary-General. UN Doc.

A/53/948, 10 May 1999.

'Namibia case'. *International Court of Justice Report*, 1971.

'NATO chief calls for a permanent peace force'. *Financial Times*, 10 November 1997.

'Nicaragua v. US'. *International Court of Justice Report*, 1984.

Peace: More Than an End to War. Selections from the Writings of Bahá'u'lláh, the Báb, 'Abdu'l-Bahá, Shoghi Effendi and the Universal House of Justice. Wilmette, IL: Bahá'í Publishing Trust, 1986.

Rastan, Rod. *State Sovereignty and the International Criminal Court.* Proceedings of the European Bahá'í Conference on International Law and World Order. Forthcoming.

Sands, Philip. 'After Pinochet: The Proper Relationship between National and International Courts', IALS Lecture Series, 4th November 1999.

Shaw, Jo. *Law of the European Union*. London: Macmillan, 1996.

Shoghi Effendi. *The World Order of Bahá'u'lláh*. Wilmette, IL: Bahá'í Publishing Trust, 1991.

The Universal House of Justice. *The Promise of World Peace*. London: Bahá'í Publishing Trust, 1985.

— Riḍván Message 153 (1996).

— Riḍván Message 155 (April 1997).

— *Wellspring of Guidance*. Wilmette, IL: Bahá'í Publishing Trust, 1976.

'US v. Flick (Flick case)'. *Law Reports of War Criminals*, vol. 9. London 1949.

Vicuña, Francisco Orrego and Christopher Pinto. *The Peaceful Settlement of Disputes: Prospects for the Twenty-First Century*. Revised report prepared for the Centennial of the First International Peace Conference, pursuant to United Nations General Assembly Resolutions A/RES/52/154 and A/RES/53/99.

Vulliamy, Ed. 'Bosnia: The crime of appeasement'. *International Affairs*, vol. 74, no. 1, 1998.

Warbrick, Colin. 'Co-operation with the International Criminal Tribunal for Yugoslavia', *ICLQ*, vol. 45, 1996.

White, N.D. *The Law of International Organizations*. Manchester: University Press, 1996.

Will, George F. 'Justice Without Borders'. *Washington Post*, 10 December 1998.

References

1. Shoghi Effendi, *World Order*, pp. 162–3.
2. See the Universal House of Justice, Riḍván Message 155 (1997):

'The acceleration of the processes [simultaneous integration and disintegration] it generates is lending impetus to developments which, with all the initial heartache attributable to them, we Bahá'ís see as signs of the emergence of the Lesser Peace.'

3. Shoghi Effendi (1897–1957), great-grandson of Bahá'u'lláh, known as the Guardian of the Bahá'í Faith. After the passing of 'Abdu'l-Bahá, he was appointed the sole interpreter of the Bahá'í scriptures and served as the Head of the Bahá'í community during his ministry.

4. Shoghi Effendi, *World Order*, p. 41.

5. ibid. p. 203.

6. ibid. p. 41.

7. 'Let there be no misgivings as to the animating purpose of the world-wide Law of Bahá'u'lláh. Far from aiming at the subversion of the existing foundations of society, it seeks to broaden its basis, to remould its institutions in a manner consonant with the needs of an ever-changing world. It can conflict with no legitimate allegiances, nor can it undermine essential loyalties. Its purpose is neither to stifle the flame of a sane and intelligent patriotism in men's hearts, nor to abolish the system of national autonomy so essential if the evils of excessive centralization are to be avoided. It does not ignore, nor does it attempt to suppress, the diversity of ethnical origins, of climate, of history, of language and tradition, of thought and habit, that differentiate the peoples and nations of the world. It calls for a wider loyalty, for a larger aspiration than any that has animated the human race. It insists upon the subordination of national impulses and interests to the imperative claims of a unified world. It repudiates excessive centralization on the one hand, and disclaims all attempts at uniformity on the other. Its watchword is unity in diversity . . .' ibid. pp. 41–2. See also Bahá'í International Community, *Turning Point for All Nations*, p. 14.

8. ibid. p. 41.

9. ibid. pp. 162–3.

10. The Universal House of Justice, Riḍván Message 153 (1996). Emphasis added.

11. *Who is Writing the Future?*, Part 2. Emphasis added.

12. John Huddleston also writes: 'For practical purposes, what is meant in this discussion [on the Lesser Peace] is the establishment of much stronger global peacekeeping institutions that will make war in the conventional sense (and later all forms of violence) increasingly unattractive and costly as a means of resolving grievances or for achieving any other purpose. In short, it is concerned with creating conditions that will result in a significant reduction in the

incidence of violence.' 'Another Look at Achieving Peace by the Year 2000', *Journal of Bahá'í Studies*, vol. 2, no. 51, June 1999.

13. *Peace Among the Nations*, para. 3.
14. ibid. para. 5.
15. ibid. para. 3.
16. ibid. para. 5.
17. 'Such a peace will result from the culmination of two distinct but simultaneous and mutually reinforcing processes: one leading to the spiritual unity of the human race, referred to as the "Most Great Peace"; the other to the political unity of nations and known as the "Lesser Peace". The former is a distant goal, requiring a monumental change in human conduct that only religious faith can ensure; the other is more immediate and can already be detected on the political horizon.' ibid. para. 2.
18. Ferencz, *An International Criminal Court*, vol. 2, p. 7.
19. These built on earlier precedents set by the Lieber Code of 1863, the Red Cross Convention of 1864 and the Brussels Declaration of 1874.
20. The Permanent Court of Arbitration built on the experiences of the United States and Great Britain under the so-called Jay Treaty of 1794, the first modern precedent of international arbitration, and the later *Alabama Claims* arbitration of 1872, under the 1871 Treaty of Washington.
21. Hudson, 'The Central American Court of Justice', *American Journal of International Law*, Special Supplement, vol. 20 (1926) ; ibid. vol. 26 (1932), ibid. vol. 29 (1935) Special Supplement. Adopted at the Central American Peace Conference in Washington (1907) to resolve 'all controversies or questions which may arise among any of them of whatever nature'. However, the Court acted by the consensus of the disputing parties and excluded matters affecting 'the vital interests, the independence or the honour' of State Parties.
22. This conflict between State sovereignty and the universality of human rights is embodied in the UN Charter itself. Compare Article 2(7) with Articles 55, 56.
23. See, e.g. *Nicaragua v. US*, *International Court of Justice Report* 1984, p. 392 or *Advisory Opinion on the Legality of the Threat or Use of Nuclear Weapons*, ILM, vol. 35, 1996.
24. *Libya v. US; Libya v. UK*, *International Court of Justice Report* 1992; also Judgement on Preliminary Objections, 27 February 1998. *Application of the Genocide Convention on the Prevention and Punishment of the Crime of Genocide (Bosnia and Herzegovina v. Federal Republic of Yugoslavia)*, Judgement on Preliminary Objections (11 July 1996). *See also* Tadic

Interlocutory Appeal Judgement, ICTY IT-94-1-AR72 (2 October 1995) where the Appeal Chamber argued an 'incidental' jurisdiction to assess the constitutionality of the Tribunal's establishment by the Security Council. On concerns raised by the binding effect of quasi-judicial decisions taken by the politically composed body of the Council see Lauterpacht, *Aspects of the Administration of International Justice* (1991), pp. 37–48. See also dissenting opinion Judges Gros and Fitzmaurice in *Namibia* case (*International Court of Justice Report* 1971); separate opinion of Judge Shahabuddeen and dissenting opinion of Judge Bedjaoui in *Lockerbie* case (*International Court of Justice Report* 1992); dissenting opinion of Judge Lauterpacht in *Genocide* case (*International Court of Justice Report* 1993). See generally White, *The Law of International Organisations*.

25. For discussion on the move back from supranational to intergovernmental proceedings, see 'Europe Survey', *The Economist*, 23 October 1999, p. 16. See generally Shaw, *Law of the European Union*.

26. *See* Sands, *After Pinochet: the Proper Relationship between National and International Courts*, IALS Lecture Series, 4th November 1999.

27. Established as a subsidiary organ of the Security Council under Resolution 692 (1991) to provide compensation for loss, damage, injury and other consequences resulting from the invasion and occupation of Kuwait.

28. See 1965 Convention on the Settlement of Investment Disputes between States and National of other States; 575 UNTS 159. See generally Lauterpacht, *Collected Papers*, vol. 1, pp. 143–7.

29. Under the Claims Tribunal, nationals of the US may bring claims against Iran and nationals of Iran against the US in respect of debts, contracts, expropriations and other measures affecting property rights; 20 ILM 230. *See* Arbitral Tribunal of Upper Silesia under the German–Polish Convention of 15 May 1922 as an early example.

30. '. . . the Committee is neither a court nor a body with a quasi-judicial mandate . . . Still, the Committee applies the provisions of the Covenant and the Optional Protocol in a judicial spirit and performs functions similar to those of the European Commission on Human Rights . . . Its decisions on the merits . . . are, in principle, comparable to the reports of the European Commission, non-binding recommendations.' HRC Report, 44 UN GAOR, Supp. (no. 40), p. 14 (1989).

31. The Assembly of Heads of States and of Governments of the Organization of African Unity (OAU) adopted the Protocol to the African Charter on Human and Peoples' Rights on the

Establishment of an African Court on Human and Peoples' Rights at its 19th Ordinary Session on 9 July 1998 in Ouagadougou, Burkina Faso. While 36 States have signed the Protocol, only five out of a required 15 have to date ratified the Protocol. Resolution of the African Commission on Human and People's Rights, 16 May 2002.

32. Shoghi Effendi, *World Order*, p. 204.
33. ibid. p. 203. This is also one of the key proposals of the Bahá'í International Community in its seminal document *Turning Point for All Nations*.
34. For the current chaotic relationship between the World Court and national jurisdiction see the recent *Breard* case [14 April 1998] US Supreme Court nos. 97–8214 (A-732), 97–1390 (A-738), 97–8660 (A-767) and no. 125, Orig. (A-771) NB: Interim measures and advisory opinions are of a legally non-binding nature under the Statute of the International Court of Justice.
35. See UN Doc. A/54/10 (1999).
36. Gilbert, *The Criminal Responsibility of States*, p. 356.
37. 'The *Flick* Case', *Law Reports of the Trial of War Criminals*, vol. 9, p. 1191.
38. Brownie, *Principles of Public International Law*, p. 304.
39. Dissenting Opinion of Judge Moore, *The Lotus Case (France v. Turkey)*, P.C.I.J. Rep., Ser. A, no. 10 (1927). See generally *Eichmann Case*, District Court of Jerusalem, *International Law Report*, no. 36 (1961), p. 5.
40. While there may be uncertainty as to the customary law definition of piracy (see Jennings and Watts, *Oppenheim's International Law*, vol. 1, section 272), its customary status is beyond doubt. For the treaty definition see Article 15, *Geneva Convention on the High Seas*, 450 UNTS 82 (1958).
41. Jennings and Watts, *Oppenheim's International Law*, n. 43, section 429.
42. *Barcelona Traction Case*, n.47; *Report of the Secretary-General pursuant to paragraph 2 of Security Council Resolution 808(1993)* [herein *Secretary-General's Report*], UN Doc.S/25704, reprinted 32 ILM 1159(1993), para. 35; Restatement of the Law: Third Restatement of US Foreign Relations Law, [herein Restatement], vol. 2 (1987), section 702,3. The 1948 Genocide Convention itself, however, confers an *aut dedere aut judicare*, not universal, based jurisdiction.
43. *Advisory Opinion on Legal Consequences for States of the Continued Presence of South Africa in Namibia*, International Court of Justice Report, no. 3 (1971), p. 57.
44. For the customary status of these provisions see *Report of the Secretary-General pursuant to paragraph 2 of Security Council Resolution*

808(1993), UN Doc.S/25704, reprinted 32 ILM 1159 (1993).

45. 1926 Slavery Convention 60 UNTS 253; and 1953 Amending Protocol, 212 UNTS 17.

46. 1958 Convention on the High Seas (Articles 14–22), 450 UNTS 82; or 1982 Law of the Seas Convention (Articles 100–7), 21 ILM 1261 (1982).

47. 1948 Convention on the Prevention and Punishment of the Crime of Genocide, 78 UNTS 277.

48. 1973 International Convention on the Suppression and Punishment of the Crime of Apartheid, Articles 2–4; 13 ILM 50 (1974).

49. 1929 International Convention for the Suppression of Counterfeiting Currency, Article 17; 112 UNTS 371.

50. Four Geneva Conventions of 1949, 75 UNTS 31, 85, 135, 287. Additional Protocol I, 1125 UNTS (1979),3–608.

51. 1961 Single Convention on Narcotic Drugs, Article 36(2)(iv), UKTS 34 (1965); 1988 Convention against the Illicit Traffic in Narcotic Drugs, Article 4(2)(b), Misc.14 (1989), Cm. 804.

52. 1970 Convention for the Suppression of Unlawful Seizure of Aircraft, Article 4; 860 UNTS 105.

53. 1971 Montreal Convention for the Suppression of Unlawful Acts against the Safety of Civil Aviation, Article 5; 974 UNTS 177.

54. 1988 Convention for the Suppression of Unlawful Acts against the Safety of Maritime Navigation (Article 3), 27 ILM 668; and 1988 Protocol for the Suppression of Unlawful Acts against the Safety of Fixed Platforms Located on the Continental Shelf (Article 2), 27 ILM 865.

55. 1973 Convention on the Prevention and Punishment of Crimes against Internationally Protected Persons, Including Diplomatic Agents, Article 2; 13 ILM 42 (1974).

56. 1979 International Convention Against the Taking of Hostages, Article 5; 18 ILM 1456 (1979).

57. 1984 Convention Against Torture and Other Cruel, Inhuman or Degrading Treatment or Punishment, Article 5(2); 23 ILM 1027.

58. Arguably, it is the prerogative of a State to punish those it will on what grounds it will but in the interests of international consensus and regularity, such treaty formulations envisage international agreement upon the grounds to do so.

59. Bhattacharyya, 'Establishing a Rule-of-Law International Criminal Justice System', *Texas International Law Journal*, vol. 31, p. 96.

60. S/RES/827 (25 May 1993).

61. S/RES/955 (8 November 1994).

62. See statement of Javier Solano, as Secretary-General of NATO:

'NATO chief calls for a permanent peace force', *Financial Times*, 10 November 1997. The article is based on the European Forum Berlin Pan-European Peacekeeping Panel, 8 November 1997, where Solano referred to the need for a permanent international police force. The idea appears to be based on the role of patrols and restructuring and retraining of local forces undertaken by the UN International Police Task Force (IPTF) in Bosnia, without any specific linkage to proactive policing duties connected with enforcing orders and warrants from the International Tribunals.

63. Shoghi Effendi, *World Order*, p. 41.

64. Jessup, *A Modern Law of Nations*, pp. 6–8.

65. Brierly, *The Law of Nations*, pp. 68–76.

66. For the full text of the reports see
    <www.minbuza.nl /English/f_sumnews14.html>

67. *See* <www.haguepeace.org>

68. 'The Millennium Summit will prove to be more than merely a celebratory event. It is essential that it should provide an opportunity for a moral recommitment to the purposes and principles laid down in the Charter of the United Nations and spur new political momentum for the international cooperation and solidarity that the peoples of the world increasingly demand.' Report of the Secretary-General, *The Millennium Assembly of the United Nations: Thematic Framework for the Millennium Summit*, UN Doc. A/53/948 (10 May 1999). *See* <www.un.org/millennium>

69. 'The Great Being, wishing to reveal the prerequisites of the peace and tranquillity of the world and the advancement of its peoples, hath written: The time must come when the imperative necessity for the holding of a vast, an all-embracing assemblage of men will be universally realized. The rulers and kings of the earth must needs attend it, and, participating in its deliberations, must consider such ways and means as will lay the foundations of the world's Great Peace amongst men. Such a peace demandeth that the Great Powers should resolve, for the sake of the tranquillity of the peoples of the earth, to be fully reconciled among themselves. Should any king take up arms against another, all should unitedly arise and prevent him. If this be done, the nations of the world will no longer require any armaments, except for the purpose of preserving the security of their realms and of maintaining internal order within their territories. This will ensure the peace and composure of every people, government and nation.' Bahá'u'lláh, *Gleanings*, p. 249.

70. Vicuña and Pinto, *The Peaceful Settlement of Disputes: Prospects for the Twenty-First Century* [herein Report], Revised report prepared for

the Centennial of the First International Peace Conference, pursuant to United Nations General Assembly Resolutions A/RES/52/154 and A/RES/53/99; <www.minbuza.nl /English/f_sumnews14.html>, p. 126.

71. ibid. See also 'Symposium Issue: The Proliferation of International Tribunals: Piecing Together the Puzzle', *Journal of International Law & Politics*, no. 31 (1999), p. 4. The whole issue is devoted to the theme.

72. Hague Centennial Report on the Peaceful Settlement of Disputes, p. 126.

73. ibid. pp. 82–107.

74. ibid. p. 82, partly citing Allott, *Eunomia: New Order for a New World*, pp. 167–8.

75. ibid. p. 99.

76. ibid.

77. ibid. See note 24 above.

78. ibid. p. 20.

79. Bahá'í International Community, *Turning Point for All Nations*, p. 13.

80. It is unlikely that the European Court would seize jurisdiction since, given the exhaustion of the legal remedies rule, it would doubtless argue that the ICC itself would be the correct and authoritative forum to raise such due process challenges. See, nonetheless, challenge brought before the European Court of Human Rights by Mladen Naletalic, accused, indicted and in custody of the ICTY.

81. Hague Centennial Report on the Peaceful Settlement of Disputes, p. 116, n52. The Report goes on to say that the negative consequences incurred by the tendency of the different principal organs of the UN to function independently of each other argues not only for greater linkages and enhanced interaction but for arrangements for sequential action in automatic reaction to the failure of a particular organ to respond during a particular phase of a dispute; ibid. p. 117.

82. Bahá'í International Community, *Turning Point for All Nations*, pp. 12–13.

83. Shoghi Effendi, *World Order*, p. 203.

84. See Marschik, *European Approaches to War Crimes*, in McCormick and Simpson, *Laws of War Crimes*, pp. 65–101, n. 10; and Warbrick, 'Co-operation with the International Criminal Tribunal for Yugoslavia', ICLQ no. 45 (1996), pp. 947–54.

85. PCNICC/1999/INF/3 (July 1999). The Rome Statute can be found at <www.un.org/icc>. See also Rastan, 'State Sovereignty and the International Criminal Court', *Proceedings of the European Bahá'í*

Conference on International Law and World Order, forthcoming.

86. This occurred on 11 April 2002 and the Treaty entered into force on 1 July 2002.

87. Aggression is yet to be defined. For jurisdictional limitations see Art. 12. *See* <www.icg.org/icc> and <www.un.org/icc> for current status of signatures and ratifications.

88. The US continues to raise particular objections that the Statute (Article 12) allows nationals of non-State Parties to be transferred to the Court. Article 98(2), however, would seem to clearly envisage mechanisms that would avert this fear. See Bergsmo, 'The Jurisdictional Regime of the International Criminal Court (part II Articles 11–19)', *European Journal of Crime, Criminal Law and Criminal Justice*, vol. 6, no. 4 (1998), pp. 350–1.

89. The passive personality (or passive nationality) principle operates where a domestic court claims jurisdiction based on the nationality of the victim, irrespective of the nationality of the accused or the territory on which the crime occurred. It is a highly contested area of the law that is only recently gaining a limited measure of international recognition. Spain, for example, claimed *inter alia*, the operation of passive personality jurisdiction in the Pinochet affair for crimes committed by Pinochet against Spanish nationals in Chile.

90. The original 1994 International Law Commission draft Statute had envisaged the inclusion of a separate category of 'treaty crimes' which would have included a number of specified international treaty crimes. See A/49/10 (1994).

91. Decision on the Objection of the Republic of Croatia to the Issuance of *subpeona duces tecum*, in *Blaskic* case, 18 July 1997. This touches the well-established principle under Article 27 of the 1969 Vienna Convention on the Law of Treaties. As Brownlie puts it: 'A state cannot plead provisions of its own law or deficiencies in that law in answer to a claim against it for an alleged breach of its obligation under international law.' Brownlie, *Principles of Public International Law*, p. 35.

92. 'Abdu'l-Bahá, *Secret of Divine Civilization*, p. 16.

93. Vulliamy, 'Bosnia: The crime of appeasement', *International Affairs*, vol. 74, no. 1 (1998), p. 75.

94. The Universal House of Justice, *Promise of World Peace*, para. 26.

95. Bahá'í International Community, *Turning Point for All Nations*, p. 22.

96. 'It seems to many that the problem is not to discover what the law is, or how to apply it to the particular case, or even whether the existing rule is "satisfactory" or not, but rather how to secure or

compel compliance with the law at all. It may be that we have now passed from a great phase of law-making to a period where the focus is not on new substantive law but on how to make existing law effective.' Sir Franklin Berman, Preface to Fox and Meyer, *Effecting Compliance*, p. xii.

97. Annan, 'Two concepts of sovereignty', in *The Economist*, 18 September 1999.

98. Shoghi Effendi, *World Order*, p. 41. See generally, *Peace: More Than an End to War*, pp. 200–6.

99. *Tadic Interlocutory Appeal*, 2 October 1995, para. 97.

100. Annan, 'Two concepts of sovereignty', in *The Economist*, 18 September 1999.

101. 'Who knows that for so exalted a conception to take shape a suffering more intense than any it has yet experienced will have to be inflicted upon humanity? . . . That so fundamental a revolution, involving such far-reaching changes in the structure of society, can be achieved through the ordinary processes of diplomacy and education seems highly improbable. We have but to turn our gaze to humanity's blood-stained history to realize that nothing short of intense mental as well as physical agony has been able to precipitate those epoch-making changes that constitute the greatest landmarks in the history of human civilization.' Shoghi Effendi, *World Order*, p. 45.

102. ibid. p. 192.

103. Franck, *Fairness in International Law and Institutions*, pp. 12–13.

104. Annan, Address at Cedar Crest College, Allentown, Pennsylvania, 13 September 1997 (SG/SM/6325).

105. Huddleston, 'Another Look at Achieving Peace by the Year 2000', *Journal of Bahá'í Studies*, vol. 2, no. 51, June 1999, p. 62, n7.

106. Will, 'Justice Without Borders', *Washington Post*, 10 December 1998, p. A31.

107. Helms, 'And After Pinochet?', ibid.

108. A sign of this new sensitivity was given a week after Pinochet was taken into custody, when Congolese President Laurent Kabila allegedly contacted Belgian authorities before heading to the country to discover whether he might face arrest on disembarking. The authorities assured him that as an *acting* Head of State, he was currently immune from prosecution.

109. *Tadic Interlocutory Appeal*, para. 58. This recalls the Nuremberg formulation that action carried out in an official capacity shall neither exclude nor mitigate responsibility.

110. 'We are told by Shoghi Effendi that two great processes are at work

in the world: the great Plan of God, tumultuous in its progress, working through mankind as a whole, tearing down barriers to world unity and forging humankind into a unified body in the fires of suffering and experience. This process will produce, in God's due time, the Lesser Peace, the political unification of the world. Mankind at that time can be likened to a body that is unified but without life. The second process,.0 0the task of breathing life into the unified body – of creating true unity and spirituality culminating in the Most Great Peace – is that of the Bahá'í's . . .' The Universal House of Justice, *Wellspring of Guidance*, pp. 133–4.

111. Allott, *International Law and International Revolution: Reconceiving the World*, Josephine Onoh Memorial Lecture 1989.

112. Allott, 'The Concept of International Law', *European Journal of International Law*, vol. 10, no. 1 (1999), p. 49.

113. 'Politics in the most socially developed national systems has recently degenerated into an impoverished debate within narrow dialectical limits, focused particularly on the manipulation of mass-opinion . . . Corrupted social consciousness fills the private minds of human beings everywhere with low values generated as systematic by-products of social systems which will soon be, if they are not already, beyond the redeeming power of higher values. ibid.

114. Bahá'u'lláh, *Tablets*, p. 69.

115. 'Abdu'l-Bahá, Talk at Church of the Ascension, New York (His first public address in the United States), 14 April 1912, in *Promulgation*, pp. 11–12.

116. Bahá'u'lláh, *Tablets*, p. 88.

117. Allott, *The Concept of International Law*, p. 50.

Global Governance:

Has a Paradigm Shift in World Government Theory Brought the Lesser Peace Closer?

Daniel Wheatley

Bahá'u'lláh: Prince of Peace

> Now that ye have refused the Most Great Peace, hold ye fast unto this, the Lesser Peace, that haply ye may in some degree better your own condition and that of your dependents.   *Bahá'u'lláh*[1]

These words were addressed to the rulers and kings of the earth in 1868 by Bahá'u'lláh, founder-prophet of the Bahá'í Faith. Peace has been the dream of every generation of humanity. The six million adherents of the Bahá'í Faith claim that the time of world peace is close at hand, a viewpoint that is open to derision and scorn in a world still scarred by seemingly endless bloody conflicts occurring with weary regularity around our planet. Bosnia, Rwanda, Somalia, Kosovo, East Timor, Chechnya. Set against this litany of warfare in just the last decade of human history, at the time this article was written, how can Bahá'ís hope to substantiate their faith that an age of universal peace, foretold by an exile, a prisoner in a remote gaol in 19th-century Palestine, is a realistic belief?

Bahá'u'lláh offered humanity two stages of peace that He promised would be realized following His divine dispensation. He offered the vision of the Most Great Peace when 'to whatsoever city a man may journey, it shall be as if he were entering his own home . . . The earth is but one country . . .'[2] Such an ideal may seem distant from the world of today, rife with religious intolerance, bigotry and a multitude of injustices. Yet Bahá'u'lláh offers the world a second level of peace, a more attainable peace that we might view as a developmental stage in our divided world of today, the Lesser Peace.

In the secular world there have been a number of organizations that have worked for a world government in the hope of securing lasting peace on earth. Their thinking emerged with some vigour after World War II and gained some following in the immediate post-war years. Throughout the period of history referred to as the 'Cold War' the world government lobby has, for the main part, seen its numbers and influence diminish. With the fall of the Berlin Wall and the massive upheaval in international politics that ensued, those who advocate world government are finding more receptive audiences again. Contemporaneous with this moderate expansion in the world government message has been a rapid growth in the debate on issues of global governance.

I intend to investigate briefly the critique of immediate post-war world government theory and then to move on to examine the newly emerging concept of 'global governance'. I wish to determine how global governance can be differentiated from world government ideology and whether it represents a new paradigm in thought or is rather a paradigm shift. Finally, I wish to investigate whether these processes bring the Lesser Peace closer.

The Lesser Peace

If we investigate the writings of Bahá'u'lláh and the two other most significant figures in the Bahá'í Faith, 'Abdu'l-Bahá and Shoghi Effendi, we can discern that the one process that will be an element of the emergence of the Lesser Peace will be the formulation of a system of world government. It is useful at this point to look into the Bahá'í writings to see how we may recognize the characteristics of the Lesser Peace. In His proclamation to the great leaders of His contemporary world, Bahá'u'lláh adjures them, 'Be reconciled among yourselves, that ye may need no more armaments save in a measure to safeguard your territories and dominions . . . Be united, O kings of the earth . . .'[3] As well as calling for disarmament, Bahá'u'lláh, 'Abdu'l-Bahá and Shoghi Effendi laid down guiding principles for a global legislature, international weights and measures, a supreme tribunal, a global peacekeeping force. Far ahead of His time, Bahá'u'lláh offered a framework for collective security. 'Should any one among you take up arms against another, rise ye all against him, for this is naught but manifest justice.'[4]

Shoghi Effendi developed the vision of the Lesser Peace in his prescient collection of letters *The World Order of Bahá'u'lláh*. In addition to the spiritual foundations of the new world that the Bahá'í dispensation heralds, such as justice, equality and unity, Shoghi Effendi expands upon the practical necessities of the Lesser Peace. These include the creation of a global executive, a global legislature, an international armed force for crisis management, a world taxation system, a global currency, global communications networks and a supreme international tribunal. There is a strong case to argue that the sum total of these institutions constitute the essential pillars of a world government, including executive, legislature, judiciary, policing and military capacity and tax-raising powers. The 1985 statement of the Universal House of Justice, *The Promise of World Peace*, foresees the establishment by stages of a world commonwealth.

One Bahá'í scholar who has devoted extensive research to the concept of world government and the Lesser Peace is J. Tyson. In his 1986 work *World Peace and World Government – From Vision to Reality*, Tyson assesses the correlation between the onset of world government and the coming of the Lesser Peace. In examining evidence in the writings of Bahá'u'lláh and 'Abdu'l-Bahá he notes: ''Abdu'l-Bahá also speaks of the organization necessary . . . in terms of a "Parliament of Man" and a "Supreme Tribunal".'[5] Having examined the Bahá'í writings, Tyson concludes that 'The

Lesser Peace is much nearer to us [than the Most Great Peace]. Its initiation would seem to require, as a bare minimum, the establishment of a true world legislature or parliament, a binding world tribunal or court, a world executive and an effective international force . . . and some form of international taxation.'[6] These elements may be viewed as part of the Lesser Peace but they do not necessarily signal the initiation of the Lesser Peace. Expectations may have been different in 1986.

Other Visions of World Government

Having laid out the foundations for the concepts of world government and the Lesser Peace, Tyson turns his attention to some of the leading theoretical structures for world government in the secular world. One of the most influential pieces of work in this field in the post-war period was *World Peace Through World Law* by Grenville Clark and Louis Sohn. Clark and Sohn offered another possible route towards world government through reform of the United Nations Organization. Their main theme was disarmament. Tyson's critique of their work is that it was a serious and detailed attempt to deal with the problem of war through the establishment of a world authority but he was concerned that the new institution they envisaged was not empowered to defend human rights. There was also little attention paid to the challenges of development.

Two other world government models worthy of note are *A Constitution for the World* and *A Constitution for the Federation of the Earth*. The former envisages a president and an elected World Council. Its remit goes wider than any institution proposed in the work of Clark and Sohn in that it would have mechanisms with the power to regulate world trade, global finances and resource distribution. The latter, *A Constitution for the Federation of the Earth*, includes all the basic tenets of world government doctrine and also proposes a three chamber World Parliament with representatives drawn from peoples, governments and universities. Interesting as this proposal is, it is difficult to see how world academia should automatically qualify for one-third of the legislative influence in a global government, as opposed to the representatives of religions, businesses, trade unions or the legal or medical professions.

Another piece of work that attracted great interest after the Second World War was *The Anatomy of Peace* by Emery Reves. Reves took as the starting point for his thinking the notion of the need for a Copernican revolution of the mind where we cease to think in nation state-centric terms and recognize globalism. This will be examined later in this article. Reves states: '. . .we are living in a geocentric world of nation states. We look upon economic, social and political problems as "national problems". . .'[7] Nearly 60 years on, as we enter the 21st century, there is a case to be argued that we no longer think in such nation-centric terms. The growth of regional trading blocs, such as the European Union and the North American Free Trade Area, as well as the series of UN conferences that began with the Rio Earth Summit, suggest that there is some evidence that people and even States are beginning to think in terms of the global interest, another concept I will return to. Perhaps the Copernican revolution Reves writes of is under way. He challenges these mental frontiers and his call to a global mind set echoes the sentiments of one of Bahá'u'lláh's most famous maxims: 'The earth is but one country, and mankind its citizens.'[8]

As Tyson observes, Clark and Sohn's seminal work *World Peace Through World Law* is one of the most highly respected works of the post-war literature on world government theory. Its primary focus is indeed concerned with abolishing the act of war. In his introduction Professor Clark states: 'The purpose [of the work] is to contribute material for the worldwide discussions which must precede the adoption of universal and complete disarmament . . .'[9] Clark and Sohn's work undoubtedly established a useful model for debate on world government but, written in an age before ozone depletion, the advent of Internet and satellite communications, the globalization of the world economy, the problem of AIDs, world debt, the trade in illegal narcotics, the rise in intra-State violence and the demise of the Cold War, its focus on traditional inter-State warfare is clearly dated. As the world has evolved in the past 50 years, there is an evident need for an evolution in the argument for a world government.

Power Politics and the Realist Critique

Critics have long dismissed advocates of world government as naïve and utopian. Even supporters of world government today admit that their early crusaders lacked realism in their approach. Two prominent British academics, Richard Mayne and John Pinder, in their book *Federal Union: The Pioneers*, chronicle the history of the early campaigns for both European and world federalism. Commenting on the 1947 Montreux Conference which saw the establishment of the World Association of World Federalists (now known as the World Federal Movement), the authors write with some frankness: 'looking back with a generation's hindsight one can wonder at such optimism'.[10] Even within the pioneering generation of world federalists in the post-war period there is evidence of internal scepticism. Describing the attitudes of Henry Usborne MP, inaugural chairman of the British Parliamentary Group for World Government, Mayne and Pinder add: 'Federal Union's Douglas Robinson thought Usborne's bull-headed approach "incredibly naïve".'[11]

Reform of the UN was regarded as a more pragmatic alternative to the ambitious aim of creating a global constitution. Emery Reves, whose work had persuaded Albert Einstein to advocate world government and who was regarded by many as the guru of the world government movement, was tempering his views with the necessity of a more realistic assessment of international politics. According to Mayne and Pinder, as early as 1948 'Reves had begun to see European Federation as a possible step towards world federation'.[12]

Academics of the 'realist paradigm' such as Hedley Bull and Hans Morgenthau have dismissed aspirations towards democratic and consensually obtained world government as incompatible with the realities of power politics. In his major work *The Anarchical Society*, Bull writes that he can conceive of a universal political organization without sovereign States, i.e. a form of world government, but he stipulates two possible paths for this event to occur. Firstly, world government by contract could come via a catastrophe such as war or ecological disaster; secondly, it could arrive from a process of UN reform.

Bull's vision for potential world government is largely a pessimistic one. World government might emerge from a policy of aggressive coercion by one powerful State or bloc or result from a global disaster of unprecedented magnitude. Only the possibility of an incremental process through reform of existing international institutions offers some hope for a peaceful path towards world unity. Tyson, writing in the 1980s, shares this pessimism, speculating that world government would only emerge after great global suffering and refers to Shoghi Effendi's prediction that the Lesser Peace might only emerge after the cities of the world have burned.[13] Perhaps we should remember that the Guardian wrote this in the 1930s and in the subsequent two decades most cities throughout Europe, Russia, China, Japan and much of Asia and North Africa have indeed burned with the fires of war. Since the end of the Second World War numerous cites across the world such as Hanoi, Phnom Penh, Kinshasa, Kigali, Baghdad, Sarajevo and others have continued to suffer the ravages of conflict. Has global apocalypse already occurred? Does it continue to occur as a localized phenomenon across the world? What worse atrocities could the people of Rwanda or Cambodia, or the survivors of Auschwitz or Nagasaki, be expected to envisage that may trigger the political will to establish the necessary mechanisms for lasting global peace?

Bull looks back to the time of the Roman Empire as a form of proto world government and asserts: 'in the 20th century there has been a revival of world government doctrine in response to the two world wars.'[14] His attitude to world government is a sceptical one, noting that 'the classical argument against world government is that, whilst it may achieve order, it is destructive of liberty and freedom, or infringes the liberties of states and nations.' Writing in 1977, he concludes that 'there is not the slightest evidence that sovereign states in this century will agree to subordinate themselves to a world government founded upon consent'.[15] Yet as the 21st century begins there is increasing evidence to challenge Hedley Bull's conclusion. Fifteen European States have by acts of conscious consent created the institutions that can be argued to constitute a European legislature, executive and judiciary. There is already a European currency and plans are well advanced to establish a European rapid reaction corps of 50,000 troops. Europe has the essential ingredients of its own continental government and 13 more States, predominantly from the former Soviet bloc, are applying for membership. World federalists argue that the European experiment offers one possible model for a process of global unification. On the global stage international treaties such as the Kyoto climate protocols and the Ottawa Convention to ban land mines demonstrate the willingness of the majority of the world governments to voluntarily submit to international conventions. The World Trade Organization has demonstrated a real capacity to enforce international economic law in the dispute between the EU and the USA over trade in bananas. In 1998 the world witnessed 120 States sign the Rome Treaty which provided the statute to establish a permanent International Criminal Court which will have the power to enforce human rights law over individuals who are citizens of State Parties to the Treaty and will have jurisdiction to investigate and prosecute individuals whether they be foot soldiers or presidents. The world has changed a great deal since 1977.

National Sovereignty after the End of the Cold War

It is perhaps more accurate to say that the world has changed a great deal since 1989. The fall of the Berlin Wall and the end of the period referred to as the Cold War has redefined international politics at a great pace and cast doubt on concepts that were previously regarded as well-established norms.

The international political system for most of the 20th century rested upon the assumption that the nation state was the primary and most significant actor in world politics. David Held, in his 1996 work *Models of Democracy* investigates this further. 'It has been assumed . . . by theorists and critics of modern democracy alike, that the fate of a national community is largely in its own hands . . .' Held is clearly critical of the overtly State-centric view of world politics and notes: 'The world putatively "outside" the nation state – the dynamics of the world economy, the rapid growth of trans-national links and major changes to the nature of international law, for example – has barely been examined, and its implications for democracy have not been thought out at all by democratic political theorists'.[16]

Keichi Ohmae's challengingly titled work *The End of the Nation State* puts forward the argument that we are living in a new era when peoples everywhere are increasingly subject to the disciplines of the global marketplace. He suggests that global accessibility to investment, industry, information technology and individual consumers make nation states obsolete in economic terms. He states: '. . . nation states have already lost their role as meaningful units of participation in the global economy of today's borderless world.'[17]

Proponents of world government have always criticized the dominance of unrestrained national sovereignty in the international political arena but Ohmae's radical thesis, which appears to regard national sovereignty as redundant, at least in the economic sphere, may overstate the case. To some degree Ohmae's work does the world government lobby no favours because he has become regarded as something like the straw man in the study of globalization and other authorities in the area have taken a critical slant on his work. In an article entitled 'Global Transformations' four leading academics, including Held, write the following: 'For the hyperglobalizers, such as Ohmae, contemporary globalization defines a new era in which peoples everywhere are increasingly subject to the disciplines of the global marketplace (1990–1995). By contrast the sceptics, such as Hirst and Thompson, argue that globalization is essentially a myth which conceals the reality of an international economy increasingly segmented into three major regional blocs in which national governments remain very powerful.'[18] The article lists a third category in the study of globalization, the transformationalists, who regard the new patterns of change as so unprecedented and profound that States are still trying to adapt to them.

The Bahá'í perspective on this issue is lucidly captured in *The Promise of World Peace*. The Universal House of Justice – the supreme governing body of the Bahá'í Faith worldwide – suggests that the international order is flawed and the impotence of sovereign States is part of the problem. The statement observes how sovereign States are unable to prevent war or the threat of a global economic collapse or to check the spread of international terrorism.

Not all analyses of our increasingly globalized world concur with the theory that the nation state and national sovereignty are in decline. In an article Jan Aart Scholte observes that a number of authors, including Thomson and Crasner, have insisted that the processes of globalization have done nothing to undermine sovereign statehood. Critics of the theory of the demise of national sovereignty point out that the very international organizations that are the engines of globalization are themselves creations of, and dependent upon, nation states. The world's largest regional trading blocs, the EU, NAFTA, ASEAN, consist of groupings of nation states. State actors sit behind closed doors around the decision-making table at the G8 and WTO, incurring the displeasure of numerous civil society organizations. The UN is a body composed of national governments and permanent membership of the Security Council is often cited as the embodiment of classic State-centric power politics.

The choice need not be as stark as the borderless world of Ohmae and the rigidity of the Westphalian model state system. Neither Bahá'ís nor world federalists have ever called for the abolition of the nation state, rather advocating an international system based on subsidiarity in which defined state authority co-exists in a rational equilibrium with bodies of global authority – limiting and defining the boundaries of state sovereignty, not abolishing it.

The polarized views that suggest the complete demise of the nation state on the one hand, or that it still reigns supreme in a different guise on the other, may not be helpful. I would suggest the academic middle ground in this field, represented by the transformationist paradigm, which recognizes that state sovereignty is at least in a period of change. This seems to be the most objective of the three schools of thought. In addition to academics, politicians have begun to recognize the changes in international politics.

Global Governance

Since 1995 there has been the emergence of a new development in internationalist thinking: global governance. That year, acting on one of the last ideas of former German Chancellor and world statesman, Willy Brandt, the Commission on Global Governance, co-chaired by Sir Shridath Ramphal and Ingvar Carlsson, produced their report, *Our Global Neighbourhood*. The report was the result of over three years' work by 28 of the world's leading international thinkers including Britain's Frank Judd, Allan Boesak of South Africa and Canada's Maurice Strong, as well as prominent UN diplomats such as Sadako Ogata and Brian Urquhart, former President of the European Commission Jacques Delors and Costa Rican Nobel Laureate Oscar Arias.

The Commission asserts that: 'The development of global governance is part of the evolution of human efforts to organize life on the planet . . .'[19] The report was published to coincide with the 50th anniversary of the United Nations and demands fresh innovation in global governance. It is interesting to note that in the co-chairmen's foreword it is clearly stated that 'global governance is not global government . . . We are not proposing movements towards world government . . .'[20] Notwithstanding such an open disavowal of the idea of world government, the report acknowledges consultations with a number of prominent organizations and individuals that openly advocate world government including the World Federalist Movement, the World Federalists of America, and world government authors John Logue, Hannah Newcombe and Harold Bidmead, as well as organizations set up with considerable input from known world government supporters including Earth Action and

Parliamentarians for Global Action. There is also an acknowledgement of the Bahá'í International Community.

In the foreword to *Turning Point for All Nations*, a statement issued by the Bahá'í International Community, also timed to coincide with the UN's 50th anniversary, the authors draw attention to the new level of scientific understanding of 'the earth's interconnected biosphere, which has in turn given a new urgency to the need for global coordination'.[21] The emerging evidence of our environmental interdependence as one planet is having profound effects on the political choices made by both individuals and States. For the first time in history some decision-makers are required to be accountable for the impact of their decisions on the global commons.

One academic who has focused his thoughts on this topic is Dr Kennedy Graham, former Secretary General of the Parliamentarians for Global Action. Also writing in 1995, Dr Graham was author of a Cambridge University occasional paper entitled *The Planetary Interest*. In his introduction the author offers his reason for writing the paper: 'the compelling need for a facilitating concept that can trigger action in a time of transition, a single interest of a magnitude commensurate with the scale of the problems faced.'[22] The concept of a period of transition would be comprehensible to members of the Bahá'í Faith who believe that this time in history is marking a change from an old world order towards a new world, a world characterized by global unity.

Graham offers a persuasive argument that decision-making in today's world is State-centric and 'top heavy' – with too much policy influence flowing from the concept of national interest. 'At present, the national interest commands the overwhelming focus of political attention in global affairs.'[23] He notes that that which he refers to as the 'supreme national interest' or 'vital national interest' effectively trumps wider human interests. He raises the need for a new normative structure in decision-making, that of the 'planetary interest'. He offers a definition of the planetary interest as follows:

. . . the interests of the planet as a whole and humanity as a single group, involving:

- maintenance of the physical integrity of Earth and the protection of its ecological system from major anthropogenic change; and
- the universal improvement in the human condition in terms of basic needs and fundamental human rights.[24]

The author concludes that the planetary interest is a new and abstract concept. He notes that 'something concerns the planetary interest if it materially affects . . . the planet, as opposed to the region or the nation-state'.[25] Perhaps the planetary interest will be the philosophical framework to guide the debate on global governance?

The development of the ideas of global governance continued in the last days of the 20th century. 1999 saw two major contributions in the United Kingdom from civil society organizations towards what may be either an emerging paradigm or a shift of thinking in the existing but dated world government paradigm. In July 1999 the influential British think-tank the Overseas Development Institute produced a briefing paper which examines *Global Governance: An Agenda for the Renewal of the United Nations*. The paper notes that: 'Global governance is a topic that waxes and wanes in the international firmament – and at present is waxing fast . . .',[26] observing that the trend has accelerated since the publication of the report of the Commission on Global Governance.

The four-page briefing goes on to argue that many new problems can only be solved at the global level, such as the depletion of the ozone layer, managing flows of speculative capital and other issues not envisaged at the time of the drafting of the UN Charter. The ODI observes one fundamental problem with global governance as it stands today. In most recent incidences of global crisis the UN 'has been side-stepped or sidelined by new membership organizations (WTO), by bodies which rich countries control (G7/IMF) or by independent organizations (NATO) . . .' [27]

On United Nations Day 1999 a worldwide coalition of individuals and organizations, initiated in the UK, published a

Charter for Global Democracy in *The Observer*, a leading British newspaper, in other press and periodicals around the globe and on the Internet. The Charter extrapolates key elements from the report of the Commission on Global Governance and argues the case for a serious debate on global policy reform. The Charter made an important intellectual departure from previous arguments in favour of global governance. Rather than argue for the creation of a world government, the Charter contends that we already live in an age of world government. Many different international, regional and national institutions wield de facto powers of world government already. When NATO took unilateral action against Serbian military policy in Kosovo, when the WTO enforced economic policy on the trade in bananas, when the UN enforced no-fly zones over areas of Iraqi air space, were these not acts of government on a global scale? We may not have a world government, in the sense of the noun, but today we do have certain actions of world government, in the sense of the act of government.

Published prior to the riots and mass protest that accompanied the Seattle round of the WTO negotiations that took place in December 1999, the Charter argues that powerful institutions have immense power but lack accountability, transparency and democracy. Signatories to the Charter argue for the right of international civil society to have, at best, a say and, at the least, transparency in global structures wielding international decision-making power. The anger and anarchy focused against the WTO, the IMF and the G8 would seem to underline the alienation and frustration civil society activists feel from their total exclusion from the deliberations on the future of world economic policy.

A New Paradigm?

Two key questions remain: Is global governance indistinguishable from world government and does its advancement bring Bahá'u'lláh's promised Lesser Peace closer? The Commission on Global Governance is unequivocal that 'global governance is not global government'. The ODI briefing paper states that: 'Successful global governance does not require monolithic world government.'[28] The global governance lobby clearly wishes to separate its ideas from the aim of establishing a world government and present itself as a new paradigm. In the secular world groups advocating world government appear to perceive global governance as a new school of world government theory that tactically sidesteps semantic problems that have dogged world government supporters for many years. Global governance avoids the two problematic words 'government' and 'federal'. In many parts of the world, not least the USA, the idea of 'big government' is the object of widespread suspicion and even anger. The concept of federalism has been a dirty word in the national politics of several States, perhaps most notably the UK, where the concept is hugely maligned in the British tabloid press.

Some critics of the report have queried what differentiates governance from government. The *Concise Oxford Dictionary* defines governance as 'act, manner, fact or function of governing'[29] whilst the *New Penguin English Dictionary* defines governance as 'governing or being governed'.[30] The Commission itself offers a more complex definition of its own, stating that governance is 'the sum of the many ways individuals and institutions, public and private, manage their common affairs'.[31] While they will not actually advocate world government, the authors of the report note that there have been great changes in the nature of international politics and acknowledge: 'These changes call for reforms in the modes of international co-operation – the institutions and processes of global governance'[32] and state that there is a need to 'weave a tighter fabric of international norms, expanding the rule of law world-wide and enabling citizens to exert their democratic influence on global processes'.[33]

Although the Commission states that it is not aiming towards world government, it is worth noting that its summary of proposals for action correlate very closely with the published manifestos of various organizations that are campaigning for world government. These proposals include:

- UN Member States accepting voluntary jurisdiction of the world court
- The establishment of an International Criminal Court
- The creation of a UN volunteer force
- Security Council enlargement and the phasing out of the veto
- A forum for civil society at the General Assembly
- Investigating the possibility of the creation of an Economic Security Council

In a 1988 pamphlet produced by the World Association of World Federalists entitled *World Federalism Today*, the organization lists a number of policy goals including limiting the use of veto at the Security Council, the creation of an Assembly of Peoples at the General Assembly, the creation of a UN force by individual recruitment and calls for a world court to enforce human rights. There is a distinctly high level of congruence between the goals of the world government lobby and the advocates of global governance. Both seek to rationalize the influence of the permanent five in the Security Council, both support movement towards greater civil society representation in the General Assembly, both advocate an independent military capacity for peacekeeping and the creation of some form of effective judicial mechanism to safeguard human rights.

In 1995 the World Federalists of Canada published *An Agenda for the Reform of the United Nations* which called for an Economic Security Council, strengthening of the International Court of Justice, creating an International Criminal Court and establishing a civil society forum. Yet again, there is a great amount of ideological territory that is common to advocates of global governance and advocates of world government.

In the same year the Bahá'í International Community (BIC) published its own document, *Turning Point for All Nations* which states the position of the Bahá'í Faith on the occasion of the 50th anniversary of the UN. The BIC document is based upon the recognition that a more intricate political landscape has emerged since the inception of the UN in 1945. The role of nation states has been compounded by the increasing relevance of transnational corporations and civil society organizations. The Bahá'í position is more visionary and is based on the underlying belief that unity is the natural state of humanity. The Bahá'í document differs from the Commission on Global Governance report in that it makes a direct and open aspiration towards world government, envisaging: 'A world Super-State in whose favour the nations of the world will have ceded every claim to make war, certain rights to impose taxation and all rights to maintain armaments except for the purposes of maintaining internal order within their respective dominions. This State will have to include an International Executive adequate to enforce supreme and unchallengeable authority on every recalcitrant member of the Commonwealth; a World Parliament whose members are elected by the peoples in their respective countries and whose election is confirmed by their respective governments; a Supreme Tribunal whose judgement has a binding effect even in cases where the parties concerned have not voluntarily agreed to submit their case to its consideration.'[34]

The reality is that the first UK launch of the report of the Commission on Global Governance was hosted by the overtly federalist Parliamentary Group for World Government, and the World Federalists of America hosted a panel discussion for four members of the Commission at a meeting during the 50th anniversary of the UN in San Francisco. The European Bahá'í Youth Council also hosted members of the Commission at a special seminar on Youth and Global Governance held at Landegg, Switzerland, in 1996. Those who do openly support world government may well view global governance as merely a development in the world government paradigm. It remains a moot point but it is my opinion that after half a century with little progress towards a world government, the faithful few are prepared to work along more strategic, incremental lines to move closer towards their ultimate goal.

Are We Closer to the Lesser Peace?

How then should Bahá'ís react to this widening debate? It has been said of 'Abdu'l-Bahá that He trod the spiritual path with practical feet and this pragmatism is evident in the statements of the Bahá'í International Community. The *Turning Point for All Nations* document recognizes that the world is not immediately ready for a planetary government and adds its voice to the wider, and more acceptable, calls for new structures of global governance. The BIC urges a convocation of world leaders to hold a world summit on global governance, with substantive input from civil society.

Measured against the structural parameters of the Lesser Peace as defined in the writings of Bahá'u'lláh, 'Abdu'l-Bahá and Shoghi Effendi, it is my contention that we are currently witnessing the emergence of new mechanisms or the reform of existing bodies that form the prototypes for a global legislature, executive and judiciary. We are evolving towards a world government and the pace of that evolution has accelerated substantially since the end of the Cold War. We learn from the Bahá'í writings that a world government will be delivered by the actions of the governments of the world and not as a result of the efforts of the Bahá'ís. Whether the advent of a global State will be part of the dawn of the Lesser Peace or the beginning of a period of dominion under a planetary hegemon, as feared by many isolationist groups, which regard the prospect of world government with great fear and suspicion, is not yet clear.

A world government remains a long-term vision but the BIC is ready to work with the global governance lobby to affect more immediate change. It notes that global integration is already a reality in the realms of business, finance and communications. Now it is beginning to materialize in the political arena. The *Turning Point* document speaks of an aggregate of international institutions, including the UN, which define the emerging international order. This idea of an aggregate of mechanisms ties in closely with the Commission's notion of global governance as a sum of many relationships involving individuals and groups in how they manage international affairs. Noting the fear of excessive centralization that is common to many critiques of world government, such as Hedley Bull's idea of world government by domination, the BIC urges that 'any new structures for global governance must . . . ensure that the responsibility for decision-making remains at appropriate levels'.[35] The document goes on to state that the Bahá'í community has investigated various mechanisms for global governance and suggests the benefit of either a federal system or a commonwealth and points out that 'Federalism has proved effective in decentralizing authority and decision-making in large, complex, and heterogeneous states'.[36]

Conclusion

The growth in the prevalence of global governance on the international policy stage is a barometer of how dramatically the world has moved in the direction of world government since 1989. In the late 20th century we witnessed a series of UN sponsored conferences such as the Rio Earth Summit, the Beijing Conference on Women and the Copenhagen Social Summit. The majority of the world's governments have signed international treaties banning the use of landmines and making provision for the creation of an International Criminal Court. The last decades of the 20th century saw a dramatic increase in the number of States which ratified all six of the major human rights conventions. There is an incremental growth in the impact of international law on the culture of the nation state.

In May 2000 the UN held a Millennium Peoples' Forum, the first occasion in UN history in which civil society had a formal channel to feed ideas and policy suggestions forward to the General Assembly and to the Inter-Governmental Summit. This event was co-chaired by the Bahá'í International Community. At the summit meeting itself, held in September of the same year, British Foreign Secretary Robin Cook gave a speech that called for universal ratification of the International Criminal Court, expansion of the Security Council and the creation of a UN Rapid Deployment Force. All of these policies have been identified earlier in this article as long-standing goals for Bahá'ís and other advocates of world government. The cusp of the 20th and

21st centuries has seen a series of unprecedented victories for the supporters of world government. Policy aims, such as the creation of an International Criminal Court, handed down from several generations of world government advocates, are actually in the process of being realized. Global governance is studied as part of degree courses in politics and international relations at universities.

There has also been an astonishing growth in the profile of global governance. Affirmations of global governance and even – astonishingly – world government have been contained in articles in mainstream British press, including *The Independent* and *The Observer*. The greatest accolade for this nascent political and social doctrine came in the autumn of 1999 when the Right Honourable Paddy Ashdown MP, outgoing leader of the British Liberal Democrat Party and a respected figure in foreign policy matters in British politics, made a farewell speech to his party conference in which he directly and strongly advocated that his party and others 'grasp the NETTLE of global governance'.[37] Mr Ashdown subsequently appeared as a guest speaker at the annual conference of the ruling Labour Party and gave the same speech there.

There seems one obvious conclusion to draw. Prominent politicians can only support global governance in their retirement speeches – and probably not go as far as world government. For those who have studied the history of the world government movement and recognize that the last time a British party leader advocated world government or global governance was in the 1950s, Mr Ashdown's endorsement, political swansong or otherwise, is a sign that the global governance movement is rising again, as noted in the ODI briefing paper.

The Bahá'í perspective on world government is born from a positive mind set and an enduring faith that a better world is close at hand. The opening words from *The Promise of World Peace* stir us to optimism for the future. 'For the first time in history it is possible for everyone to view the entire planet, with all its myriad diversified peoples, in one perspective. World peace is not only possible but inevitable. It is the next stage in the evolution of this planet . . .'[38] Perhaps the worldwide Bahá'í community should set practical feet on the path towards world government to assist their fellow human beings to recognize the current and forthcoming upheavals in social and political dynamics for the deeper transition that Bahá'u'lláh promises His followers it will surely be.

Bibliography

'Abdu'l-Bahá. *Paris Talks*. London: Bahá'í Publishing Trust, 1967.

Bahá'í International Community. *Turning Point for All Nations*, Bahá'í International Community, New York, 1995

Bahá'u'lláh. *Gleanings from the Writings of Bahá'u'lláh*. Wilmette, IL: Bahá'í Publishing Trust, 1983.

Bull, Hedley. *The Anarchical Society*. London: MacMillan, 1977.

Clark, G. and L. Sohn. *World Peace Through World Law*. Cambridge, MA: Harvard University Press, 1966.

The Commission on Global Governance. *Our Global Neighbourhood*. Oxford: Oxford University Press, 1995.

The Concise Oxford Dictionary. Oxford: The Clarendon Press, 1964.

Global Governance: An Agenda for the Renewal of the UN. Overseas Development Institute briefing paper. London, July 1999.

Graham, Kennedy. *The Planetary Interest*. Padstow: UCL Press, 1999.

Held, David. *Models of Democracy*. Cambridge: Policy Press, 1996.

— Antony McGrew, David Goldblatt and Jonathon Perraton. *Global Transformations: Politics, Economics and Culture*. Cambridge: Polity Press, 2000.

The New Penguin English Dictionary. Harmondsworth, Middx.: Penguin Books, 1986.

Ohmae, Keichi. *The End of the Nation State*. London: Harper Collins, 1995.

Pinder, J. and R. Mayne. *Federal Union: The Pioneers*. London: MacMillan, 1990.

Reves, Emery. *The Anatomy of Peace*. New York: Harper and Brothers, 1945.

Scholte, Jan Aart. 'Globalization: A Critical Introduction'. Basingstoke: Palgrave, 2000.

Shoghi Effendi. *Citadel of Faith*. Wilmette, IL: Bahá'í Publishing Trust, 1965.

— *The World Order of Bahá'u'lláh*. Wilmette, IL: Bahá'í Publishing Trust, 1991.

Tyson, J. *World Peace and World Government: A Bahá'í Approach*. Oxford: George Ronald, 1986.

The Universal House of Justice. *The Promise of World Peace*. London: Bahá'í Publishing Trust, 1985.

World Association of World Federalists. *World Federalism Today*. Leliegracht, Netherlands: World Association of World Federalists, 1988.

World Federalists of Canada. *An Agenda for Reform of the United Nations*. Ottawa: World Federalists of Canada, 1995.

References

1. Bahá'u'lláh, *Gleanings*, p. 254.
2. ibid. p. 250.
3. ibid. p. 254.
4. ibid.
5. Tyson, *World Peace and World Government*, p. 57.
6. ibid. pp. 59–60.
7. Reves, *Anatomy of Peace*, p. 26.
8. Bahá'u'lláh, *Gleanings*, p. 250.
9. Clark and Sohn, *World Peace Through World Law*.
10. Pinder and Mayne, *Federal Union: The Pioneers*, p. 62.
11. ibid. p. 63.
12. ibid. p. 62.
13. See Shoghi Effendi, *Citadel of Faith*, p. 125.
14. Bull, *The Anarchical Society*, p. 244.
15. ibid. p. 245.
16. Held, *Models of Democracy*, p. 336.
17. Ohmae, *The End of the Nation State*, p. 11.
18. Held, McGrew, Goldblatt and Perraton, *Global Transformations: Politics, Economics and Culture*.
19. The Commission on Global Governance, *Our Global Neighbourhood*, p. xvi.
20. ibid.
21. Bahá'í International Community, *Turning Point for All Nations*, pp. 1–2.
22. Graham, *The Planetary Interest*, p. 4.
23. ibid.
24. ibid. p. 7.
25. ibid.
26. *Global Governance: An Agenda for the Renewal of the UN*, Overseas Development Institute briefing paper.
27. ibid.
28. ibid.

29. *The Concise Oxford Dictionary.*
30. *The New Penguin English Dictionary.*
31. The Commission on Global Governance, *Our Global Neighbourhood,* p. 2.
32. ibid. p. xiv.
33. ibid.
34. Bahá'í International Community, *Turning Point for All Nations,* p. 6.
35. ibid. p. 5.
36. ibid. p. 6.
37. Rt Hon Paddy Ashdown MP, Speech to Liberal Democrat Party Conference, 1999.
38. The Universal House of Justice, *The Promise of World Peace,* p. 1.

'Everything That Rises Must Converge'[1]

Global Governance and the Emergence of the Lesser Peace

Charles Lerche

World unity is the goal towards which a harassed humanity is striving. Nation-building has come to an end. The anarchy inherent in
state sovereignty is moving towards a climax. A world, growing to
maturity, must abandon this fetish, *recognize the oneness and wholeness of
human relationships, and establish once for all the machinery that best incarnate
this fundamental principle of its life.*[2]

WTO Director-General Renato Ruggiero said that globalization
required the construction of a new international architecture to
manage the linkages not only between trade and the environment
but among all policies that spill over national borders.[3]

Introduction

Efforts by politicians, scholars and journalists to figure out what
is happening in our world reflect some consensus about the con-
tours of change but little agreement about what the patterns
mean. Though conflicting views are to be expected in our shrinking but diverse global village, there is a real need for more clarity,

for a conceptual framework within which to dispassionately assess current trends. In recent years we have seen opportunities for ameliorative action emerge suddenly, and vanish just as suddenly; but neither leadership nor citizens have seemed able to respond adequately to the challenges of the last years of the 20th century.

To act decisively requires the ability to distinguish threats from opportunities and such distinctions are a function of the values brought to bear on a given situation. It is in this connection that the Bahá'í Faith makes a significant contribution to thinking about world order. It has been distinguished from other religions since its foundation in the mid-19th century by its spiritual commitment to globalist[4] values, its promotion of a just and participatory world federalism, and, more generally, by its optimistic, coherent and far-reaching vision of where current events are leading. From a Bahá'í perspective current trends are viewed as indicators of an unprecedented change in human affairs called the 'Lesser Peace'. This is seen as a necessary and divinely-ordained stage in the evolution of world order and is described in various letters from both Shoghi Effendi, the Guardian of the Faith, and the Universal House of Justice, as coming about 'through the political efforts of the states and nations of the world'[5] and involving increasing 'unity of nations',[6] decreasing arms expenditures and the application of the principle of collective security to threats to international peace.[7] More recently the Bahá'í International Community (BIC)[8] has explained that this 'political unity of nations' 'implies the achievement of a relationship among them that will enable them to resolve questions of international import through consultation rather than war and that will lead to the establishment of a world government'.[9] Furthermore, they declare that an irreversible process towards peace was well under way at century's end, and they list some of its more important aspects:

- The birth of the League of Nations and the United Nations
- The frequency with which world leaders come together to resolve global issues and their call for a 'global order'
- The multiplication of civil society organizations

- The widespread debates on the need for global governance
- The emergence of global tribunals
- The rapid developments in communications technology

Finally, they reiterate the warning that such a momentous change in human affairs can come about only through 'a universal fermentation and horrendous social upheavals.'[10] Thus, for Bahá'ís, the evolution and character of global governance at this early stage of its development are issues of great significance and interest.

In this paper an effort is made to draw on both the values and vision found in the Bahá'í writings, as given expression by the BIC in various documents prepared in the course of its work at the UN, to assess the current state and processes of global governance. First, the concept of global governance is defined and a number of viewpoints about its scope and implications considered; then, a perspective for assessing new dimensions of global governance is derived from three recent BIC statements; and, finally, this framework is used to assess a few specific cases.

Contemporary Global Governance: A Definition and Some Implications

The concept of 'global governance' figures with increasing prominence in the discussion of world affairs and evokes a wide latitude of reactions in public opinion. People love and hate it; proclaim it as an idea whose time has come and dismiss it as completely unrealistic; fear it; promote it; understand and misunderstand it; and even theologically condemn it. The oft-cited definition of the Commission on Global Governance reflects how diffuse the concept is:

> Governance is the sum of the many ways individuals and institutions, public and private, manage their common affairs . . . It includes formal institutions and regimes empowered to enforce compliance, as well as informal arrangements that people and institutions either have agreed to or perceive to be in their interest . . . At the global level, governance has been viewed primarily as intergovernmental

relationships, but it must now be understood as also involving non-governmental organizations (NGOs), citizens' movements, multinational corporations, and the global capital market. Interacting with these are global mass media of dramatically enlarged influence.[11]

Still, extremist and paranoid reactions notwithstanding, there seems to be no getting away from global governance. 'Globalization' seems to be well under way and we have reached a point when the majority of the planet's inhabitants are aware of themselves *as* inhabitants of the planet; when the world is becoming one place and we are increasingly aware of it as such.[12] Global governance can, in fact, be seen as the sum of humanity's collective efforts to cope with the enfolding processes of globalization. In effect, all politics are becoming planetary (in implication if not always in scope), aspects of what physicist and philosopher Carl-Friedrich von Weizsacker called 'global domestic politics'.[13] Therefore, as globalization intensifies, there is increasing interest in and concern about the direction, institutions and processes of global governance.

But aren't there still separate sovereign States? Don't these States still make the primary claims on most people's loyalties? Aren't nations distinguishable one from the other and don't they have unique and endogenously defined political identities and futures? These notions, taken as a whole, have become paradigmatic to politics and political thinking during the post-Westphalian era and, as such, are still most frequently invoked to explain and understand contemporary events. However, they don't entirely 'work' any more as a basis for public policy. The fundamental economic and social forces shaping our present possibilities and our future expectations are those which transcend borders, revealing the limitations of this inherited mind set. Again, as the Commission on Global Governance definition indicates, States, great and small, constitute only one set of actors in a world system which transcends and imposes priorities on them.

There are already people in prominent places who see the world as one. Unfortunately, their intentions, while perhaps well-meaning in many cases, may not prove entirely benign. To the extent that they have the means to do so, they try to steer the processes of globalization in directions which reflect their interests. Prominent among such actors are those firms and individuals responsible for maximizing the return on large amounts of capital. Whatever one may think of contemporary international business and finance, they have knit the world together as never before and provided the technology which keeps us aware that the world is an interdependent system. Many of these people and firms seem to be doing quite well in the world as it is but they would like the global status quo to become more stable and they would like to see trends that promote their interests intensified.[14] Furthermore, they exercise, through various channels, a major, if not determinant, influence on government policies in most parts of the globe; with the result that, as one Central American scholar puts it: 'Governments . . . are pressured by capital itself to provide securities against systemic risk, protection for investors, policing of state and firm insolvency, and the like.'[15] This accounts, in large measure, for the increasing impact of multilateral institutions such as the International Monetary Fund (IMF), World Bank, Group of Seven Leading Industrialized Countries (G7), and most recently, the World Trade Organization (WTO).

These points lead us to an initially startling conclusion: despite the persistence of provincialism, jingoism and xenophobia, a steady extension and consolidation of global governance, in some form, is really the most likely scenario for the immediate future. Richard Falk is one prominent analyst who makes a very forceful case for the emergence of what he calls 'geogovernance':

> The globalizing trends are moving so rapidly in integrative directions, especially with respect to economic, environmental, and cognitive dimensions of reality, that it seems almost inevitable that some form of geogovernance will take shape. Prevailing tendencies suggest that geogovernance will be achieved by a coalition between leading states in the West (possibly including East and South Asia) and transnational capital as deployed by corporate managers and banking operatives. These state and market forces will, in turn, wire the world for purposes of advertising, indoctrination, and administration.[16]

Claude Ake, a leading African critical thinker, feels the process is already well under way:

> Economic forces are constituting the world into one economy and, to a lesser extent, one political society. Nations participate in global governance according to their economic power, which is coextensive with their rights. The global order is ruled by an informal cabinet of the world's economically most powerful countries; its law is the logic of the market, and status in this new order is a function of economic performance.[17]

This vision of global governance is decidedly negative, since it is elitist, interventionist, coercive and little concerned with issues of social justice or environmental quality; but these analysts are convinced that it is already coming into being and, is 'the most plausible scenario' for the future.[18]

Multilateralism of this kind could expand for some time without overtly or directly challenging the dominant statist political myths. After all, theorists across the board insist that 'global governance' is not 'world government', and that national sovereignty remains the dominant principle, and limiting parameter, of international cooperation. One might argue, therefore, that when the 'sovereignty threshold' is passed, meaning when national sovereignty is 'given up' or 'alienated' to higher bodies, an international regime passes from 'governance' to 'government' – from something less formal to something more formal. But in practice it is not that simple. Consider, for instance, the UN Security Council (discussed further below). All signatories to the Charter are legally bound to accept Council decisions. However, the Permanent Members can avoid this by exercising their veto. Is this an example of government or governance? The easy answer is to call it governance but it could just as well be seen as an example of weak and inequitable government. Another example is the European Union (EU). A little effort invested in studying the treaties which define its current structure reveals that the EU has, at a regional level, the most developed supranational institutions on the planet today. However, the predominant discourse and practice of EU politics tend to downplay and obfuscate this fact, primarily because the supranational dimensions of the EU are neither well understood nor much appreciated by the citizens of member States. Finally, as Ake indicates, sovereignty has done little to prevent the majority of countries in the Global South being subject to policies imposed on them by the global financial institutions.

What we have experienced so far could be seen as more of a 'parameter' shift than a 'paradigm' shift: same 'players', same 'game', just a wider 'field'. Admittedly, the players (whether private or public) find new possibilities and new strategies in the wider field and there is much re-shuffling of hierarchies and coalitions. But as Neorealists have been arguing for close to two decades, you can still pursue power and wealth in an interdependent international environment – you just have to do it differently. There is no reason to assume that a world organized as one system will be inherently more fulfilling for more people in the long run than a world divided into relatively autonomous communities. Rather, global governance is, as the definition above indicates, completely open-ended. Any new development in this diffuse aggregate – such as the creation of the World Trade Organization, for example – should be primarily understood as a pragmatic effort by decision-making elites to create institutional means with greater scope to respond to the political, economic and social demands made on them in their official capacities. Like any other policy output of an 'open' political system, these initiatives can and should be assessed and, if necessary, modified in response to questions such as: Is the new institution/procedure necessary? What values underpin it? Does it do what it says it will do? Who benefits?

This should be straightforward, but it isn't. Rather, the policy environment is clouded with alienation and distrust. As nation states' capacity to cope with transnational forces diminishes, they lose autonomy and effectiveness, causing governments to lose credibility. People all over the world, already sceptical of leaders' motives, have little reason to believe that complicated new international agreements are formulated with their needs in mind. This suspicion is reinforced by the steady increase in the extremes of wealth and poverty which has gone hand in hand with neo-liberal economic policies. Furthermore, as natural and man-made disasters multiply,[19] technocrats' claims to the expertise necessary to solve complex social problems seem increasingly hollow. Simply put, leadership often seems remote, manipulated by special interests and of questionable competence.

The masses of humanity are currently caught in a dilemma: they don't want to go 'forward' towards a world 'globalized' according to elite preferences and they can't go 'back' to the 'good old days' of feeling secure 'at home'. There is a need to somehow reconcile the priorities of leaders who must respond to transnational forces and citizens who need to feel a part of the decisions that are shaping their lives. Otherwise, even the elite agenda will not be realized since the gap which is growing between popular and elite perceptions of globalization must ultimately undermine the stability decision-makers seek. In this context, it seems reasonable to predict both that there will be more global governance initiatives and that they will not be supported by the general public to the extent they are perceived (rightly or wrongly) as threats to people's needs for security, identity or community – no matter how rational they appear to the technocrats.

This may be the principle tension and limitation in the emerging pattern of global governance, and it arises at least partly because there is no unifying vision of where the process should be going. The global 'consensus' over liberalism, always more rhetoric than reality, has brought to light the inefficiency of various restrictive policies and institutions but it doesn't help much in defining longer term goals and priorities. As hard as it may have been to gain, 'freedom from' is only useful to the extent that it allows you to define your 'freedom to'. Furthermore, the famous 'end of history' argument is really too statist to be of long-term use. The benefits of political and economic reform at the national level cannot ultimately be secured unless and until the same values are institutionalized at the global level. Thus, rather than having arrived safely at the 'end of history' in our various liberal nation states, we find that the age-old questions of political philosophy about such things as 'justice', 'community' or 'obligation', need to be re-opened, re-formulated and re-addressed in terms of the planet as a whole.

At the moment, to the extent that this debate goes on, it takes the form of an often acrimonious exchange between governments, multinational corporations and their various institutions on the one hand; and on the other, the growing network of non-governmental organizations and other elements of 'global civil society' which give a 'voice' to causes and peoples often overlooked by the powerful. Though the Commission on Global Governance gives the impression that global governance is somehow a *sum* of the actions of all these participants, the process has actually emerged as a *conflict* between the 'top down' elite agenda and the 'bottom up' popular agenda. This has been increasingly evident at high profile United Nations sponsored conferences in recent decades where the official government representatives' conference and the NGO forum have had divergent priorities and have competed for media attention in defining the parameters of global policy. Predictably, under these conditions most new policy initiatives are contested, controversial and enjoy only limited and variable support – hardly a satisfactory result, given the urgency of the need for change in so many areas.

Bridging the Gap: A Bahá'í Perspective on Global Governance

Both because its ethics are globalist in orientation and because its world community presents a working participatory model of unity in diversity, the Bahá'í Faith is making an important contribution to the evolving discourse on global governance. While most of the other engaged groups and organizations of civil society are focused on single issues or issue areas, the BIC has over the years articulated views on a wide variety of world problems.[20] These documents provide insights into what might be called a Bahá'í vision of global governance and in this section principles and prescriptions from three of the BIC's recent statements will be drawn upon to highlight the positive and negative aspects of the contemporary state of global governance.

Speaking about the concept of 'governance', the BIC affirms that it is 'essential to social progress' and that it 'occurs on all levels and encompasses the ways that formal government, non-governmental groups, community organizations and the private sector manage resources and affairs'.[21] They also argue that the state of governance is principally determined by three factors: 'the quality of leadership, the quality of the governed and the quality of the structures and processes in place', and that there is 'an emerging international consensus on the core characteristics of good governance' which includes 'democracy, the rule of law, accountability, transparency and participation by civil society'.[22]

However, the BIC feels that good governance should encompass even more than this:

> This consensus must be enlarged, however, to encompass an appreciation of the role that governance must assume in promoting the spiritual and material well-being of all members of society. Governance must be guided by universal values, including an ethic of service to the common good. It will need to provide for the meaningful participation of citizens in the conceptualization, design, implementation and evaluation of programmes and policies that affect them. It should seek to enhance people's ability to manage change and should offer opportunities to increase their capacities and sense of worth. It will need to provide mechanisms for equitable access to the benefits of programmes and policies, to education and information, and to opportunities for lifelong learning. Moreover, it must help to ensure that the news media are active, vibrant and truthful. *At the global level, a truly participatory system of governance will also need to be established.*[23]

The Prophet-Founder of the Faith, Bahá'u'lláh, and 'Abdu'l-Bahá, the principal Interpreter of its teachings, both emphasized the need for stronger authoritative global institutions and elsewhere the BIC elaborates on the need for the process of governance to expand greatly in scope and intensity at the global level. In its detailed statement prepared for the 50th anniversary of the founding of the United Nations, *Turning Point for All Nations*, the BIC joined other globalist organizations (like the Commission on Global Governance) in calling for a dramatic step forward in the institutionalization of global governance:

> We urge leaders at all levels to take a deliberate role in supporting a convocation of world leaders before the turn of this century to consider how the international order might be redefined and restructured to meet the challenges facing the world. As some have suggested, this gathering might be called the World Summit on Global Governance.[24]

All three of the documents cited in this section pinpoint the emerging gap between the elites and masses of global society as a problem which must be overcome if global governance is to truly succeed. The BIC argues that the energy necessary for positive global change is latent in the masses of humankind and that to be effective global governance must stimulate and channel this energy in creative directions. However, to date, the connection between global institutions and the average person has been far too weak to accomplish this task:

> With a focus on building institutions and creating a community of nations, international bodies have historically remained distant from the minds and hearts of the world's people . . . International institutions will succeed in eliciting and directing the potentialities latent in the peoples of the world to the extent that their exercise of authority is moderated by their obligation to win the confidence, respect, and genuine support of those whose actions they seek to govern and to consult openly and to the fullest extent possible with all those whose interests are affected.[25]

The BIC also attributes much of the tension between elites and the grassroots of society to the prevalent conception of 'power' in social relations:

> Throughout history . . . power has been largely interpreted as advantage enjoyed by persons or groups. Often, indeed, it has been expressed simply in terms of means to be used against others. This interpretation of power has become an inherent feature of the culture of division and conflict that has characterized the human race during the past several millennia, regardless of the social, religious, or

political orientations that have enjoyed ascendancy in given ages, in given parts of the world. In general, power has been an attribute of individuals, factions, peoples, classes, and nations . . . Its chief effect has been to confer on its beneficiaries the ability to acquire, to surpass, to dominate, to resist, to win.[26]

However, times have changed and this 'inherited understanding and use of power' seems increasingly dysfunctional:

Today, in an era most of whose pressing problems are global in nature, persistence in the idea that power means advantage for various segments of the human family is profoundly mistaken in theory and of no practical service to the social and economic development of the planet. *Those who still adhere to it – and who could in earlier eras have felt confident in such adherence – now find their plans enmeshed in inexplicable frustrations and hindrances.*[27]

The BIC sees this as one of a number of indications that the human race has to leave behind habits associated with earlier stages in its development and begin to work out patterns of collective action more suitable to new social conditions; a change which involves 'a radical rethinking of most of the concepts and assumptions currently governing social and economic life'.[28] Central to this effort are the qualities of 'unity' and 'justice', which must be at the heart of any plans for successful efforts at social change. With regard to unity, the BIC argues that:

Only through the dawning consciousness that they constitute a single people will the inhabitants of the planet be enabled to turn away from the patterns of conflict that have dominated social organization in the past and begin to learn the ways of collaboration and conciliation.[29]

This echoes the argument made 60 years ago by Shoghi Effendi, the Guardian of the Bahá'í Faith, when he explained that unity is not just an ideal for a rapidly maturing human race but a necessity if its increasingly disordered collective life is ever to stabilize.[30] At the close of a century of unprecedented violence, several analysts argued that globalization was unleashing yet another wave of destructive conflict around the planet, as communal groups responded atavistically to perceived threats of economic and cultural imperialism,[31] a trend which further emphasizes the urgency of imbuing the peoples of the world with a much more profound sense of common, rather than competing, identity.

The promotion of unity among the world's peoples depends, in turn, on finding ways to respond to the increasingly strident cries for justice from those who feel they have 'fallen through the cracks' of global change. Again, it is hard to imagine any globalization scenario which systematically ignores concerns about social justice and equity bringing in its wake anything but suffering, alienation and conflict. This is particularly true since the very technologies which have 'wired' the world for globalization have also provided marginalized groups with the means to become informed about the reasons for their plight and to band together and mobilize to articulate their concerns to a world audience:

> An age that sees the people of the world increasingly gaining access to information of every kind and to a diversity of ideas will find justice asserting itself as the ruling principle of successful social organization. With ever greater frequency, proposals aiming at the development of the planet will have to submit to the candid light of the standards it requires.[32]

A sincere commitment to global social justice can help to counter 'the temptation to sacrifice the well-being of the generality of humankind – and even of the planet itself – to the advantages which technological breakthroughs can make available to privileged minorities'[33] and implies that only those global initiatives which 'are perceived as meeting their needs and as being just and equitable in objective can hope to engage the commitment of the masses of humanity, upon whom implementation depends'.[34] Ultimately, only trust in the fairness of rulers' motives and policies can elicit the support those policies require to succeed:

> The relevant human qualities such as honesty, a willingness to work, and a spirit of cooperation are successfully harnessed to the accomplishment of enormously demanding collective goals when every

member of society – indeed every component group within society –
can trust that they are protected by standards and assured of benefits
that apply equally to all.[35]

Progress in this direction requires new leadership in both the
public and private sectors and the BIC again joins with other concerned organizations, such as the Commission on Global
Governance, to suggest a new model of leadership for the next
millennium, a leadership which shuns elitism, adheres scrupu-
lously to high moral and ethical standards and thinks and acts
globally.

> Above all else, leaders for the next generation must be motivated by
> a sincere desire to serve the entire community and must understand
> that leadership is a responsibility; not a path to privilege. For too
> long, leadership has been understood, by both leaders and followers,
> as the assertion of control over others. Indeed, this age demands a
> new definition of leadership and a new type of leader.
>   This is especially true in the international arena. In order to estab-
> lish a sense of trust, win the confidence, and inculcate a fond affinity
> in the hearts of the world's people for institutions of the interna-
> tional order, these leaders will have to reflect on their own actions.
>   Through an unblemished record of personal integrity, they must
> help restore confidence and trust in government. They must embody
> the characteristics of honesty, humility and sincerity of purpose in
> seeking the truth of a situation. They must be committed to and
> guided by principles, thereby acting in the best long-term interests of
> humanity as a whole.[36]

The principles for global governance derived from these texts,
might be summarized as follows:

1) The planet has to be reconstructed as one system.

2) Leaders should articulate and act in the global interest – and
should expect to be judged on how well they succeed in this
effort.

3) People everywhere need to be assisted to acquire an identity as

human beings which is as deeply felt as any communal or national identity.[37]

4) People's needs for personal security, community and self-realization should have a higher priority on the global policy agenda, relative to issues of economic growth and technological advancement.

5) To be effective over the long term, global governance should become truly democratic, creating the means for the masses of humanity to participate in and contribute to the formulation and execution of world-embracing policies.

6) The global policy-making process should be more transparent and more comprehensible to the public.

All three documents go on to discuss other issues such as human rights, development planning and the need for world federalism. No matter what specific measures are undertaken, the principles above will remain relevant to the evolution of global governance, and indeed to governance generally, for the foreseeable future. It should be added that, though quite optimistic about humanity's long-term future, the BIC does not assume their prescriptions will be implemented, even in part, in the short term. Rather: 'The precise speed and cost of this progress will be determined largely by the actions, in the years immediately ahead, of governments, multilateral organizations, the private sector, organizations of civil society, and key individuals.'[38] However, if and when leadership emerges which feels inspired or compelled to act, creative alternatives to the disruption and alienation of the present have already been pointed out by the BIC and other forward-looking elements of global civil society.

Some Applications

In 1985, in a letter 'To the Peoples of the World', widely distributed on the occasion of the UN International Year of Peace,[39] the

Universal House of Justice mentioned by name a list of nine regional international organizations and stated categorically that 'all the joint endeavours represented by such organizations prepare the path to world order'.[40] This observation can be extended to most, if not all, the multilateral institutions which have been created in subsequent years, in that they provide proof that sustained international cooperation is possible in an ever-widening range of areas and that its benefits outweigh its costs. Those international regimes which have formulated effective rules and decision-making structures, particularly regulatory authorities, can also be seen as pointing the way towards supranationalism.

All of the existing institutions, from the United Nations itself to the regional functional organizations, could benefit from the application of the principles listed above, and as argued earlier, their ultimate success or failure may well depend on the extent to which they develop in this direction. Thus, these principles can be used to highlight strengths and weaknesses in contemporary world and regional institutions and agreements. Since a full analysis of even one institution or process would exceed the scope of this paper, all that is attempted here is to provide a few examples, selected from different dimensions of global governance, of how the principles might be usefully applied.

The United Nations Security Council

Arguably the most powerful and authoritative international institution, the Security Council is an interesting mix of new and old in international relations. On the one hand, it embodies the desire of the founders of the United Nations to institutionalize the principle of collective security in order to 'save future generations from the scourge of war'. On the other hand, it accords primacy to the victorious allies of World War II, and in so doing, resembles as much the 19th-century Concert of Europe as it does the executive branch of an embryonic world government. The obvious anachronisms in the Charter, such as references to 'enemy powers', and the radical changes in world affairs generally, have served to highlight the need for rethinking the membership and responsibilities of the Council.

In *Turning Point for All Nations*, the BIC limited its suggestions in this area to the question of the veto:

> The original intention of the UN Charter in conferring veto power on the five Permanent Members was to prevent the Security Council from authorizing military actions against a Permanent Member or requiring the use of its forces against its will. In fact, beginning with the Cold War, the veto power has been exercised repeatedly for reasons that have to do with regional or national security.
>
> In its 1955 submission on UN reform, the Bahá'í International Community argued for the gradual elimination of the concepts of 'permanent membership' and 'veto power' as confidence in the Security Council would build. Today, forty years later, we reaffirm that position. However, we also propose that, as a transitionary step, measures be introduced to curb the exercise of the veto power to reflect the original intention of the Charter.[41]

Though first priority is given here to preventing veto abuse and returning to the original purpose of the Charter in granting that prerogative to the Council's Permanent Members, the BIC is also looking further ahead to a time when these distinctions might be eliminated altogether. This is a very important idea, since it represents the full extension of the democratic principle to the conduct of relations between and among States. Such a suggestion runs contrary to the entire logic of power politics in that it denies the most powerful States any privileged status in world affairs – even though this status has been a constant in the history of the States-system since its inception and has even been regarded by some as an 'institution of international society'.[42]

Without suggesting that such a step will either come soon, or be straightforward to implement, it would seem to be inevitable. An elitist 'Concert' really has no place at the heart of the world's supreme multilateral institution in an age which is characterized by a worldwide process of 'democratization'. As argued above, in the long run the contradiction between a preferred, and frankly prescribed, democratic model of governance at the national level and a hegemonic or oligarchic international system has to be resolved through the formulation and implementation of more democratic processes at the global level. If not, the agenda of democratic reform will be perceived by weaker peoples as just another imposition of the 'centre' on the 'periphery'.

The International Monetary Fund

One institution which has acquired enormous influence of a quasi-supranational character is the International Monetary Fund. Though created immediately after World War II for the purpose of assisting States to cope with short-term imbalances in their current accounts, the IMF has come to be the primary institution in charge of guiding countries with long-term monetary problems through the contemporary process of liberal economic reform. Without going into detail about the controversy surrounding the Fund's 'Structural Adjustment Policies' (SAPs), it has to be admitted that this institution does have an 'image' problem among many governments and peoples. There seem to be a few principal reasons for this, not all of which stem directly from the hardship caused by the policy changes required for Fund assistance:

1) The Fund's influence extends to many countries which have no representation on its Board of Governors. Though there is a case to be made that those who contribute most to the organization's resources should have most to say about how those resources are used, one can understand why Fund policies might be resented by those millions of people who feel quite rightly that they have not had the opportunity to participate, even indirectly, in decisions which have caused them substantial hardship. Experts in social and economic development know that 'top-down' development projects don't work; why should 'top-down' fiscal reform 'projects' be any different?

2) At times, the Fund gives the impression of being reluctant to acknowledge that its policy prescriptions may not be suitable to

all economies, may be in need of some revision or may simply not work in certain cases. After several decades of SAPs, more open consultation on their strengths and weaknesses could do much to increase support for economic reform – but this would require a willingness to take seriously opposing views. It should be added that the IMF's 'sister' institution, the World Bank, has shown itself more willing to recognize that its policies have not always been effective. Most recently, the World Bank has suggested that economic reform should include provision for improvements in education, health and infrastructure, as well as assistance for the poor and helpless.[43] To date, the IMF has yet to echo this theme.

3) The language of the institution is very technical and difficult for non-experts to understand. A certain amount of jargon is justified in any specialized field but given that the decisions of this institution have an impact on so many people, more effort could be made to make the rationale for policy changes accessible to the people directly affected.

4) Finally, there is an impression in the Global South that the North, through the medium of IMF SAPs, imposes more rigorous liberal standards of market openness and government deregulation on the Fund's 'clients' than are actually applied in the Northern economies themselves. Whether true or not, such perceived discrimination can do little to enhance the Fund's credibility among the poor and weak and reinforces the plausibility of Ake's image of global governance directed by an 'informal cabinet of the world's economically most powerful countries'.

Free Trade Area of the Americas (FTAA)

A series of negotiations to bring this organization into being were begun at the 1994 Summit of the Americas and over the last few years there have been signs that Western hemisphere leaders are aware of the need to address mass as well as elite concerns in their effort to further expand free trade in the region. The background to this development is instructive. Economic integration is already well under way in North and South America, primarily through the North American Free Trade Association (NAFTA), Mercado Común del Sur (MERCOSUR, i.e. Southern Common Market), the Andean Pact and the Caribbean Community (CARICOM). However, there seems little question that the masses, particularly in North America, are highly sceptical that the process is to their benefit. For instance, a Bank of Boston poll in 1996 showed that 51 per cent of US citizens believed free trade pacts cost US jobs and 57 per cent opposed any new trade agreements with Latin America.[44] The most concrete effect of the discontent indicated by these poll results was the Clinton administration's withdrawal, in the face of overwhelming Congressional opposition, of its request for 'fast-track' authority to negotiate further agreements. Apparently this trend, and other dramatic events such as the Zapatista uprising in the Chiapas region of Mexico, are bringing home the message that:

> There is little evidence that a hemisphere-wide trade agreement based on the NAFTA/MERCOSUR model would establish a solid foundation for economic relationships that foster sustainable development and economic progress in member countries. The NAFTA experience has demonstrated that the benefits of trade will not automatically trickle down to the population as a whole. Instead, trade agreements must be specifically designed to serve as tools for development that benefits everyone, not just those at the top.[45]

The formal talks to establish the FTAA were launched at the second Summit of the Americas in Santiago, Chile, during April 1998. Though it is difficult to assess the effectiveness of measures adopted at this meeting, there is, at least, a new concern about the distribution effects of globalization being expressed in the discourse of hemispheric free trade. For instance, the American president stated to business leaders while in Chile for the Summit that: 'Harnessing the forces of globalization to work for all our citizens is literally a challenge to every nation in the world . . . A rising tide does not necessarily lift all boats. People without the right education, without training, without bargaining power can be stranded on yesterday's shore.'[46] And, at a more substantive level, by the end of the gathering the Heads of State collectively admitted they had 'fallen short on the social agenda since the first Summit of the Americas in 1994' and announced 'a four-part action plan that seeks to correct the lack of progress on social issues by targeting education, democracy, economic integration and the eradication of poverty' for which they promised US$45 billion worth of funds from various sources, such as the Inter-American Development Bank, World Bank and US Agency for International Development.[47]

To suggest that the elite-civil society 'gap' has been closed in this area would still be quite premature. Parallel to the Presidential Summit in Santiago was a 'People's Summit', in which all the grassroots concerns about globalization mentioned above were expressed in connection with the hemispheric free trade regime. The entire Summit and negotiation process was deemed 'undemocratic and unrepresentative' and 'incompatible with the principles and criteria of sustainable development'. In response to these perceived shortcomings, the People's Summit proposed 'that all free trade agreements be approved by a plebiscite in each country' and that 'any trade agreement must be conditioned on ratification of a social, labour and environmental rights charter for civil society, and on the inclusion in this charter of provisions on ethics and on respect for ethnic minorities and women'.[48] This shows that further measures to enhance transparency and to foster more inclusive consultation on relevant social issues could do much to create that popular support for free trade which is essential if it is to fulfil its potential as a force for stability and well-being in the hemisphere and, indeed, the world.

Conclusion

The thesis of this paper is quite simple: globalization has put global governance on everybody's agenda and progress in global governance is as much about values as it is about interests and institutions. As the BIC has written elsewhere:

The negative effects of globalization can be softened only through new and higher levels of international cooperation and consultation, filtered through a new system of moral values that puts human welfare and social justice ahead of the predominantly materialistic paradigm currently in vogue. Call this global governance. Call it world government. But one way or another, the forces of globalization will require the creation of some sort of international super authority, one that can ensure that human rights and workers' prerogatives are upheld, and that the environment is protected, as globalization proceeds.[49]

As we enter the millennium a patchwork of global governance processes exists, and, as stated by the BIC in *Peace Among the Nations*, there is evidence of increasing coordination among organizations, convergence at the level of ideas and growing input from civil society in planning and executing multilateral initiatives – trends which contribute directly to the development of a more democratic global public policy process. However, there are many areas of global governance where such principles as unity, justice and consultation could be more thoroughly and consistently applied and in which it is becoming increasingly urgent to do so. However a Bahá'í vision of global governance sees burgeoning multilateralism as part of a greater and more far-reaching change in human affairs:

> . . . beyond the political peace reluctantly entered into by suspicious rival nations, beyond pragmatic arrangements for security and coexistence, beyond even the many experiments in cooperation which these steps will make possible lies the crowning goal: *the unification of all the peoples of the world in one universal family.*[50]

In the final analysis, all aspects of global governance can be judged according to whether they hasten or hinder progress toward this goal. That we cannot realistically expect progress in this direction to be linear indicates the extent to which the Lesser Peace is a significant and challenging evolutionary threshold for the human race. However, the Bahá'í writings state unequivocally that humanity is currently passing over this threshold, that more effective and equitable international institutions are emerging and that the general pattern of world affairs will become more orderly and progressive.

Bibliography

Ake, Claude. 'The New World Order: A View from Africa', in Holm, and Sørensen (eds.). *Whose World Order: Uneven Globalization and the End of the Cold War.* Boulder: Westview, 1995.

Bahá'í International Community Office of Public Information. *Peace Among the Nations.* Statement in response to a question about the Lesser Peace and the catastrophic events of the end of the Twentieth Century, 8 March 1999. Haifa: Bahá'í International Community Office of Public Information, 1999.

— *The Prosperity of Humankind.* New York: Bahá'í International Community United Nations Office, 1995. First distributed at the United Nations World Summit on Social Development, Copenhagen, Denmark, March 1995.
<www.bic-un.bahai.org /95-0303.htm>

— *Turning Point for All Nations: A Statement of the Bahá'í International Community on the Occasion of the 50th Anniversary of the United Nations.* New York: Bahá'í International Community United Nations Office, 1995. <www.bic-un.bahai.org/95-1001.htm>

— *Valuing Spirituality in Development: Initial Considerations Regarding the Creation of Spiritually Based Indicators for Development.* London: Bahá'í Publishing Trust, 1998. A concept paper presented to the 'World Faiths and Development Dialogue' hosted by the President of the World Bank and the Archbishop of Canterbury at Lambeth Palace, London, 18–19 February 1998. <www.bic-un.bahai.org/98-0218.htm>

Barber, Benjamin R. 'Jihad vs. McWorld', *The Atlantic Monthly*, March 1992.

BRIDGES Weekly Trade News Digest, vol. 2, no. 11, 30 March 1998.

Bull, Hedley. *The Anarchical Society.* New York: Columbia University Press, 1977.

Commission on Global Governance. *Our Global Neighbourhood.* New York: Oxford University Press, 1995.

Compilation of Compilations, The. Prepared by the Universal House of Justice 1963–1990. 2 vols. [Sydney]: Bahá'í Publications Australia, 1991.

Falk, Richard. *On Humane Governance: Toward a New Global Politics.* University Park, PA: Pennsylvania State University Press, 1995.

Fuller, Graham. 'The Next Ideology', *Foreign Policy*, Spring 1995.
Hansen-Kuhn, Karen. 'Free Trade Area of the Americas', *The Progressive Response*, 13 April 1998, vol. 2, no. 11, <www.zianet.com/infocus>
Lippman, Thomas W. 'Clinton Stresses Benefits of Open Markets', *Washington Post*, Friday, 17 April 1998, p. A25.
NAFTA & Inter-American Trade Monitor, 14 November 1996. <trade-news@igc.apc.org>
— vol. 5, no. 9, 1 May 1998. <iatp@iatp.org>
O'Connor, Flannery, in R.V. Cassill (ed.). *The Norton Anthology of Short Fiction*. New York: W.W. Norton & Co., 1990.
One Country: The online newsletter of the Bahá'í International Community, vol. 9, no. 2, July–September 1997, <www.onecountry.org /oc92/oc9209as.html>
Ritchie, Mark. 'Globalization vs. Globalism: Giving Internationalism a Bad Name'. Conference 'trade-strategy'. <trade-strategy @igc.apc.org>. 26 February 1996.
Robertson, Roland. *Globalization: Social Theory and Global Culture*. London: Sage, 1992.
Shoghi Effendi. *The World Order of Bahá'u'lláh*. Wilmette, IL: Bahá'í Publishing Trust, 1991.
The Universal House of Justice. *The Promise of World Peace*. London: Bahá'í Publishing Trust, 1985.
World Development Report 1997: The State in a Changing World. <www.worldbank.org/html/extpb/wdr97/english/>

References

1. Title of a short story by Flannery O'Connor, in Cassill, *The Norton Anthology of Short Fiction*, p. 1280.
2. Shoghi Effendi, *World Order*, p. 202. Emphasis added.
3. *BRIDGES Weekly Trade News Digest*, vol. 2, no. 11, 30 March 1998.
4. 'Globalism' can be defined as 'the belief that we share one fragile planet whose survival requires mutual respect and careful treatment of all its people and its environment. Globalism is also a set of values and ethical beliefs requiring active practice in our day-to-day lives. Active communications to foster understanding, the sharing of resources on the basis of equity and sustainability, and mutual aid in times of need are three central activities that undergird globalism.' Ritchie, 'Globalization vs. Globalism, Conference 'trade-strategy'. <trade-strategy@igc.apc.org>. 26 February 1996.
5. From a letter written on behalf of Shoghi Effendi to the National Spiritual Assembly of the United States and Canada and to an

individual, 14 March 1939, in *Compilation*, vol. 2, p. 194.

6. From a letter written on behalf of the Universal House of Justice, 31 January 1985, in ibid. p. 199.

7. In this regard, Shoghi Effendi wrote:

> . . . that 'Lesser Peace' to which the Author of our Faith has Himself alluded in His writings. 'Now that ye have refused the Most Great Peace', He, admonishing the kings and rulers of the earth, has written, 'hold ye fast unto this the Lesser Peace, that haply ye may in some degree better your own condition and that of your dependents'. Expatiating on this Lesser Peace, He thus addresses in that same Tablet the rulers of the earth: 'Be reconciled among yourselves, that ye may need no more armaments save in a measure to safeguard your territories and dominions . . . Be united, O kings of the earth, for thereby will the tempest of discord be stilled amongst you, and your peoples find rest, if ye be of them that comprehend. Should any one among you take up arms against another, rise ye all against him, for this is naught but manifest justice'. Shoghi Effendi, *World Order*, p. 162.

8. The Bahá'í International Community is an international non-governmental organization that both encompasses and represents the worldwide membership of the Bahá'í Faith. Registered with the UN Department of Public Information (UNDPI) since 1948, the Bahá'í International Community was granted consultative status (category II) with the UN Economic and Social Council (ECOSOC) in 1970, consultative status with the United Nations Children's Fund (UNICEF) in 1976, and working relations with the World Health Organization (WHO) in 1989.

The Bahá'í International Community has offices at the United Nations in New York and Geneva and representations to regional United Nations offices in Addis Ababa, Bangkok, Nairobi, Rome, Santiago, and Vienna. Its United Nations Office now includes an Office of the Environment and an Office for the Advancement of Women'. <www.bic-un.bahai.org/bic-e.htm>

9. Bahá'í International Community Office of Public Information, *Peace Among the Nations*, para. 3.

10. ibid. para. 5.

11. Commission on Global Governance, *Our Global Neighbourhood*, pp. 2–3.

12. In regard to the role of consciousness in globalization, see Robertson, *Globalization*.

13. In the original German: *Weltinnenpolitik* – coined in 1963. <www.sonntagsblatt.de/1995/ds-30/weizsae.htm>

14. International business generally favours stability because it reduces the 'transaction costs' of business dealings across borders.
15. Alejandro Bendana, director of the Centro de Estudios Internacionales in Managua, cited in *The Progressive Response*, 13 April 1998, vol. 2, no. 11.
16. Falk, *On Humane Governance*, p. 13.
17. Ake, 'The New World Order: A View from Africa', in Holmand and Sørensen, *Whose World Order*, p. 26.
18. Falk, *On Humane Governance*, p. 13.
19. A brief list might include such things as increasing numbers of hurricanes, war in the Balkans, terrorist activities, suicide bombings and ecological emergencies.
20. A complete list of BIC statements in English can be found at: <www.bic-un.bahai.org/i-e-com.htm>
21. Bahá'í International Community, *Valuing Spirituality in Development*, p. 23.
22. ibid. p. 24.
23. ibid. Emphasis added.
24. Bahá'í International Community, *Turning Point for All Nations*, p. 4.
25. ibid. pp. 13–14.
26. Bahá'í International Community. *The Prosperity of Humankind*, p. 28.
27. ibid. p. 28. Emphasis added.
28. ibid. p. 32.
29. ibid. p. 8.
30. Referring to Bahá'u'lláh's proclamation of the oneness of mankind, Shoghi Effendi wrote that: 'It implies at once a warning and a promise – a warning that in it lies the sole means for the salvation of a greatly suffering world, a promise that its realization is at hand.' Shoghi Effendi, *World Order*, p. 47.
31. See, among others Barber, 'Jihad vs. McWorld', *The Atlantic Monthly*, March 1992; and Fuller, 'The Next Ideology', *Foreign Policy*, Spring 1995.
32. Bahá'í International Community, *The Prosperity of Humankind*, p. 9.
33. ibid. p. 10.
34. ibid.
35. ibid.
36. Bahá'í International Community, *Turning Point for All Nations*, p. 22.
37. The BIC has suggested some steps which could be taken in this direction:

An educational programme to promote such a consciousness might include, but not be limited to, cultivating an appreciation for the richness and importance of the world's diverse cultural, religious and social systems, and nurturing the feeling of belonging to and responsibility toward the world community. It might also include study of the significant contributions that the nations of the world are making to humanity's collective progress through participation in such international fora as the United Nations, through such agreements as the numerous human rights treaties and UN global action plans, and through such international initiatives as the World Heritage Sites. Bahá'í International Community, *Valuing Spirituality in Development*, p. 25.

38. ibid. p. 7.
39. The Universal House of Justice, *The Promise of World Peace*. <www.bahai.org/bworld>
40. ibid. para. 27.
41. Bahá'í International Community, *Turning Point for All Nations*, p. 11.
42. Bull, *The Anarchical Society*, see chapter 9, 'The Great Powers and International Order'.
43. *World Development Report 1997: The State in a Changing World*. <www.worldbank.org/html/extpb/wdr97/english/>
44. *NAFTA & Inter-American Trade Monitor*, 14 November 1996. <trade-news@igc.apc.org>
45. Hansen-Kuhn, 'Free Trade Area of the Americas', *The Progressive Response*, 13 April 1998, vol. 2, no. 11. <www.zianet.com /infocus>
46. Lippman, 'Clinton Stresses Benefits of Open Markets', *Washington Post*, Friday, 17 April 1998, p. A25.
47. 'FTAA Talks Launched', *BRIDGES: Weekly Trade News Digest*, vol. 2, no. 14, 20 April 1998. <tradedev@igc.apc.org>
48. *NAFTA & Inter-American Trade Monitor*, vol. 5, no. 9, 1 May 1998. <iatp@iatp.org>
49. *One Country: The online newsletter of the Bahá'í International Community*, vol. 9, no. 2, July–September 1997. <www.onecountry.org /oc92/oc9209as.html>
50. The Universal House of Justice, *The Promise of World Peace*, para. 54. Emphasis added.